Assessment of Writing

THE ASSOCIATION FOR INSTITUTIONAL RESEARCH

Printed in the United States

ISBN 978-1-882393-18-3

Table of Contents

FOREWORD

This volume is the fourth in a series sponsored by the Association for Institutional Research (AIR) focused on assessment in the disciplines. The first year was dedicated to employing assessment in the teaching of business, the second year to the teaching of mathematics and related fields, and the third year to the best practices for assessment in engineering. Future volumes will focus on assessment of the teaching of chemistry and of arts- and design-related fields of study.

Traditionally, the assessment of writing has been considered to be a matter of concern for English professors and especially those teaching composition courses, normally in the first year of college. Some academic programs might also have technical writing courses concerned with a more specialized version of communication in the professional field, which would address assessment as well. As the chapters in this volume suggest, if this was ever the prevailing wisdom, times have definitely changed. Today, the concern about writing is throughout the curriculum, hence, assessment of Writing Across the Curriculum or WAC and extensive use of electronic portfolios to assist with such efforts. Increased collaboration among scholars from multiple disciplines is another common feature of the current ethos in writing assessment. Not only are writing experts collaborating with assessment experts, but they are also collaborating with content area experts in the other disciplines in which students are expressing themselves. It is only through such collaboration that a truly comprehensive assessment of student writing can occur across an entire curriculum.

It is no accident that the editors of this volume, Marie Paretti and Katrina Powell, exemplify the kinds of scholarship so necessary in this new environment in writing assessment. Not only are both writing scholars in the traditional sense, but both also have extensive experience working with those who are not traditional writing scholars. In fact, Marie is currently employed in a College of Engineering, not the traditional home of an English Ph.D. but one, I predict, that will be less uncommon in the future as all disciplines recognize the necessity of improving communication within their own fields by collaborating with experts in written and oral communication from other fields.

I want to take this opportunity to thank Marie and Katrina for their tireless efforts at pulling the chapters together and editing them. Only those who have tackled such a task have an appreciation for the difficulties involved. I would also like to thank Lisa Gwaltney of the AIR staff for her editorial assistance, Gary Pike, chair of the Editorial Board, for his support, and Randy Swing, the Executive Director of AIR, for his continuing support and guidance. Volumes of this type, and the series in assessment, are only possible because of many people such as these.

We in institutional research continue to cherish our role as partners with faculty in improving higher education through assessment. This volume and series are tangible evidence of that continuing commitment.

John A. Muffo
John A. Muffo & Associates, Inc.

EDITORS' PROFILES

Assessment of Writing

Dr. Marie C. Paretti

Assistant Professor

Engineering Education

Virginia Tech

Blacksburg, Virginia

and

Dr. Katrina M. Powell

Associate Professor of Rhetoric and Writing

English

Virginia Tech

Blacksburg, Virginia

Dr. Paretti is the director of the nationally recognized Materials Science and Engineering Communications Program, as well as co-director of the Virginia Tech Engineering Communications Center. She has been actively involved in assessing professional and workplace writing, with a particular emphasis on engineering. Her current research projects include developing and validating assessment methods for writing in the discipline programs.

Dr. Powell is Associate Professor of Rhetoric and Writing at Virginia Tech. She teaches courses in Contemporary Composition Theory, Research Methodology, and Feminist Autobiography. Her forthcoming book, *The Anguish of Displacement*, analyzes a collection of letters written by mountain families who were forced to move from their homes in order to form Shenandoah National Park. In addition to serving as Assistant Editor for the journal, *Assessing Writing,* Powell also helped design the recent change in first-year writing at Louisiana State University, where the second semester writing course was shifted to the second or third year. The requirements of this course were revised to account for the WPA Outcomes Assessment and the University's assessment study of writing.

CHAPTER 1

BRINGING VOICES TOGETHER: PARTNERSHIPS FOR ASSESSING WRITING ACROSS CONTEXTS

Marie C. Paretti and Katrina M. Powell
Virginia Tech

Introduction: Research and Practice in Writing Assessment

Writing assessment, perhaps unlike a number of other domains in the *Assessment in the Disciplines* series, has long been a field in its own right, emerging primarily within the larger discipline of composition and writing studies. Writing faculty and writing program directors, not surprisingly, have a passionate interest in writing assessment; theoretical rationales, methodologies, questions of reliability and validity, practical examples, and uses to which assessment is directed have all been studied and debated in the literature with increasing attention over the past few decades. Landmark texts such as Brian Huot's *(Re)Articulating Writing Assessment for Teaching and Learning* (2002), Richard Haswell's *Beyond Outcomes: Assessment and Instruction Within a University Writing Program* (2001), Kathleen Blake Yancey and Brian Huot's *Assessing Writing Across the Curriculum* (1997), Edward White's (1996) *Teaching and Assessing Writing* (now in its second edition), and most recently Brian Huot and Peggy O'Neill's *Assessing Writing: A Critical Sourcebook* (2008) are notable not simply for the number of times they are referenced by the authors in this volume, but for the ways in which they have shaped the practice of writing assessment at colleges and universities across the country over the past 20 years. In addition to these landmark volumes, however, the scholarship of writing assessment includes dedicated journals such as *Assessing Writing* and the *Journal of Writing Assessment*, both of which emerged in the 1990s, along with numerous articles in other premier journals such as *College Composition and Communication, Writing Program Administration,* and *Technical Communication Quarterly*, and presentations and special sessions at the Conference on College Composition and Communication, the Association of Teachers of Technical Writing, the International Writing Across the Curriculum Conference, the Society of Technical Communication Conference. CompPile (http://compile.org), an online searchable database of publications dating back to 1939 on "post-secondary composition, rhetoric, technical writing, ESL, and discourse studies" includes almost 3,000 books and articles that use *assessment* as a keyword.

The field is even so rich and well-established as to have produced its own histories. For example, Yancey (1999) offers an overview of writing assessment since the 1950s for a special retrospective issue of *College Composition and Communication*, in which she traces the movement from objective testing on grammar, mechanics, and related skills to holistic scoring of individual essays (often timed writing samples) and finally to the emergence of portfolio assessments, in which evaluators examine not one essay but multiple documents by each student. More recently, Norbert Elliot's book-length study, *On a Scale: A Social History of Writing Assessment in America* (2005) details much of the earlier history, describing the shift during the early 20th century from assessment by individual faculty to large-scale standardized assessment by the College Board and the Educational Testing Service (see Mary Trachsel's *Institutionalizing Literacy* [1992] for additional detail on this issue). In addition, several major professional organizations associated with teaching writing—the National Council of Teachers of English (NCTE), Conference on College Composition and Communication (CCCC), and the Council of Writing Program Administrators (WPA)—all have position statements regarding appropriate practices for developing writing assessments, which are described in detail in Chapter 2 of this volume.

As a result, readers who wish to find both theoretical frameworks and practical examples for developing a writing assessment process face no shortage of available resources. In fact, the opposite may be true: with such an abundance of scholarship, it may be difficult to locate a starting point. That, we hope, is where this volume comes in. *Assessment of Writing* covers a vast territory that includes placement of incoming students, first-year programs, writing across the curriculum, writing in specific disciplines, and outcomes of assessments of graduating seniors. In selecting contributors for this volume, we have attempted to bring all of these voices together to provide a starting point for anyone charged with assessing student writing. We have invited authors from a full range of institutions to address the full range of assessment contexts, from the first year (e.g., Edgington; Phillips & Ahrenhoerster) to writing in the disciplines (e.g., Schneider et al.; Zawacki & Gentemann; House et al.). The volume, moreover, includes not only practical advice but also critical frameworks for understanding writing assessment (e.g., Janangelo & Adler-Kassner; O'Neill & Moore) as well as discussions of the role of current technologies (e.g., Herrington & Moran; Yancey). Readers have an opportunity not only to find assessment practices applicable to their own contexts, but to understand the rationales behind those practices to enable them to develop locally appropriate strategies. Each of the chapters in this volume includes a strong list of references that will serve to guide readers to additional resources.

Outcomes Assessment and Student Learning: Bringing Together Writing and Assessment Experts

In addition to providing what we hope is a useful starting point for those charged with writing assessment, we also see this volume as an important site of collaboration among professionals in writing and professionals in institutional research—collaboration that is, we believe, essential to the successful implementation of any writing assessment program. As Huot (2002) points out in his discussion of the emergence of writing assessment as a field of study, the field's history has two independent and unfortunately often unconnected strands: institutional researchers and measurement specialists have been part of one ongoing conversation, with standardized language/writing tests such as the SAT being one of the more prominent outcomes, while writing specialists have been part of another ongoing conversation, resulting in portfolio assessment protocols (see also Huot & Neal, 2006). Too often, these two conversations met only when writing specialists have rallied to critique and oppose the kinds of standardized, computerized testing that has emerged from the measurement community (Huot, 2002), Les Perelman's work castigating the new SAT writing exam being one of the more high-profile examples of late (Anson, Perelman, Poe, & Sommers, 2008; Perelman, 2007).

Huot's argument, however, and one which we hope this volume furthers, is that successful assessment—that is, assessment that not only evaluates student performance but also meaningfully supports teaching and learning—requires collaboration across disciplinary and professional lines. As outcomes assessment has become an increasingly powerful force in education, writing program faculty, with their broad subject area knowledge, and institutional research, with their broad expertise in measurement and evaluation, need to understand one another and work together. Such collaborations, when supported by mutual respect and ongoing dialogue, work to ensure that assessment becomes not an end in itself undertaken merely to fulfill requirements for an external body such as state legislatures or accreditation agencies, but rather a dynamic and valuable tool to further the core mission of colleges and universities—the education of students. The essays in this volume consistently emphasize this collaboration; several are co-authored by writing faculty and institutional researchers, while others describe a variety of processes for establishing successful collaborations. In addition, those authors who focus on assessing writing within disciplinary contexts also stress the need to include faculty from those disciplines along with the writing and measurement experts. While the impetus for outcomes assessments may arise from external drivers, it becomes meaningful for universities when, as all of our authors emphasize, that impetus and its results are used as tools to support students, faculty, and programs.

Understanding What Are We Assessing: Writing as a Social Act

As noted above, a number of scholars have traced the history of writing assessment, tracking moves from standardized tests of grammar and mechanics to holistic scoring of individual essays and portfolios. At the core of these shifts is the central question of what, exactly, we are evaluating when we "assess writing." Tests of vocabulary, grammar, punctuation, and related skills position writing as primarily the mechanical skill of forming sentences that conform to standard academic English. The move to assess student writing samples, however, emerged from the deep understanding that these mechanical skills are not the same as the ability to write—the ability to combine sentences together in ways that effectively make meaning for both the writer and the reader. This emphasis on making meaning implies that writing is always a social act and that definitions of "good" depend more on context (which writers, which readers, and in which social or professional settings) than on some mythical archetypal construct of "good writing" that "everyone" agrees on. Evidence for understanding writing in this way is abundant in research on composition, rhetoric, and professional writing; Thaiss and Zawacki (2006), for example, in their book-length study of writing in academic disciplines, illustrate that not only do definitions of "good" vary across disciplines, but even within a given department faculty often have contradictory standards. Carolyn Miller's (1984) seminal article, "Genre as Social Action," traces the ways in which various document structures and styles (a proposal, a progress report, a journal article) are intimately tied to the ways in which the documents are used by those who need the information they present. Dias, Freedman, Medway, and Pare (1999), Beaufort (1999), Artemeva, Logie, and St-Martin (1999), and others have traced the kinds of problems students face when they move from academic to workplace writing, noting the ways in which the forms, styles, and strategies learned in one context do not always easily translate to new environments. Differences across contexts can range from appropriate organizational strategies to type and level of detail expected, accepted sources of evidence, legitimate logical moves used to connect evidence to claims, and even preferred stylistic, linguistic, and digital choices.

Hence the production of a perfect essay in a given format may or may not reflect a student's "ability to write" in some broad, generic sense. Many students who successfully pass the SAT writing exam still struggle in their college writing courses; many who master their first-year English class are still the source of much despair in disciplinary courses as upper-level faculty wonder "why students can't write"; students who succeed in academic writing still emerge as poor communicators in professional settings; and employers constantly bemoan students' weakness in this core area. Unfortunately, particularly for those concerned with outcomes assessment, research demonstrates over and over that the ability to write one type of document does not automatically guarantee the ability to write another kind of document; the successful completion of a generic "research paper" does not ensure the successful completion of a journal article or a business proposal or a laboratory report. In part, this issue of transfer results from the social, contextual nature of writing discussed above; what constitutes "good" in one setting for one audience does not necessarily constitute "good" in another setting. Moreover, writers' understanding of the material is also closely tied to their ability to write about that material successfully. Students who are habitually "good" writers and have learned to successfully negotiate differences in context often still produce "bad" writing when they are working with information or ideas that they themselves do not fully grasp. In such cases, even the "basics" of grammar and mechanics can fall apart as students struggle with their conceptual understanding of the subject matter.

Equally important, research on student writing provides some cautionary insights into the limitations of outcomes assessment as a means to understand the ways in which students develop as writers and the ways in which education affects students' roles as both writers and readers. Drawing on the work of the Harvard Study, which followed 400 students through their college experience to "observe undergraduate writing through the eyes of students," Nancy Sommers argues that "to reduce the story of an undergraduate education to a single question—do students graduate as stronger or better writers than when they entered?—is to miss the complexity of a college education" (Anson et al., 2008, p. 155). In exploring the complex nature of students' experiences with writing, always inflected with their development as thinkers, professionals, and engaged citizens, Sommers notes the ways in which writing development does not always reflect a clear and steady march of progress, nor is it often characterized by huge gains in small spans of time (a semester, a year, or even four years). She argues persuasively that "the problem with measuring writing development by any set of outcomes is that 'outcomes' reduce education to an endpoint, transferring the focus on instruction from students to written products and leaving both students and teachings behind in the process" (Anson et al., 2008, p. 162). Thus, even as we offer a volume dedicated to writing assessment based on well-defined learning outcomes grounded in the work of professionals in a range of writing contexts, Sommers' work, as well as the findings of other longitudinal studies of students' development as writers, reminds us that assessing writing may only provide one very small glimpse into the process of education.

Implications for Assessment: Location, Location, Location (and Time)

With Sommers' cautionary work in mind, the imperative to conduct meaningful writing assessment remains a powerful force in higher education. The nature of writing as a socially constructed, socially mediating tool rather than an isolated artifact, has a number of significant implications for both teaching and assessing writing that are explored in detail in the following chapters. Here we summarize the salient points as a way to help readers frame the discussions that follow.

First, the inextricable connection between "good" writing and the context in which that writing emerged means that writing assessment is always a localized project. Even while assessment methods such as holistic scoring and portfolio assessment can be used across contexts, the standards used to evaluate writing must always be developed locally and take into consideration the course, the discipline, and the faculty expectations that guided the writing. The chapters that follow offer a variety of examples for developing these standards, but in each case the emphasis is on a localized, collaborative approach among writing experts and measurement specialists, along with disciplinary faculty when assessment occurs in upper-level courses. Assessment practices and evaluation standards need to take into account the context in which students were taught, the goals of the writing instruction, definitions of "good writing" at work for both teachers and students, and the technology available to and used by students as they compose.

Second, this emphasis on localization means that discussions of assessment are always tied to discussions of teaching. We cannot talk about how to assess writing without understanding how writing is being taught and evaluated in individual classes. The kinds of teaching and feedback and grading in those courses affects the ways in which assessment operates; furthermore, the results of the assessment need to feed back into those sites of instruction in ways that are productive and meaningful to ensure that improvements in students' learning and development are at the heart of this work.

Third, the social, localized nature of writing means that those engaged in writing assessment need to be very clear about what kinds of claims they can make about students' writing abilities. In some cases, portfolio approaches, particularly when they include students' reflections on writing as well as sample documents, can enable evaluators to assess meta-knowledge and determine what students understand about the writing they've done and what principles they've learned that can transfer to other settings. In other cases, however, the claims resulting from the assessment may be much more narrow; we may not be able to affirm that students are "good writers" in a universal sense, but only that they are "good writers" in this context, of this particular set of genres, in this knowledge domain.

Finally, because writing is a social act, a mode of both thinking and communicating, writing assessment is time-intensive, and the time required for effective assessment must always be included in the design. While machine-grading may seem like an inviting idea because of its labor-saving capabilities, the essays that follow demonstrate the limitations of this approach. "Good writing" is good precisely because it achieves a specific human effect; the primary way to assess this effect is to involve human readers. And human reading of student essays requires time—time to bring evaluators together to develop and/or understand the assessment standards, time to reach agreement, time to read and evaluate the documents, and time to find the resources in order to conduct such work.

Writing Assessment in Theory and Practice: Navigating This Volume

As noted, the chapters in this volume elaborate on the issues raised in this introduction and provide multiple practical examples for developing effective writing assessments, along with the theoretical grounding needed to ensure those assessments are adapted and implemented appropriately.

In Chapter 2, **Janangelo and Adler-Kassner** present and discuss the position statements on writing assessment from several major professional organizations. These position statements help frame the nature of both writing and assessment that informs the chapters that follow; each of these organizations maintains its own public website that provides additional resources and information for readers. By drawing together the position statements from various organizations, these authors help locate a set of common guidelines for implementing and using writing assessments in university settings.

In Chapter 3, **O'Neill and Moore** offer theoretical explanations that both underpin the guidelines in the previous chapter and help account for the disconnect between institutional assessment offices and writing faculty. In doing so, they provide a call for the respectful understanding of the underlying ideological differences between the two groups. Offering strategies for working together, they articulate clearly and carefully the ways in which writing professionals and assessment professionals can and should be responsible for understanding these differences, valuing the practice of assessment, and collaborating successfully.

In Chapter 4, **Zawacki and Gentemann** provide the first of several examples of such collaborations as they present a detailed model for developing departmentally based assessment practices. They first position their assessment efforts within the larger framework of state-mandated assessment, and demonstrate the importance of tailoring the response to those mandates to the needs and mission of the university. They then describe ways to bring department faculty together to discuss and reach consensus on evaluation standards and provide models for conducting meaningful assessment and putting the results to work to improve student learning, exemplifying the model with cases from government and international affairs, biology/ecology, and business.

Where Zawacki and Gentemann describe a process for assessment in the disciplines, in Chapter 5, **Schneider, Leydens, Olds, and Miller** draw on their experiences of developing assessments to meet disciplinary accreditation standards in science and engineering. They identify principles that guide writing assessment in the disciplines that reflect both the position statements of Chapter 2 and the theoretical framework of Chapter 3. Their work provides numerous examples of ways to enact those principles in different contexts, including engineering courses and curricula at various levels, and provides a strong example of the link between how writing is assessed and how it is taught.

Similar to Zawacki and Gentemann, in Chapter 6, **Phillips and Ahrenhoerster** describe their program's response to institutionally based demands of assessment. They focus on the assessment of first-year writing courses and describe the process of negotiating with assessment imposed "from the top down" to develop an approach that would meet both the needs of the program and the institution. Their work demonstrates the ways in which assessment, even if it is required from the "top down," can be considered as research and contributes to the scholarship of teaching, thereby serving the specific needs of programs. Phillips and Ahrenhoerster provide specific tools for conducting this kind of research and its usefulness for individual programs.

Edgington's Chapter 7 highlights the kinds of problems described by O'Neill and Moore, where institutional demands may conflict with programmatic values. He, therefore, provides a series of practical strategies designed to help writing program administrators take a proactive approach to the assessment of first-year student in terms of both placement at the beginning of the year and outcomes at the end of the program. He, too, stresses the need to negotiate programmatic and administrative needs and develop assessments that benefit student learning.

In Chapter 8, **House, Livingston, Minster, Taylor, Watt, and Williams** describe the bridges between a large-scale institutional assessment of student portfolios and the work of individual faculty teaching writing in disciplinary classrooms. Like Schneider et al., their work is situated at a small private institution with a focus on engineering, science, and mathematics, one that has been a leader in the use of portfolios for programmatic assessment on an institutional scale. Their chapter not only enacts principles similar to those developed by the preceding authors, but takes those principles into classroom teaching practices to help close the assessment loop and provide a holistic account of the educational cycle. At the same time, by linking writing assessment to a much larger institutional assessment program directed towards accreditation, they demonstrate the ways in which multiple strands of assessment can work together in a holistic fashion to support an entire curriculum.

In Chapter 9, **Herrington and Moran** provide an overview of online assessment packages, including both the theoretical and practical implications of employing these techniques. Their chapter can help readers understand both the uses and the limitations of these packages as a component of a comprehensive approach to writing assessment. A key issue for Herrington and Moran is that while they may not completely "rule out" standardized instruments for assessing "some aspect" of the writing, they emphasize that they do not see the use of them as "central" to assessing the complexities of critical thought and writing. Like Edgington, and O'Neill and Moore, Herrington and Moran clearly place the ownership of writing assessment with the teaching faculty, as those best equipped to determine the benefits of particular assessment practices.

In Chapter 10, **Yancey** addresses the challenge of electronic portfolios, examining the ways they are both like and unlike their paper counterparts. Her work examines the ways in which the electronic, hyper-textual nature of these multi-media artifacts raises additional questions about good writing and the need for e-portfolio assessment to develop standards appropriate to digital compositions. Like Herrington and Moran, Yancey emphasizes the ways that digital composing affects the ways writing is taught and understood. As the recent CCCC "Position Statement on Teaching, Learning, and Assessing Writing in Digital Environments" suggests, the 21st century poses new challenges as digital composing and its assessment practices become more and more expected across colleges and universities (CCCC, 2004).

Finally, in Chapter 11, **Huot and Dillon** look both back at the development of writing assessment over the past few decades and forward to the next steps in this important field. As they note, the chapters in this volume reflect the strong movement away from writing assessment as only the stories of individual teachers and students and toward a more systematic, research-based approach to analyzing student writing that involves collaborations across a range of academic disciplines. At the same time, they point the way forward in suggesting that assessment is not yet a fully regularized component of most writing programs, nor has it yet fully engaged with issues of validity and measurement as those concepts are understood within educational research. They remind us of both how far we've come and what work still lies before us.

Each of these chapters, as we noted at the beginning of this introduction, is valuable both for the practical and theoretical framework it offers to readers and for the rich references it provides for readers who wish to learn more about specific types of writing assessments. A number of the authors include links to websites that offer additional assessment tools and practices, and many have related publications that provide more detail than a single chapter affords. We hope that this volume provides a valuable starting point for those charged with developing meaningful assessments of student writing, and that it leads to collaborations that, most importantly, support students' development as writers and learners.

REFERENCES

Anson, C. M., Perelman, L., Poe, M., & Sommers, N. (2008). Symposium on assessment. *College Composition and Communication, 60*(1), 113-164.

Artemeva, N., Logie, S., & St-Martin, J. (1999). From page to stage: How theories of genre and situated learning help introduce engineering students to discipline-specific communication. *Technical Communication Quarterly, 8*(3), 301-316.

Beaufort, A. (1999). *Writing in the real world: Making the transition from school to work.* New York: Teachers College.

Conference on College Composition and Communication (CCCC). (2004). Position statement on teaching, learning, and assessing writing in digital environments. *College Composition and Communication, 55*(4), 785-790.

Dias, P., Freedman, A., Medway, P., & Pare, A. (1999). *Worlds apart: Acting and writing in academic and workplace contexts.* Mahwah, NJ: Lawrence Erlbaum.

Elliot, N. (2005). *On a scale: A social history of writing assessment in America.* New York: Peter Lang.

Haswell, R. H. (Ed.). (2001). *Beyond outcomes: Assessment and instruction within a university writing program.* Westport, CT: Ablex.

Huot, B. (2002). *(Re)Articulating writing assessment for teaching and learning.* Logan, UT: Utah State University.

Huot, B., & Neal, M. (2006). Writing assessment: A techno-history. In C. A. MacArthur, S. Graham, & J. Fitzgerald (Eds.), *Handbook of writing research* (pp. 417-432). New York: Guilford.

Huot, B., & O'Neill, P. (2008). *Assessing writing: A critical sourcebook.* Boston: Bedford/St. Martins.

Miller, C. (1984). Genre as social action. *Quarterly Journal of Speech, 70*(2), 151-167.

Perelman, L. C. (2007, March). *Teacher-based, technology assisted writing assessments: Test to the teaching.* Paper presented at the Conference on College Composition and Communication, New York, NY.

Thaiss, C., & Zawacki, T. M. (2006). *Engaged writers and dynamic disciplines: Research on the academic writing life.* Portsmouth, NH: Heinemann.

Trachsel, M. (1992). *Institutionalizing literacy: The historical role of college entrance examinations.* Carbondale, IL: Southern Illinois University.

White, E. M. (1996). *Teaching and assessing writing* (2nd ed.). San Francisco: Jossey-Bass.

Yancey, K. B. (1999). Looking back as we look forward: Historicizing writing assessment. *College Composition and Communication, 50*(3), 483-503.

Yancey, K. B., & Huot, B. (Eds.). (1997). *Assessing writing across the curriculum: Diverse approaches and practices.* Greenwich, CT: Ablex.

CHAPTER 2

COMMON DENOMINATORS AND THE
ONGOING CULTURE OF ASSESSMENT

Joseph Janangelo, Loyola University (Chicago)
and
Linda Adler-Kassner, Eastern Michigan University

Assessment has become a "beltway conversation" that occurs both in and out of academe (Paul Bodmer, personal interview, July 8, 2007). That beltway traverses classrooms, programs, institutions, scholarly journals, and listservs. It also fuels conversations held among policy makers. The expanded, and expansive, nature of these discussions is reflected in the 2006 publication of *A Test of Leadership* (U.S. Department of Education), the report of the Commission on the Future of Higher Education (also known as the Spellings Report). A cursory search illustrates the point: an online search of *The Chronicle of Higher Education* using the keyword *Spellings* turns up 185 stories focusing on the potential, promise, and/or threat of the report; *Inside Higher Education* lists 301 stories under the search term *Spellings*. But while *A Test of Leadership* calls for "transparency" and "accountability" in assessment, such calls are not new. Instead, they echo calls that began in public policy institutes such as the RAND Corporation, the National Commission on Writing (which is funded, in part, by the College Board), and even ACT and SAT. Those conversations have been rehearsed through stories in mainstream media and political arenas such as discussions currently surrounding the reauthorization of the Higher Education Act.

The intense attention given to assessment has met with critical response by a number of faculty and scholarly organizations. Among the concerns is that, as it is cast in the conversations listed above, assessment is seen as a myopic, unilateral, and ineffective activity. Such conceptions are compounded by a competing experiential base that perpetuates assessment's dubious reputation. Simply put, assessment is sometimes seen as involving practices and activities that are perceived by students and teachers as fearful and ferreting, intrusive and ineffective, and mandatory and punishing. Some have grown to see it as a kind of tithe that is as compulsory as it is cyclical. For others, even the term *assessment* can evoke a sense of tedium or dread. This perception is complicated by the reputation of assessment as something that is separate from, and at times antithetical to, effective teaching, something that is overseen by an assessment office and/or an assessment expert who is outside of the classroom and often outside of the teaching faculty of an institution. This conception of assessment stands in stark contrast to the definition offered by Catherine Palomba and Trudy Banta (1999), who define assessment as "the systematic collection, review, and use of information about educational programs undertaken for the purpose of improving student learning and development" (p. 4).

Within the discipline of Rhetoric and Composition, there are certainly those who subscribe to both of these perceptions of assessment—and, we argue, with good reason. Writing, the primary focus of our work, is always included in cries for assessment, which are often preceded by descriptions of what teachers and/or students cannot do well enough, or are not doing, or should not be doing. *Ready or Not* (2006), a report published by the American Diploma Project (an organization formed as collaboration among Achieve, Inc., The Education Trust, and the Thomas B. Fordham Foundation that is attempting to develop and implement national curriculum standards at the secondary level which could then form the foundation for post-secondary standards), notes that

> More than 70 percent of graduates enter two- and four-year colleges, but at least 28 percent of those students immediately take remedial English or math courses. Transcripts show that during their college careers, 53 percent of students take at least one remedial English or math class. (p. 3)

The report goes on to note that while instructors (high school and post-secondary) may be well-intended, they do not understand what, in the authors' estimation, students need to know. "The academic standards that states have developed over the past decade generally reflect a consensus in each discipline about what is *desirable* for students to learn," the report explains, "but not necessarily what is *essential* for them to be prepared for further learning, work, or citizenship after completing high school" (p. 8).

To remedy this situation, *Ready or Not* recommends that, at the secondary level, states should ensure "that schools and students participating in them are held to the same state English and mathematics standards and are assessed using the same [NCLB mandated] state standards-based tests" (p. 10). Additionally, those tests should be consistent from state to state. "Although high school graduation requirements are established state by state, a high school diploma should represent a common currency nationwide.... States owe it to their students to set expectations for high school graduates that are portable to other states" (p. 4). According to the report, such "currency" should be used for college admission and placement: "Little justification exists for maintaining completely separate standards and testing systems for high school graduation and college admissions and placement..." (p. 15). "Postsecondary institutions need to reinforce efforts to raise standards in K-12 by making use of standards-based assessment data for admissions, for course placement, and/or for the awarding of merit based scholarships" (p. 15).

In response to, and often in anticipation of such recommendations, writing scholars have long been involved with assessment that is designed to improve teaching and learning (see, for example, Broad, 2003; Huot, 2002; Lynne, 2004; and White, 1984 for explanations and examples of different assessment practices; Yancey, 1999, for a to-date historical overview; and McLeod, 2007, for a discussion of accountability, of how Writing Program Administrators [WPAs] have broached assessment in their scholarship, and of how assessment can inform decisions about placement, proficiency, and program review).

Recently, three of our discipline's scholarly organizations—the Conference on College Composition and Communication (CCCC), the Council of Writing Program Administrators (WPA), and the National Council of Teachers of English (NCTE), have argued for alternative conceptualizations of assessment. This argument is grounded in the belief that assessment can provide valuable, ongoing opportunities for faculty members to proactively educate stakeholders about the central values of our disciplinary practices, and then to systematically investigate whether or not the practices emanating from these values are achieving their desired effects. The term "stakeholders" includes colleagues, campus administrators, and community members who, with a subject like writing, are very interested in what students are learning, how they are learning it, and to what effect it is being learned.

This approach toward assessment is rooted in research-based practices at the core of our discipline. It is also outlined in our discipline's three germinal statements about assessment: the "CCCC Writing Assessment: A Position Statement" (2006), the "NCTE Framing Statements on Assessment" (2004), and "The NCTE-WPA White Paper on Writing Assessment in Colleges and Universities" (2008) and associated resources. These documents make the point that good assessment is consistent at the level of conceptualization. Assessment activities must be *valid, appropriate, and fair*; they must be situated in local contexts, locally determined, and used to improve teaching and learning at the local level.

We present these statements because they reflect the combined wisdom of experienced teachers, scholars, and writing program administrators. We will conclude by offering a distillation and a discussion of important points of congruence among them.

Conference on College Composition and Communication
Writing Assessment : A Position Statement

Prepared by CCCC Committee on Assessment
November 2006
Copyright © 2006 National Council of Teachers of English.
All Rights Reserved.

Introduction

Writing assessment can be used for a variety of appropriate purposes, both inside the classroom and outside: providing assistance to students, awarding a grade, placing students in appropriate courses, allowing them to exit a course or sequence of courses, and certifying proficiency; and evaluating programs—to name some of the more obvious. Given the high stakes nature of many of these assessment purposes, it is crucial that assessment practices be guided by sound principles to insure that they are valid, fair, and appropriate to the context and purposes for which they designed. This position statement aims to provide that guidance. In spite of the diverse uses to which writing assessment is put, the general principles undergirding it are similar:

Assessments of written literacy should be designed and evaluated by well-informed current or future teachers of the students being assessed, for purposes clearly understood by all the participants; should elicit from student writers a variety of pieces, preferably over a substantial period of time; should encourage and reinforce good teaching practices; and should be solidly grounded in the latest research on language learning as well as accepted best assessment practices.

Guiding Principles for Assessment

1. Writing assessment is useful primarily as a means of improving teaching and learning. The primary purpose of any assessment should govern its design, its implementation, and the generation and dissemination of its results.

As a result...

A. Best assessment practice is informed by pedagogical and curricular goals, which are in turn formatively affected by the assessment. Teachers or administrators designing assessments should ground the assessment in the classroom, program or departmental context. The goals or outcomes assessed should lead to assessment data which is fed back to those involved with the regular activities assessed so that assessment results may be used to make changes in practice.

B. Best assessment practice is undertaken in response to local goals, not external pressures. Even when the external forces require assessment, the local community must assert control of the assessment process, including selection of the assessment instrument and criteria.

2. Writing is by definition social. Learning to write entails learning to accomplish a range of purposes for a range of audiences in a range of settings.

As a result...

A. Best assessment practice engages students in contextualized, meaningful writing. The assessment of writing must strive to set up writing tasks and situations that identify purposes appropriate to and appealing to the particular students being tested. Additionally, assessment must be contextualized in terms of why, where, and for what purpose it is being

14

undertaken; this context must also be clear to the students being assessed and to all stakeholders.

B. Best assessment practice supports and harmonizes with what practice and research have demonstrated to be effective ways of teaching writing. What is easiest to measure—often by means of a multiple choice test—may correspond least to good writing; choosing a correct response from a set of possible answers is not composing. As important, just asking students to write does not make the assessment instrument a good one. Essay tests that ask students to form and articulate opinions about some important issue—for instance, without time to reflect, talk to others, read on the subject, revise, and have a human audience—promote distorted notions of what writing is. They also encourage poor teaching and little learning. Even teachers who recognize and employ the methods used by real writers in working with students can find their best efforts undercut by assessments such as these.

C. Best assessment practice is direct assessment by human readers. Assessment that isolates students and forbids discussion and feedback from others conflicts with what we know about language use and the benefits of social interaction during the writing process; it also is out of step with much classroom practice. Direct assessment in the classroom should provide response that serves formative purposes, helping writers develop and shape ideas, as well as organize, craft sentences, and edit. As stated by the CCCC Position Statement on Teaching, Learning, and Assessing Writing in Digital Environments, "we oppose the use of machine-scored writing in the assessment of writing." Automated assessment programs do not respond as human readers. While they may promise consistency, they distort the very nature of writing as a complex and context-rich interaction between people. They simplify writing in ways that can mislead writers to focus more on structure and grammar than on what they are saying by using a given structure and style.

3. Any individual's writing ability is a sum of a variety of skills employed in a diversity of contexts, and individual ability fluctuates unevenly among these varieties.

As a result...

A. Best assessment practice uses multiple measures. One piece of writing—even if it is generated under the most desirable conditions—can never serve as an indicator of overall writing ability, particularly for high-stakes decisions. Ideally, writing ability must be assessed by more than one piece of writing, in more than one genre, written on different occasions, for different audiences, and responded to and evaluated by multiple readers as part of a substantial and sustained writing process.

B. Best assessment practice respects language variety and diversity and assesses writing on the basis of effectiveness for readers, acknowledging that as purposes vary, criteria will as well. Standardized tests that rely more on identifying grammatical and stylistic errors than authentic rhetorical choices disadvantage students whose home dialect is not the dominant dialect. Assessing authentic acts of writing simultaneously raises performance standards and provides multiple avenues to success. Thus students are not arbitrarily punished for linguistic differences that in some contexts make them more, not less, effective communicators. Furthermore, assessments that are keyed closely to an American cultural context may disadvantage second language writers. The CCCC Statement on Second Language Writing and Writers calls on us "to recognize the regular presence of second-language writers in writing classes, to understand their characteristics, and to develop instructional and administrative practices that are sensitive to their linguistic and cultural needs." Best assessment practice responds to this call by creating assessments that are sensitive to the language varieties in use among the local population and sensitive to the context-specific outcomes being assessed.

C. Best assessment practice includes assessment by peers, instructors, and the student writer himself or herself. Valid assessment requires combining multiple perspectives on a performance and generating an overall assessment out of the combined descriptions of those multiple perspectives. As a result, assessments should include formative and summative assessments from all these kinds of readers. Reflection by the writer on her or his own writing processes and performances holds particular promise as a way of generating knowledge about writing and increasing the ability to write successfully.

4. Perceptions of writing are shaped by the methods and criteria used to assess writing.

As a result...

A. The methods and criteria that readers use to assess writing should be locally developed, deriving from the particular context and purposes for the writing being assessed. The individual writing program, institution, or consortium should be recognized as a community of interpreters whose knowledge of context and purpose is integral to the assessment. There is no test which can be used in all environments for all purposes, and the best assessment for any group of students must be locally determined and may well be locally designed.

B. Best assessment practice clearly communicates what is valued and expected, and does not distort the nature of writing or writing practices. If ability to compose for various audiences is valued, then an assessment will assess this capability. For other contexts and purposes, other writing abilities might be valued, for instance, to develop a position on the basis of reading multiple sources or to compose a multi-media piece, using text and images. Values and purposes should drive assessment, not the reverse. A corollary to this statement is that assessment practices and criteria should change as conceptions of texts and values change.

C. Best assessment practice enables students to demonstrate what they do well in writing. Standardized tests tend to focus on readily accessed features of the language (grammatical correctness, stylistic choices) and on error rather than on the appropriateness of the rhetorical choices that have been made. Consequently, the outcome of such assessments is negative: students are said to demonstrate what they do wrong with language rather than what they do well. Quality assessments will provide the opportunity for students to demonstrate the ways they can write, displaying the strategies or skills taught in the relevant environment.

5. Assessment programs should be solidly grounded in the latest research on learning, writing, and assessment.

As a result...

A. Best assessment practice results from careful consideration of the costs and benefits of the range of available approaches. It may be tempting to choose an inexpensive, quick assessment, but decision-makers should consider the impact of assessment methods on students, faculty, and programs. The return on investment from the direct assessment of writing by instructor-evaluators includes student learning, professional development of faculty, and program development. These benefits far outweigh the presumed benefits of cost, speed, and simplicity that machine scoring might seem to promise.

B. Best assessment practice is continually under review and subject to change by well-informed faculty, administrators, and legislators. Anyone charged with the responsibility of designing an assessment program must be cognizant of the relevant research and must stay abreast of developments in the field. The theory and practice of writing assessment is continually informed by significant publications in professional journals and by presentations at regional and national conferences. The easy availability of this research to practitioners makes ignorance of its content reprehensible.

Applications to Assessment Settings

The guiding principles apply to assessment conducted in any setting. In addition, we offer the following guidelines for situations that may be encountered in specific settings.

Assessment in the Classroom

In a course context, writing assessment should be part of the highly social activity within the community of faculty and students in the class. This social activity includes:

- a period of ungraded work (prior to the completion of graded work) that receives response from multiple readers, including peer reviewers,
- assessment of texts—from initial through to final drafts—by human readers, and
- more than one opportunity to demonstrate outcomes.

Self-assessment should also be encouraged. Assessment practices and criteria should match the particular kind of text being created and its purpose. These criteria should be clearly communicated to students in advance so that the students can be guided by the criteria while writing.

Assessment for Placement

Placement criteria in the most responsible programs will be clearly connected to any differences in the available courses. Experienced instructor-evaluators can most effectively make a judgment regarding which course would best serve each student's needs and assign each student to the appropriate course. If scoring systems are used, scores should derive from criteria that grow out of the work of the courses into which students are being placed.

Decision-makers should carefully weigh the educational costs and benefits of timed tests, portfolios, directed self placement, etc. In the minds of those assessed, each of these methods implicitly establishes its value over that of others, so the first cost is likely to be what students come to believe about writing. For example, timed writing may suggest to students that writing always cramps one for time and that real writing is always a test. Portfolio assessment may honor the processes by which writers develop their ideas and re-negotiate how their communications are heard within a language community. And machine-scored tests may focus students on error-correction rather than on effective communication.

Students should have the right to weigh in on their assessment. Self-placement without direction, sometimes touted as a student right, may become merely a right to fail, whereas directed self-placement, either alone or in combination with other methods, provides not only useful information but also involves and invests the student in making effective life decisions.

If for financial or even programmatic reasons the initial method of placement is somewhat reductive, instructors of record should create an opportunity early in the semester to review and change students' placement assignments, and uniform procedures should be established to facilitate the easy re-placement of improperly placed students. Even when the placement process entails direct assessment of writing, the system should accommodate the possibility of improper placement. If assessment employs machine scoring, whether of actual writing or of items designed to elicit error, it is particularly essential that every effort be made through statistical verification to see that students, individually and collectively, are placed in courses that can appropriately address their skills and abilities.

Placement processes should be continually assessed and revised in accord with course content and overall program goals. This is especially important when machine-scored assessments are used. Using methods that are employed uniformly, teachers of record should verify that students are appropriately placed. If students are placed according to scores on such tests, the ranges of placement must be revisited regularly to accommodate changes in curricula and shifts in the abilities of the student population.

Assessment of Proficiency

Proficiency or exit assessment involves high stakes for students. In this context, assessments that make use of substantial and sustained writing processes are especially important.

Judgments of proficiency must also be made on the basis of performances in multiple and varied writing situations (for example, a variety of topics, audiences, purposes, genres).

The assessment criteria should be clearly connected to desired outcomes. When proficiency is being determined, the assessment should be informed by such things as the core abilities adopted by the institution, the course outcomes established for a program, and/or the stated outcomes of a single course or class. Assessments that do not address such outcomes lack validity in determining proficiency.

The higher the stakes, the more important it is that assessment be direct rather than indirect, based on actual writing rather than on answers on multiple-choice tests, and evaluated by people involved in the instruction of the student rather than via machine scoring. To evaluate the proficiency of a writer on other criteria than multiple writing tasks and situations is essentially disrespectful of the writer.

Assessment of Programs

Program assessment refers to evaluations of performance in a large group, such as students in a multi-section course or majors graduating from a department. Because assessment offers information about student performance and the factors which affect that performance, it is an important way for programs or departments to monitor and develop their practice.

Programs and departments should see themselves as communities of professionals whose assessment activities reveal common values, provide opportunities for inquiry and debate about unsettled issues, and communicate measures of effectiveness to those inside and outside the program. Members of the community are in the best position to guide decisions about what assessments will best inform that community. It is important to bear in mind that random sampling of students can often provide large-scale information and that regular assessment should affect practice.

National Council of Teachers of English
Framing Statements on Assessment

Revised Report of the Assessment and Testing Study Group
of the NCTE Executive Committee
November 2004
Copyright © 2004 National Council of Teachers of English.
All rights reserved.

NCTE holds the following beliefs about assessment:

- Assessment must include multiple measures and must be manageable.
- Consumers of assessment data should be knowledgeable about the things the test data can and cannot say about learning.
- Teachers and schools should be permitted to select site-specific assessment tools from a bank of alternatives and/or to create their own.

Based on these beliefs, NCTE upholds the following vision regarding assessment. We want:

- To help teachers develop competence in using various forms of data about how students are doing and what they need in order to continue to grow—assessment for both formative and summative purposes.
- Teachers to be knowledgeable about many forms of assessment and to be able to use these data-collection tools in order to articulate what students have learned and their growth in using strategies for further learning. We also want teachers to be able to provide appropriate parties purposeful accounting for student learning (e.g., descriptive narratives).
- Teachers to use collections of assessment strategies appropriate in their settings. We also want teachers to be knowledgeable about the appropriate uses and limitations of use for each of these assessments.
- Conversations in schools, businesses and communities to be focused on "assessment" as an ongoing part of how we educators do our work—taking stock of what students have accomplished and making plans for what needs to come next for continued learning.
- Parents to be knowledgeable and involved in the assessment process for their children and their schools. We also want parents to have a voice in establishing the criteria by which their schools will be judged.

To attain our vision, NCTE will act on the following Guiding Principles when taking action regarding Assessment. NCTE:

21

- Intends to work PreK – University in our efforts to influence assessment practices.
- Will send a consistent message opposing sole reliance on standardized tests.
- Will help teachers cope with the reality they currently have while helping them critique current testing mandates and forms and propose alternatives to the current reality.
- Believes parents should be knowledgeable and involved in the assessment process, including establishing the criteria by which their schools will be judged.
- Wants to influence the way "mid course corrections" are approached, particularly the ways data are used in the process.

Ultimately our goal will be that those involved in and affected by assessment will attain the following ends.

In Knowledge and Disposition

- ELA [English and Language Arts] teachers' decisions regarding assessment are trusted by parents, administrators, and other interested stakeholders.
- ELA teachers are knowledgeable about assessment principles and implement assessment strategies that make sense in light of their daily instructional practice.
- ELA teachers help students understand how to become (appropriately) self-critical and reflective so that they can take these "habits of mind" to other disciplines and the workplace.
- ELA teachers are confident and skillful in articulating specific details about student growth in areas of reading, writing, literature response, use of oral and written language for learning, etc.
- Assessment Coordinators assume primary responsibility for communicating classroom assessment information to groups outside the school building.
- Teachers, administrators, and school communities work together to change school culture, to shift the assessment paradigm such that learning theory matches assessment theory.
- Assessment Coordinators are able to translate and communicate assessment information to school officials, community members, and legislators.
- Teachers are free to focus on teaching and learning—and assessment is an integral part of the process, not something set aside from the process.
- Assessment Coordinators provide regular, cohesive information sessions for parents and other stakeholders, helping them

learn how to prepare their children for tests, how to work for their children as learning advocates, and how to be active participants in ongoing assessment conversations about their children's learning.

In Environment and Materials (how/when do assessments take place)

- ELA teachers—in collaboration with students—have primary control over the types of assessment data that are gathered about students, and how these data are analyzed and interpreted and most important, used in any decision-making process.
- ELA teachers have time during the school day to develop, interpret, and use assessment information to guide their planning.
- ELA teachers feel a sense of "spaciousness" with time and creativity to work with students.
- ELA teachers select their own assessment programs from various options, and/or create their own.
- ELA teachers work with a steady stream of low-stakes assessment of day-to-day learning, rather than decoding high stakes "end point" assessment numbers. This stream of data informs differentiated practice.
- ELA teacher study groups have assessment conversations focused on "significant" learning—learning that is significant in both the in-school and out-of-school lives of students, as well as what can be done better.
- Classroom assessments developed by teachers feed directly into district assessments—are an integral part of how the district establishes the effectiveness of its programs.
- Assessment practices embrace diversity in terms of learning styles, rates and routes of learning, and languages for learning. "One size fits all" assessments are not used by schools or imposed by legislators and policymakers.
- Assessment practices are well integrated with instruction and produce a stream of feedback that is useful to teachers in planning learning engagements. This integration eliminates a separate time for "test prep."
- Where tests with writing prompts are used, students have an opportunity to identify a range of interests or matters that they consider themselves to have expertise in, and are then be presented with prompts designed to match these interests (so that they can write about what they know, rather than an issue or subject that means nothing to them).

- All student writing, including college entrance exams, are evaluated by knowledgeable humans rather than scored by machines.
- Literacy assessments are situated in the classroom learning context and will help stakeholders focus on strengths, areas of concern, goals to improve, and actions to be taken. Assessments are only valid to the extent that they help students learn.
- Assessments include both content-specific goals as well as "habits of mind" and assessment of growth in "learning how to learn."

In Student Impact

- Students value assessment and have a better sense of why it's important (for learning) and why and how it works.
- Students participate in ongoing, multiple, authentic means of assessment of their learning, as they learn to be self-assessors.
- Students participate in and/or lead learning conferences about their work.
- Students monitor and assess their own learning with guidance.
- Classroom assessment data are used to inform others about the learning success of students and schools.
- All stakeholders contribute to decisions about how their schools will be judged.

These two documents have been synthesized into a white paper jointly developed and published by NCTE and the Council of Writing Program Administrators (WPA) provided below.

NCTE-WPA White Paper on Writing Assessment in Colleges and Universities

Adopted by the NCTE Executive Committee, April 2008 and the Council of Writing Program Administrators, February 2008. National Council of Teachers of English and Council of Writing Program Administrators. All rights reserved.

The National Council of Teachers of English and the Council of Writing Program Administrators offer this statement, a white paper, on writing assessment in postsecondary education. This white paper is meant to help teachers, administrators, and other stakeholders articulate the general positions, values, and assumptions on writing assessment that both the National Council of Teachers of English and the Council of Writing Program Administrators jointly endorse. What follows is an articulation of common understandings and general agreements in the membership of both organizations on the following:

- The connections among language, literacy, and writing assessment
- The principles of effective writing assessment
- The appropriate, fair, and valid use of writing assessment
- The role and importance of reliability in writing assessment

Connections: Language, Literacy, and Writing Assessment

Writing instruction and literacy education at all levels are formal ways in which societies build citizens, and in which citizens develop reading and communication behaviors and competencies in order to participate in various communities. Learning to write better involves engaging in the processes of drafting, reading, and revising; in dialogue, reflections, and formative feedback with peers and teachers; and in formal instruction and imitative activities. A preponderance of research argues that literacy and its teaching are socially contextualized and socially constructed dynamics, evolving as people, exigency, context, and other factors change. The varied language competencies and experiences with which students come to the classroom can sometimes conflict with what they are taught or told to value in school. The assessment of writing, therefore, must account for these contextual and social elements of writing pedagogy and literacy.

Principles of Effective Writing Assessment

The principles of effective writing assessment that can take the form of classroom tests and grades or extracurricular exams measuring student writing ability are highly contextual, and should be adapted or modified in accordance with local needs, issues, purposes, and concerns of stakeholders. These assessments function across large-scale and classroom contexts and are used to make important decisions about students, curriculum, and teachers. Generally, there is agreement about the following principles that tend to be a part of effective, meaningful, and responsible writing assessment:

- Writing assessment should place priority on the improvement of teaching and learning.
- Writing assessment responds to student, teacher, institutional, and other stakeholder needs. It should be used to foster environments for student learning. In placement testing, this

25

principle might demand that administrators consider the local classroom conditions students will be entering after they have been placed into a writing course, or the places in the local communities from which students come.

- Writing assessment should demonstrate that students communicate effectively.
- The effectiveness of student performance should be connected to criteria relevant to the educational decisions the assessment is designed to facilitate. For example, in placement testing, student performance should indicate a readiness for the curriculum of the course in which the student is placed. In exit testing, student performance should indicate the completion of course goals and objectives and a readiness to write for the next course or courses in the curriculum. We acknowledge that writing assessment must communicate to a variety of stakeholders the essence of what we want students to learn and the evidence of such learning.
- Writing assessment should provide the foundation for data-driven, or evidence-based, decision making.
- In some cases, assessment is designed to improve student performance, and in others to improve teaching and curricula. The purposes for assessment differ depending on the desired results of the assessment project. Programs may assess end products of a student's semester-long work to consider how and whether that work demonstrates the outcomes for the course. Depending on the purpose of the assessment, results can be used to improve instruction at multiple points in the curriculum.
- Writing assessment should be informed by current scholarship and research in assessment.
- While writing assessment should be locally grown and implemented, those designing, implementing, and validating writing assessments should also stay informed of current developments in the fields of writing assessment, composition theory, and literacy studies. This means that those involved in writing assessment should be supported (financially and otherwise) to share and disseminate their own assessment and validation findings and work.
- Writing assessment should recognize diversity in language.
- The methods and language that teachers and administrators use to make decisions and engage students in writing, reading, responding, and revising activities should incorporate meaningfully the multiple values and ways of expressing knowledge by students present in the classroom and local communities. Assessments and the decisions made from them

26

should account for students' rights to their own languages (see the Guideline approved by the Conference on College Composition and Communication in 1974 and reaffirmed in 2003).

- Writing assessment should positively impact pedagogy and curriculum.
- Curriculum designers and teachers should attempt to understand and incorporate into instruction the ways in which the assessments can improve the curriculum and instruction in classrooms. Positive writing assessment takes into account the nature of writing as a social process and product, situated within particular contexts (e.g., classrooms or timed environments), and limited or shaped by these factors.
- Writing assessment should use multiple measures and engage multiple perspectives to make decisions that improve teaching and learning.
- These multiple measures and perspectives can include the use of several readers and the perspectives they bring to student texts. A single off-the-shelf or standardized test should never be used to make important decisions about students, teachers, or curriculum.
- Writing assessment should include appropriate input from and information and feedback for students.
- Students should have access to the goals, purposes, and scoring criteria for required assessments. Students should also receive appropriate feedback for any important decisions made about them.
- Writing assessment should be based on continuous conversations with as many stakeholders as possible.
- Developing, researching, and validating a writing assessment is a constant process, and one should expect the assessment, its results, and its products to change over time. Thus, it is important to have conversations about the assessment (e.g., dialogue about the features particular teachers notice in student portfolios in various courses).
- Writing assessment should encourage and expect teachers to be trusted, knowledgeable, and communicative.
- Teachers should be the primary agents in writing assessment, and therefore need to be continually educated in writing assessment, to engage in dialogue with one another locally, and to find ways to gain the trust of the other stakeholders. Additionally, other stakeholders should support teachers in their efforts to become more knowledgeable about writing assessment and to communicate to all stakeholders involved.

- Writing assessment should articulate and communicate clearly its values and expectations to all stakeholders, especially students and, if applicable, parents.
- Assessment should not be invisible, mysterious, or elusive to any stakeholders. There should be a variety of ways stakeholders can understand and be informed about the local writing assessment and its methods, findings, and products.

Appropriate, Fair, and Valid Use of Writing Assessment

The Appropriate use of writing assessment, whether in a classroom or large-scale context, means that it fits the context and decisions that will be made based on it. Appropriateness can also be understood as a measure of the decisions made. For example, when placing students into courses based on portfolio readings, one might ask—and measure in some way—how appropriate the decisions are (do students and teachers later find that the placements put students in the right places?). Appropriateness might also be considered regarding the kinds of evaluation/feedback provided, based on their purpose or use (e.g., grades, summative feedback, formative feedback, recorded audio responses, no responses, detailed annotations/marginalia, responses offered to the entire class and not individual students, etc.).

The Fair use of writing assessment is crucial, since it can be used to make important decisions about individuals. A concern for fairness should guard against any disproportionate social effects on any language minority group. Writing assessments that are used to make important decisions about individuals and the material and educational conditions that affect these individuals should provide an equal opportunity for students to understand the expectations, roles, and purposes of the assessment. For instance, if students have no recourse, or opportunities to respond to evaluations or judgments of their writing, or if they do not have any access to the criteria used to evaluate their writing or to the uses of the assessments of their writing, then those assessments may be unfair. Considering the fair use of power does not mean giving equal power to decide to all stakeholders in an assessment. It means all stakeholders should have as much power over the assessment as their particular roles and positions dictate they can have, considering the ethical and expedient administration of the assessment, and the purposes of judgments.

The Valid use of writing assessment decisions and evaluations is a complex and technical activity. "Validity refers to the degree to which evidence and theory support the interpretations of test scores entailed by proposed uses of tests" (American 9). Every use of an assessment requires a validation inquiry in which an argument is made that the theoretical understanding of the assessment and the evidence the assessment generates support the decisions being made on behalf of the assessment. For example, if we use any method to place students into first-year writing courses, we must provide evidence that students are being correctly placed and profit from the educational experience. Questions such as how well students learn in each course of the curriculum must be answered in order to validate placement decisions. This inquiry-driven, researched-based activity is a required part of the appropriate, fair, and valid use of writing assessment.

Reliable Assessment

A reliable assessment provides consistent results, no matter who conducts the assessment. Because writing assessment often involves more than one rater scoring student performances, it can also involve interrater reliability, a measure of the degree of consistency from one rater judgment to another. A student's score thus might depend upon the bias of the reader rather than upon the document or product being assessed. Attention to reliability is an integral part of any responsible validity argument.

Common Denominators

Having studied those documents, we see that they are underscored by some important common denominators which, we argue, serve as discussion points for, and as hallmarks of, valid, fair, and generative assessment. Collective wisdom and experience point to the things outlined below.

1. Assessment should take into account the ideas, interests, and expertise of stakeholders. This means including students, teachers, administrators, and other community members in the design, implementation, and examination of assessment practices. For example, in "Assessment without Angst" (2008), Susan Wells advises colleagues to "start small" by designing a sustainable pilot project. She adds that "Such a pilot project helps faculty members see assessment as an extension of normal reflection on teaching; it helps a department identify resources in the institution for doing more ambitious projects" (p. 15).
2. Project design should be grounded in, and informed by, exemplary and evolving research in assessment. Insights gleaned from that research should inform the questions used to frame the assessment and the methods used to undertake investigations of those questions.

3. Assessment should attend to language diversity. That involves considering the relationships among students' language backgrounds and literacy practices. It also informs the framing of the study and the ways in which "data" and "outcomes" are defined and analyzed.
4. While assessment should respond to institutional context and to programmatic mission, it should not be unilaterally encompassed by, or tethered to, them. Issues of transferability and replication should be considered. Key questions are: How and what can faculty and schools learn from assessments conducted at their own schools and at other institutions? What can be learned from assessment practices that can help us understand how students are best taught?
5. Assessment should use multiple measures (e.g., primary trait scoring, holistic reading, portfolios) and analyze multiple artifacts of student writing. It is not enough to focus exclusively on students' formal, school-sponsored writing. Studying students' self-sponsored literacy practices reveals important facets of contemporary communication that examining only essayistic or research-based writing do not.
6. In classrooms where students write with contemporary technologies, assessment should study texts composed in, and read on, new media. Those conducting assessment should consider the media in which texts are created and circulated (e.g., wikis, blogs, web sites, video-sharing sites) and develop criteria that is responsive and pertinent to those mediums. That means designing questions that pay attention to evolving technologies, genres, and definitions of texts. This especially includes the self-sponsored, and often public, writing that many students do.
7. Assessment inquiry and findings should take into account the contexts in which learning take place. These contexts include, but are not limited to, pedagogical approach, delivery venue (physical and online classroom, writing center), curriculum, teacher preparation and mentoring, placement, and class size. Valuable information about situated assessment activities can be found online at CompPile at http://comppile.org/search/comppile_main_search.php and the WAC (writing-across-the-curriculum) Clearinghouse at http://wac.colostate.edu/.
8. Assessment should inform teaching and learning by incorporating regular opportunities for reflection and action based on processes and findings. For instance, students, teachers, and administrators should be given significant opportunities to reflect on their learning and on their work, and to explain whether and how well the assessment projects and processes are supporting their best work. As Beth Kalikoff (2007) argues, "The act of assessment is invariably rhetorical because it involves written or oral articulation of a judgment" and "interdisciplinary assessment that uses a mosaic of methodologies and emerges from shifting social, political, and cultural contexts—can play a valuable role in teaching and learning across the curriculum" (p. 95).

9. Assessment should evince transparency in its delineation of goals, roles, and processes. That is, those designing and implementing assessments should be able to define the questions that interest them, and explain their rationale for asking them. Those conducting assessments should explicate the thinking behind the terms in which their questions are framed, the methods they are using to investigate those questions, the language and genres in which they will memorialize and disseminate their findings, and the actions they envision taking as a result of those findings.

10. Colleagues should ensure that that the *terms* used in assessment projects are subject to the same critical discussion as the *processes* and the results themselves. In practical terms, that means working collaboratively with colleagues to define and delineate the issues, problems, strategies, and goals. Those who introduce and frame the project should take care to explain why change is sought and seen (e.g., "constructed") as vital and necessary. That means:

   - explaining why and how samples and assessment methods were selected;
   - defining performance criteria and the writing where they will be examined (e.g., specific, repeated, rehearsed, impromptu, reflective writing);
   - explaining why and how these criteria and study samples are appropriate; and
   - making sure that terms are not just inherited and deployed by rote. Subject them to critical discussion. Such scrutiny should be put to words like: *feedback, implementation, local, discipline-specific, abilities, data, samples, authentic, judgment, experience, learning, information, resources, value, validity, reliability, performance, situated, transferable, measurement, skills,* and *proficiency.*

The goal is develop coherent and shared, if variously contested, definitions of key concepts and terms.

11. Those who conduct assessment should design and employ systematic processes (informed by research, programmatic, and institutional self-study) to ensure that proper preparation, controls, and instruments are incorporated and evaluated. Viable assessment does not just import models uncontested because someone influential on campus has read or heard about them in or at a prominent venue, or because one's peer institutions have profitably used that model.

12. Assessment should contribute to a program's growth, history, health, and efficacy. The purpose is not just to observe, scrutinize, and judge. For example, assessment can pertain to institutional research and to the allocation of resources. Some questions might be: What should change? What is working well now? What could work even better with a sustained infusion of resources?

13. Because human beings write to and for other human beings, writing assessment should be conducted by human readers, not machines.
14. Conducting responsible assessment means recognizing and valuing colleagues' input, especially their feelings of vulnerability and expressions of resistance. It is important to find out from where, philosophically and pedagogically, that resistance emanates. The task is then to view disagreement not as an obstacle to assessment, but as a viable and critical lens through which to view and understand it. To that end, those conducting assessment should seek collegial involvement and reward participants' investment. They should take seriously the concerns, qualifications, and fears of colleagues without labeling or dismissing those individuals as paranoid, naïve, or self-interested. All phases of assessment (from preparatory to reflective), should address questions like: Who is made vulnerable? Who might feel that way? What is their tolerance for, and experience with, risk? What are their definitions of successful, valid assessments? What are your own, your institution's, and your discipline's ideas about valid assessment?

Conclusion

We believe that, when mindful of these points, participants can ensure that assessment becomes an ongoing (rather than zenithal) project that is inclusive of diverse perspectives, scrupulous in its concern for accuracy, and cognizant of its own specificity. Valid assessment also cultivates useful data that offers discernible value to community members and offers "rolling returns" to participants and their programs. At its best, assessment is cognizant of, and contributory to, an institutional and a disciplinary database that can help students, teachers, and administrators learn more about the work they endeavor to do.

To that end, when reflecting on "the culture of assessment" we recommend thinking of *culture* as a verb, not just as a noun. To culture something is to be intentional, invitational, ethical, and participatory. Moreover, it involves being careful and communicative. The activity is a deliberate group effort in which participants are discerning about, and accountable for, their plans, roles, and responsibilities. If participants are really invested (and vested) community members, then no one is entitled or exempt. Thus, one would not say, hear, or imply that "you produce the data and I/we/they will interpret it." Within an evolving culture of knowledge and discernment, assessment can become a call to leadership because it teaches us ways of triangulating responsibly and productively with community members in order to frame the issues, discern the stakes, and give and receive valuable direction and support. The common denominators among the documents we have cited indicate a shared desire to conduct assessment with probity, skill, conscience, and accuracy. We suggest that culturing assessment will help participants do just that because it invites them to reflect on their goals, attend to language diversity, and give serious thought to evolving media as well as the texts and literate activities they sponsor and encourage. Most of all, culturing assessment reminds us that whatever it is we think we "see," find, and notice can tell us something important about what we may be missing and ignoring.

REFERENCES

American Diploma Project/Achieve, Incorporated. (2006). *Ready or not: Creating a high school diploma that counts.* Retrieved July 20, 2009, from http://www.achieve.org/node/552

Broad, B. (2003). *What we really value: Beyond rubrics in teaching and assessing writing.* Logan, UT: Utah State University Press.

Conference on College Composition and Communication. (2006). *Writing assessment: A position statement.* Retrieved July 20, 2009, from http://www.ncte.org/cccc/resources/positions/writingassessment

Huot, B. (2002). *(Re)Articulating writing assessment for teaching and learning.* Logan, UT: Utah State University Press.

Kalikoff, B. (2007). The new assessment and the new rhetoric. In S. E. Thomas (Ed.), *What is the new rhetoric?* (pp. 94–103). Newcastle, UK: Cambridge Scholars Publishing.

Lynne, P. (2004). *Coming to terms: A theory of writing assessment.* Logan, UT: Utah State University Press.

McLeod, S. (2007). *Writing program administration.* West Lafayette, IN: Parlor Press.

National Council of Teachers of English. (2004). *Framing statements on assessment.* Retrieved July 20, 2009, from http://www.ncte.org/positions/statements/assessmentframingst

National Council of Teachers of English and Council of Writing Program Administrators. (2008). *NCTE-WPA white paper on writing assessment in colleges and universities.* Retrieved July 20, 2009, from http://wpacouncil.org/whitepaper

Palomba, C. A., & Banta, T. W. (1999). *Assessment essentials: Planning, implementing, and improving assessment in higher education.* San Francisco: Jossey-Bass.

U.S. Department of Education. (2006). *A test of leadership: Charting the future of U.S. higher education.* Retrieved July 20, 2009, from http://www.ed.gov/about/bdscomm/list/hiedfuture/reports/final-report.pdf

Wells, S. (2008). Assessment without angst. *ADE Bulletin, 144,* 14–16.

White, E. (1984). Holisticism. *College Composition and Communication, 35,* 400–409.

Yancey, K. (1999). Looking back as we look forward: Historicizing writing assessment. *College Composition and Communication, 50,* 483–503.

CHAPTER 3

WHAT COLLEGE WRITING TEACHERS VALUE AND WHY IT MATTERS

Peggy O'Neill and Cindy Moore
Loyola College in Maryland

Much of the stress over college-level assessments of writing these days can be traced to misunderstandings between those charged with collecting and reporting data at the university level and those responsible for these activities at the departmental or program level. Institutional research personnel, trained in areas such as psychometrics or quantitative research methods, though sensitive to disciplinary differences, often have trouble seeing the assessment landscape the way faculty in the humanities see it. At the same time, writing administrators and faculty, who typically get their professional training in English departments, struggle with research methodologies and reporting conventions that seem oriented toward the social sciences. Since we have written elsewhere about what writing-program administrators and faculty can do to anticipate and address the unfamiliar perspectives of people outside their departments,[1] we will focus this chapter on what people trained outside of English departments and, perhaps, outside the humanities, need to know about writing faculty in order to support assessments that satisfy the needs of both universities and writing-based programs.

How We Look at Writing

For writing faculty, especially those with advanced course work and/or degrees in Composition and Rhetoric, writing is a complex activity that both fosters and reflects thinking.[2] In fact, for us, writing is so intertwined with thinking that, as teachers and researchers, we cannot easily focus on a particular aspect of writing (whether that be idea development, organization, or syntax) without acknowledging the impact of cognitive development, learning style, and/or authorial intent. That is, when considering a piece of writing, we tend to think not just about what is there, on paper, but what the words may tell us about the writer.

Though we understand that writing is, in many ways, an individual enterprise, requiring personal engagement with subjects, ideas, and words, we also see it as

---

[1] The article "Creating a Culture of Assessment in Writing Programs and Beyond," by Moore, O'Neill, and Huot is currently in press.

[2] See McCutchen, Teske, and Bankston (2008) for a review of the research on writing and cognition.

highly social. We assume that writing, like any act of communication, is context-dependent—influenced by who the reader or perceived audience is, what the purpose is, and the particular social conditions in which it occurs. Meaning-making depends not only on the relationship between the writer and the subject matter, but on the relationship between the writer and reader—what James Moffett (1968) terms the "I-you" relationship. In other words, the meaning of a text does not reside in the text itself—or even in the writer himself/herself—but in the interaction of the writer, the text, the reader and the context. Similarly, the "whole" of the text is not equal to the sum of its discrete parts, but is, rather, the result of how the reader puts the parts together to make meaning from the text.

This rhetorical view is supported by scholarship and research in reading over the last several decades, which shows how readers construct a text's meaning, relying on individual experiences and knowledge (Nelson, 2008) and/or processes of interpretation valued by a particular discourse group or community. This perspective is also supported by the work of sociolinguists such as James Paul Gee (1996) who argue that the meaning of language cannot be determined outside of context. Gee explains that language and literacy only make sense within "Discourses," which include ways of behaving, valuing, thinking, believing, speaking, reading and writing (p. viii). Understanding and interpreting language requires knowledge beyond the linguistic code (letters, words, grammar). It is impossible to communicate in a decontextualized way because "all communication is rooted in sociocultural identities and based on shared knowledge and understandings" (Gee, 1996, pp.156–157). In other words, we should not look at a word or sentence outside the particular situation because meaning can only be determined in context. For example, a simple question like "Did you clean your room this morning?" could have multiple meanings depending on many other factors surrounding its utterance. Who is asking the question—and to whom? A parent to a child? To a teenager? A sibling to another sibling? A friend to a friend? A Resident Advisor to a college student? A police officer to a suspect? What is meant by "clean"? Pick up the clothes on the floor? Take out the trash? Vacuum and dust? Scrub the floor? And which "room" is being referenced? Bedroom? Dorm room? Hospital room? Work room? The question may also be functioning as something besides a request for information: a reminder to a child from a parent; a polite form of a command; or something else depending on the tone of the utterance, when it is spoken, where it is uttered, and a multitude of other factors. As native language speakers, we navigate these issues every day as we interpret meanings based on the context of the language act, typically without consciously thinking about it.

Additionally, in the school setting, research shows that developing language and literacy competencies requires the acquisition of not just cognitive skills but also the social processes for "demonstrating knowledgeability"(Cook-Gumperz, 2006, p. 3; also see, for example, Cazden, 2001; Gee, 1996; Heath, 1983). School discourse often has established protocols and expectations, so effective communication requires understanding those discourse conventions. For instance, Heath (1983) found that in the communities she studied, elementary students from working-class African American families did not understand how questioning functioned in school. Typically, teachers ask questions for which they already know the answers, as a method of evaluating students' understanding of the material being taught. In Heath's subjects' home cultures, however, questioning functioned differently—as requests for unknown information, based on the assumption that one would not ask a question if one knew the answer. Because the students were confused and did not understand the conventions and discourses associated with school, teachers often misinterpreted the students' responses to their questions.

In writing assessment, these same kinds of misunderstandings can occur. Sandra Murphy (2007) summarized several studies that demonstrated how misfires can happen in writing assessment when tests are not sensitive to the particular students and their context. She relates one example, published by Keech (1982), who reports on problems with a familiar prompt that asked students to write a letter to the principal about a problem in the school. Keech (1982) explains that at one school, students responded to the prompt with laughter, complaints, and even refusals to write because they did not think the principal would listen to anything they said. At another school, the students struggled because they could not find any problem in the school to write about. This prompt misfired because the particular climate and culture of these schools made the given rhetorical situation seem unimaginable to students who did not understand the discourse conventions of testing and, thus, took the task literally. Murphy (2007) argues that these kinds of misunderstandings are more likely to occur for students with linguistic and/or cultural backgrounds different from the dominant or mainstream culture (including non-native speakers of English and international students).

This basic theoretical tenet about the sociality of literacy is also supported by dominant theories concerning genre. As rhetorician Carolyn Miller (1984) has argued, genre is best defined not as a fixed set of conventions but as a "social action." From this perspective, genres are complex, situated language acts, not pre-determined formats or structures that exist in isolation from the motives and expectations of writers and readers in a given communicative context. In addition, studies reported by scholars such as Ruth and Murphy (1988), and Witte and Cherry (1994) demonstrate that both writing processes and the quality of the product change as the writing task is varied. In other words, a writer's performance is not stable across genres and tasks; multiple writing samples that represent multiple tasks are needed to determine writing competency. Writing teachers familiar with such scholarship realize that students need a variety of writing assignments that vary in terms of audience, purpose, and genre so that they (the students) can develop the breadth and depth needed to satisfy the diverse writing tasks they will encounter in school and beyond.

Finally, for writing teachers and scholars, writing development is closely linked with the development of other abilities, including reading, listening, and speaking. It is no coincidence, for example, that strong writers are often strong readers, as research by Witte (1983) and Shanahan and Lomax (1986) demonstrates. While it is true that some people may be born with a natural inclination toward writing, everyone can develop his or her writing abilities unless a mental impairment interferes with cognition or neurological processes. Like all language development, writing is best learned by engaging in authentic communication activities—not decontextualized drills and skill exercises. It is an ability that can be strengthened through continuous practice, useful feedback, regular reading, and discussion. And, like development of other skills, writing is fostered in an environment that allows for risk taking but that ultimately supports high expectations.

How We Look at Writers

Just as writing faculty see the human act of writing as complex, so too do we try to see writers in all of their complexity. Writing development, we believe, depends very heavily not only on cognitive development, but also on environmental factors such as the degree to which parents and teachers supported early childhood literacy activities including reading, speaking, and writing. In fact, as Deborah Brandt (1998) explains, the range of social influences on literacy learning is extensive, including "the people, institutions, materials, and motivations involved in the process" (p. 167). Within this framework of "literacy sponsorship," assessment can be considered a powerful literacy "agent," working to "enable, support, teach, model . . . recruit, suppress, or withhold literacy," in much the same way that the more obvious influences Brandt identifies (e.g., relatives, teachers, priests, supervisors) might work (pp. 166-167).

Consequently, tests, depending on their design and content, encourage the development of certain types of writers. For example, impromptu essay exams reward—and, therefore, encourage the development of—writers who are able to develop ideas and draft quickly, and who, without response or revision, can produce first drafts that are clear, concise, organized, and relatively correct. Based on the results of these writing assessments, student writers are labeled in static and one-dimensional ways—e.g., basic, developmental, standard, or honors. Writing teachers, however, prefer to highlight the multiplicity of positions student writers may occupy—a novice or basic writer in one situation may be considered a much more accomplished, experienced writer in other circumstances. Writing teachers also attempt to appreciate the particular experiences of individual writers. For example, though we may all agree that certain types of early childhood literacy experiences can be traced to parents' educational level and social class (see, for example, Heath, 1983), we also understand that individuals within those groups will develop and perform in ways uncharacteristic of the group as a whole. It is the acknowledgement of these individual differences that helps us meet the needs of all of our students—and not just specific groups of students.

How We Look at Writing Assessment, Generally

The way writing specialists look at writing assessment is informed by how we view writing and writers. This may seem a simple concept, but it is often not acknowledged by institutional research personnel who may see our resistance to top-down assessment directives as attempts to protect territory and autonomy, when, in most cases, it is a resistance based in the perception that these directives do not support our values.[3]

Because we view writing as a complex act, any assessment that simplifies writing—or boils it down to one element, such as mechanical correctness—will not fit with our values. This is why we resist any assessment mechanism that correlates writing ability with achievement on a multiple-choice grammar or usage test. For us, if the assessment does not involve students actually writing, in ways that will help them develop their thinking abilities and communication skills, then we will assume that it can not give us the information we need to make decisions about students and programs.

Similarly, since writing, from our perspective, is a rhetorical, and thus context-dependent activity, we will object to assessments that ask us to consider student writing out of the context in which it was written—or to consider one part of a text outside of the context of the full piece of writing. If we are charged with evaluating student writing ability or achievement, we generally prefer reading student texts holistically, as we would read any other piece of writing—and not assigning separate points or values to discrete aspects of texts. However, we also see value in analytic or primary trait scoring in certain situations such as when trying to identify the strengths and weaknesses of a program in meeting its outcomes.

Likewise, if the assessment calls for a single measure of writing ability, even if it is a writing sample, we will be wary of using it to make judgments about students and programs. Because writing is a complex activity, it cannot adequately be demonstrated by one measure—especially if that measure involves a timed activity—or one sample, as research demonstrates. This is why writing faculty promote the use of portfolios, whose contents are diverse (in terms of genre, purpose, and audience) and collected over time, as a way for students to more fully demonstrate their abilities and progress—and for us to better judge their capabilities.

Because, as writing teachers, we recognize the differences within groups of students, we resist assessments that will not help us teach the students who are at our particular schools and in our particular classrooms. If, for example, we are working with students who have a hard time quickly gathering their thoughts together and getting them down on paper, information gleaned from a timed writing exam will not help us teach these students. This is why we tend to argue for the right to design our own assessments that provide us with information about how our particular curriculum at our particular school is working for our students.

Which brings us to our last point: if the information gleaned through an assessment will not help us teach better, then we will not pay much attention to it.

---

[3] See Murphy and Yancey (2008) for a review of research on writing assessment. See Huot (2002) and White (1994) for an overview of writing assessment presented from the writing teacher's perspective.

How We Understand Key Assessment Concepts

We have observed that much of the tension over assessment is inspired by traditional assessment terminology and/or differing definitions of the terminology. First, it is important to know that people trained in the humanities often become uneasy when they are confronted with concepts and terms that are associated with social science research. Because of its complexity, writing cannot be researched—or measured—in the same way that physical traits such as height or weight might be measured. It is not easy to use control groups or to set up lab conditions in which the complex human act of writing can be separated from the human actor—or where the act or actor can be easily distinguished from influences outside of the immediate writing context. While we value many qualitative social science research methods for their ability to capture the dynamics of writing, we are less likely to endorse quantitative methods, especially if they lead to interpretations that over-simplify writers, writing, and teaching.

This preference for qualitative research methods translates to assessment. Because we are uncomfortable with objectivist, quantitative approaches to or perspectives on writing, we also feel uneasy about the terms associated with these approaches—terms like *validity* and *reliability*. In fact, some people in our field feel so strongly about the inappropriateness of using scientific terms to talk about writing that they are proposing ways of not using them. Patricia Lynne (2004) has proposed, for example, using more composition-friendly terms like *meaningfulness* and *ethics* instead of terms such as *validity* and *reliability*. While we do not advocate this particular position, we do think that much can be done to alleviate the tension caused over traditional assessment terminology. In fact, many writing assessment scholars, some within the college composition and rhetoric tradition and others in education, are working to integrate theories of writing and literacy with psychometric theories.

In the last decade writing assessment scholars in composition—most notably Huot (2002) and Broad (2003)—have looked to measurement scholars such as Lee Cronbach (1988), Samuel Messick (1989a, 1989b), and Pamela Moss (1992, 1994) for insights about validity that are aligned with our theories of writing. Validity, after all, is the critical concept in testing and assessment, as explained in the *Standards on Psychological and Educational Testing* (American Educational Research Organization, American Psychological Association, & National Council on Measurement in Education, 1999). Sometimes, however, the concept of validity is over-simplified in a way that not only makes it unpalatable to people who teach writing and administer writing programs but also misrepresents what measurement scholars and professional organizations actually support. For example, instead of discussing the validity of the test results in the particular situation, as the *Standards* (AERA, APA, & NCME, 1999) advocates, institutional testing personnel or representatives of testing companies will claim that a test is or is not "valid." At other times, psychometricians, often working for testing organizations, assert validity by demonstrating a correlation to another performance indicator such as grades or test results. However, validity as represented in the most recent issue of the

Standards (AERA, APA, & NCME, 1999) is a much richer and complex concept than measurement practitioners sometimes admit.

Writing teachers and scholars are more likely to accept explanations of validity and validity inquiry that acknowledge its complexity as well as its social and rhetorical aspects (e.g., Kane, 2006; Messick, 1989a, 1989b; Moss, 1992, 1994, 2007; Murphy, 2007; Shepard, 1993). Messick, for example, argued in the 1989 edition of *Educational Measurement* that validity is "an integrated evaluative judgment of the degree to which empirical evidence and theoretical rationales support the adequacy and appropriateness of inferences based on test scores and other modes of assessment" (1989b, p. 13). Michael T. Kane (2006), in the chapter on validity in the latest edition of *Educational Measurement,* also explains that validation addresses the use and consequences as well as the plausibility of the inferences and assumptions. He writes: "Validation focuses on interpretations, or meanings, and on decisions, which reflect values and consequence. Neither meanings nor values are easily reduced to formulas, literally or figuratively. . . ." (p. 18). In other words, validation is a complex concept that is not a property of the test itself and cannot be reduced to a statistical formula or correlation. As Messick (1989b), Kane (2006), and others agree, validity is usually considered along a continuum and not simply perceived in either/or (valid versus invalid) terms. Validation is also about using evidence to construct an argument, which draws on both empirical and theoretical evidence, about the interpretation of the assessment's results rather than a simple correlation to another measurement. These approaches to validity and validation, which are also supported by the latest edition of the *Standards* (AERA, APA, & NCME, 1999) and the work of measurement theorists, acknowledge the socially situated-ness of validity and, in effect, assessment design, use, and interpretation. Just as important, they coincide with the basic theoretical perspectives that writing teachers and scholars hold about language and literacy.

This approach to validity has implications for writing assessment. For example, Murphy (2007), drawing on the work of Messick (1989a, 1989b) and others, looks specifically at how validity, conceived in complex, context-sensitive terms, is threatened when culture and consequences are ignored in writing (and other literacy) assessments. Other writing assessment scholars, such as Huot (2002), Haswell (1998) and O'Neill (2003), show how a more nuanced sense of validity can be used to justify locally designed and implemented writing assessments in colleges and universities.

While validity is the critical concept in assessment, as the *Standards* (AERA, APA, & NCME, 1999) make clear, in writing assessment reliability often gets over-emphasized, sometimes at the expense of validity (Williamson, 1994). In writing assessment, reliability has tended to focus on consistency in the scoring of writing samples (Cherry & Meyer, 1993). In the mid-20th century, test developers focused on creating procedures that would produce reliable scores on timed impromptu essay exams (e.g., Diederich, French & Carlton, 1961; Godshalk, Swineford, & Coffman, 1966). Holistic scoring and primary trait scoring, which grew out of this work, have been popular methods of scoring writing, especially for standardized tests. While these procedures are accepted as methods for prompting scorers to agree on a score, the assumptions that inform them often do not make sense to writing specialists who are grounded in current theories of writing instruction and development. Scoring, after all, is not the same as reading. In fact, holistic scoring actually requires that the raters suppress their own individualized reading processes and interpretations and focus on sorting the texts. Research shows that raters do not necessarily agree on the reason for the scores and that other factors (such as background and experience) can influence their decisions (e.g., Huot, 1993; Pula & Huot 1993; Smith, 1993; Weigle, 2002). As teachers of writing, we are more interested in the rationale—the response a reader has to a text—than the score itself—because this is where we can address instructional needs of the student related to audience, purpose, and context.

Another reason we find holistic scoring troubling is that the same score may be assigned to two texts for very different reasons. So in terms of psychometric reliability, the scoring is reliable, but in practical terms, it is not very interesting or useful. Broad (1994) actually argues that the differences in readings provide important insights that should not be minimized or discouraged. Ignoring points of conflict among readers does not help writing instructors understand the needs of particular students or how to help individual students improve as writers (versus test-takers). At a programmatic level, it does not help us determine the strengths and weaknesses of the program because the information is too generic. While many writing specialists will agree to use a holistically scored impromptu writing sample in some situations, it is usually seen as a compromise and not based on a belief that the process will yield truly helpful information.

For most writing instructors, reliability is not the primary rationale for determining or designing a writing assessment. The most "reliable" method, after all, may not produce very useful information as we have already discussed. Additionally, Cherry and Meyer (1993) demonstrate that many claims about reliability associated with writing assessments are questionable because of the methods used to determine reliability. Finally, reliability does not guarantee the validity of the results and interpretations, which should ultimately improve teaching and learning. Moss (1994) argues that "continued reliance on reliability, defined as quantification of consistency among independent observations, requires a significant level of standardization" (p. 6). However, according to Moss (1994), less standardized forms of assessment are often preferable "because certain intellectual activities" cannot be documented through standardized assessments (p. 6). Writing specialists tend to see writing as this kind of complex activity that does not lend itself very well to standardization. Moss (1994) suggests that we look beyond psychometric theories and practices in cases where acceptable reliability rates are difficult or impossible to achieve. She recommends a hermeneutic approach, explaining how this methodology would work:

> A hermeneutic approach to assessment would involve holistic, integrative interpretations of collected performances that seek to understand the whole in light of its parts, that privilege readers who are most knowledgeable about the context in which the assessment occurs, and that ground those

interpretations not only in textual and contextual evidence available, but also in a rational debate among the community of interpreters. (1994, p. 7)

Key features of this approach include the recognition of disagreement or difference in interpretations as evaluators bring their expertise and experience to bear on the work. Through the debate and discussion, individual evaluators may change their position or interpretation with the final decision the result of consensus or compromise. An example of this approach is Washington State University's Junior Writing Portfolio, which relies on the judgment of experienced writing instructors to make the decisions, and it encourages discussion and debate especially for difficult cases (Haswell, 2001). This approach reinforces our commitment to critical dialogue and desire to meet the needs of individual students. Because of these types of values, writing teachers are likely to agree with Moss (1994) who reminds readers that reliability and objectivity are no guarantors of truth and that they can, in fact, work against "critical dialogue" and can lead "to procedures that attempt to exclude, to the extent possible, the values and contextualized knowledge of the reader and that foreclose on dialogue among readers about specific performances being evaluated" (p. 9).

More recently, Parkes (2007) contends that reliability should be considered as argument—in much the same way that validation involves constructing an argument. In this view, the focus is not on the methods of gathering reliability evidence (for example, calculating co-efficients and standards of errors) but on the values that reliability represents—accuracy, dependability, stability, consistency, and precision (Parkes, 2007, p. 2). Finding appropriate methods for gathering evidence as well as the appropriate level of reliability needed, according to Parkes (2007), would depend on the purpose and context of an assessment, including how the scores are to be used. Like Moss's (1994) discussion of reliability, Parkes's (2007) position is more closely aligned with what writing faculty value and how we approach assessment.

How to Negotiate Diverse Perspectives

We are writing this article because writing is frequently used across the university in general education assessments as well as in more focused situations from placement into the first-year writing curriculum to assessment of majors as they near graduation. In many of these situations, composition and rhetoric faculty are either not involved or must work with IR staff (as well as other faculty or staff) to design, plan, execute and evaluate writing assessments. In attempting to work together, confusion, resentment, and frustration often result because of a lack of understanding—maybe even a lack of respect—of the multitude of perspectives and expertise that each party brings to the table. After all, while many composition and rhetoric faculty are not experts in writing assessment, they are experts in writing practice and theory. As Messick (1989a, 1989b) explains, in order for an assessment to truly be valid, we must take this kind of information into account—not only as we design assessments, but as we interpret data, use results, and reflect on the implications of our decisions.

We all can do some concrete things to create a situation in which all of us get what we want: assessments that generate data that we can use to improve our programs and show that our students are learning what we say they are learning. Faculty in English can start by articulating for all participants their beliefs and assumptions about writing and learning to write, the learning goals for courses and programs, and the evaluation criteria for student writing—and by listening to the other institutional participants with thoughtfulness and respect. Those responsible for college-level and university-level assessment can help by first becoming aware of the reasons for resistance, outlined in this article, re-thinking how they present requests for assessment data and reports, and perhaps reading some key articles on assessment from our discipline. It can help, for example, to consider whether institutional research documents and directions are as sensitive to disciplinary differences as personnel may think. Perhaps the presentation of the materials does privilege a scientific or social-scientific perspective when viewed by someone coming from a humanities perspective. By anticipating questions and concerns from humanities faculty, acknowledging the legitimacy of differing views, and patiently explaining how university requirements can be met through various types of assessments, IR personnel will be in a better position to support faculty as they take on the difficult work of evaluating the success of their curricula. Often there is room for compromise and negotiation if all parties come to the table with open minds, respecting the different perspectives and approaches each brings with them.

REFERENCES

American Educational Research Association, American Psychological Association, & National Council on Measurement in Education. (1999). *Standards for educational and psychological testing*. Washington, DC: American Educational Research Association.

Brandt, D. (1998). Sponsors of literacy. *College Composition and Communication, 49*, 164–185.

Broad, B. (2003). *What we really value: Beyond rubrics in teaching and assessing writing*. Logan, UT: Utah State University Press.

Broad, R. L. (1994). Portfolio scoring: A "contradiction of terms." In L. Black, D. A. Daiker, J. Sommers, & G. Stygall (Eds.), *New directions in portfolio assessment: Reflective practice, critical theory, and large-scale scoring* (pp. 263–277). Portsmouth, NH: Boynton/Cook.

Cazden, C. (2001). *Classroom discourse: The language of teaching and learning* (2nd ed.). Portsmouth, NH: Heinemann.

Cherry, R., & Meyer, P. (1993). Reliability issues in holistic assessment. In M. M. Williamson, & B. A. Huot (Eds.), *Validating holistic scoring for writing assessment: Theoretical and empirical foundations* (pp. 109–141). Cresskill, NJ: Hampton Press.

Cook-Gumperz, J. (2006). *The social construction of literacy* (2nd ed.). Cambridge, UK: Cambridge University Press.

Cronbach, L. J. (1988) Five perspectives on validity argument. In H. Wainer, & H. Braun (Eds.), *Test validity* (pp. 3–17). Hillsdale, NJ: Erlbaum.

Diederich, P. B., French, J. W., & Carlton, S. T. (1961). *Factors in judgments of writing quality* (RB No. 61-15 ED 002 172). Princeton, NJ: Educational Testing Service.

Gee, J. P. (1996). *Social linguistics and literacies: Ideology in discourses* (2nd ed.). London: Taylor & Francis.

Godshalk, F. I., Swineford, F., & Coffman, W. E. (1966). *Measurement of writing ability* (CEEB RM No. 6). Princeton, NJ: Educational Testing Service.

Haswell, R. H. (1998). Multiple inquiry into the validation of writing tests. *Assessing Writing, 5*, 89–110.

Haswell, R. H., (Ed.). (2001). *Beyond outcomes: Assessment and instruction within a university writing*. Greenwich, CT: Ablex.

Heath, S. B. (1983). *Ways with words: Language, life, and work in communities and classrooms*. Cambridge, UK: Cambridge University Press.

Huot, B. (2002). *(Re)Articulating writing assessment for teaching and learning*. Logan, UT: Utah State University Press.

Huot, B. A. (1993). The influence of holistic scoring procedures on reading and rating student essays. In M. M. Williamson, & B. A. Huot (Eds.), *Validating holistic scoring for writing assessment: Theoretical and empirical foundations* (pp. 206–236). Cresskill, NJ: Hampton Press.

Kane, M. T. (2006). Validity. In R. L. Brennan (Ed.), *Educational measurement* (4th ed.). Westport, CT: American Council on Education, Praeger Series on Higher Education.

Keech, C. (1982). Practices in designing writing test prompts: Analysis and recommendations. In J. R. Gray, & L. P. Ruth (Eds.), *Properties of writing tasks: A study of alternative procedures for holistic writing assessment* (pp. 132–214). Berkeley, CA: University of California, Graduate School of Education, Bay Area Writing Project. (ERIC Document Reproduction Service No. ED230576).

Lynne, P. (2004). *Coming to terms: A theory of writing assessment.* Logan, UT: Utah State University Press.

McCutchen, D., Teske, P., & Bankston, C. (2008). Writing and cognition: Implications of the cognitive architecture for learning to write and writing to learn. In C. Bazerman (Ed.), *Handbook of research on writing: History, society, school, individual, text* (pp. 451–470). New York: Lawrence Erlbaum Associates.

Messick, S. (1989a). Meaning and value in test validation: The science and ethics of assessment. *Educational Researcher, 18*(2), 5–11.

Messick, S. (1989b). Validity. In R. Linn (Ed.), *Educational measurement* (3rd ed.) (pp. 13–103). Washington, DC: American Council on Education and National Council on Measurement in Education.

Miller, C. R. (1984) Genre as social action. *Quarterly Journal of Speech, 70*(2), 151–167.

Moffett, J. (1968). *Teaching the universe of discourse—a rationale for English teaching used in a student-centered language arts curriculum.* Boston: Houghton Mifflin.

Moore, C., O'Neill, P., & Huot, B. (in press). Creating a culture of assessment in writing programs and beyond. *College Composition and Communication.*

Moss, P. A. (1992). Shifting conceptions of validity in educational measurement: Implications for performance assessment. *Review of Educational Research, 62*(3), 229–258.

Moss, P. A. (1994). Can there be validity without reliability? *Educational Researcher, 23*(4), 5–12.

Moss, P. A. (2007). Joining the dialogue on validity theory in educational research. In P. O'Neill (Ed.), *Blurring boundaries: Developing writers, researchers, and teachers* (pp. 91–100). Cresskill, NJ: Hampton.

Murphy, S. (2007). Culture and consequences: The canaries in the coal mine. *Research in the Teaching of English, 42*(2), 228–244.

Murphy, S., & Yancey, K. B. (2008). Construct and consequence: Validity in writing assessment. In C. Bazerman (Ed.), *Handbook of research on writing: History, society, school, individual, text* (pp. 365–386). New York: Lawrence Erlbaum Associates.

Nelson, N. (2008). The reading-writing nexus in discourse studies. In C. Bazerman (Ed.) *Handbook of research on writing: History, society, school, individual, text* (pp. 435–450). New York: Lawrence Erlbaum Associates.

O'Neill, P. (2003). Moving beyond holistic scoring through validity inquiry. *Journal of Writing Assessment, 1,* 47–65.

Parkes, J. (2007). Reliability as argument. *Educational Measurement: Issues and Practice, 26*(4), 2–10.

Pula, J., & Huot, B. A. (1993). A model of background influences on holistic raters. In M. M. Williamson, & B. A. Huot (Eds.), *Validating holistic scoring for writing assessment: Theoretical and empirical foundations* (pp. 237–265). Cresskill, NJ: Hampton Press.

Ruth, L., & Murphy, S. (1988). *Designing writing tasks for the assessment of writing.* Norwood, NJ: Ablex.

Shanahan, T., & Lomax, R. G. (1986). An analysis and comparison of theoretical models of the reading-writing relationship. *Journal of Educational Psychology, 78,* 116–123.

Shepard, L. A. (1993). Evaluating test validity. *Review of Educational Research in Education 19,* 405–450.

Smith, W. L. (1993). Assessing the reliability and adequacy of using holistic scoring of essays as a college composition placement technique. In M. M. Williamson, & B. A. Huot (Eds.), *Validating holistic scoring for writing assessment: Theoretical and empirical foundations* (pp. 142–205). Cresskill, NJ: Hampton Press.

Weigle, S. C. (2002). *Assessing writing.* Cambridge, UK: Cambridge University Press.

White, E. M. (1994). *Teaching and assessing writing* (2nd ed.). San Francisco: Jossey-Bass.

Williamson, M. M. (1994). The worship of efficiency: Untangling theoretical and practical considerations in writing assessment. *Assessing Writing, 1*(2), 147–174.

Witte, S. (1983). Topical structure and revision: An exploratory study. *College Composition and Communication, 34,* 313–341.

Witte, S., & Cherry, R. (1994). Think-aloud protocols, protocol analysis, and research design: An exploration of the influence of writing tasks on writing processes. In P. Smagorinsky (Ed.), *Speaking and writing: Reflection on research methodologies* (pp. 20–54). Thousand Oaks, CA: Sage.

CHAPTER 4

MERGING A CULTURE OF WRITING WITH A CULTURE OF ASSESSMENT:

EMBEDDED, DISCIPLINE-BASED WRITING ASSESSMENT

Terry Myers Zawacki
and
Karen M. Gentemann

George Mason University

It is no secret that the federal government, state governments, regional accrediting agencies, and specialized accrediting agencies all believe that assessment will address the apparent demand for "accountability." Never mind that "assessment" is not the equivalent of "testing," but is rather a philosophy about education, albeit accompanied by an emerging consensus of what constitutes good methodology and best practice. The philosophy, simply stated, is that student learning is the purpose of teaching and that much of student learning can be demonstrated, and, further, if a good assessment is conducted, corrections or changes can be made to enhance the learning experience for students. Central to assessment is the concept that faculty own the curriculum. The individual instructor in his or her classroom does not stand alone, however. Program faculty must establish coherence in the curriculum by agreeing upon the contribution of each part and sharing a sense of direction and purpose for the student and the learning experiences.

So, it is ironic that those who are calling for accountability are championing assessment, and those who have so much to gain from it are so much less enthusiastic. The purpose of this article, then, is to demonstrate that, given an approach developed by faculty to improve the educational experience for students, assessment can lead to greater understanding among faculty about their goals and expectations for student writers, which provides, in turn, an impetus to improve teaching and student learning.

George Mason University (or Mason), home to both of the co-authors, is situated in Fairfax, Virginia, a state that very early on embraced the idea that assessment could be used for improvement purposes while also providing information to state legislators and to the public that would demonstrate that publicly supported institutions were fulfilling their obligations to its citizens. In 1985, Virginia legislators directed SCHEV, the State Council of Higher Education for Virginia, to investigate means to measure student achievement. Shortly thereafter, SCHEV directed Virginia's public institutions to develop plans for assessing institution-defined student outcomes. More than a decade later, in 2001, SCHEV issued new guidelines that required all institutions to develop

49

definitions of six specific learning competencies and plans for assessing them, with reporting to begin two years later.

What made both mandates unusual, if not unique, is that both allowed each institution to develop its own assessment plans; the mandate, then, was designed with great flexibility so that plans could match assessment procedures with institutional missions and cultures. There were no demands for standardized testing and no one method was identified as the norm for the state. Even when the State Council determined that assessment in the state needed to be refocused on six competencies—written communication, oral communication, information technology, scientific reasoning, quantitative reasoning, and critical thinking—SCHEV continued to allow institutional flexibility in defining these skills and determining how best to assess them. In this article, we will provide the specific context and motivations for creating an assessment of writing that is discipline-based and embedded in the curriculum, and that is congruent with the George Mason culture.[1]

Course-embedded Assessment and Mason's Culture of Writing in Disciplines

The commitment to course-embedded assessment is both practical and philosophical. From a practical perspective, removing assessment from the curriculum proved not to work at Mason. Early attempts to have students take standardized tests, specifically the Academic Profile and Major Field Achievement Tests (MFAT)[2] failed, chiefly because of the demographics of our student population and the use value for our faculty. Of the over 17,000 undergraduate students Mason enrolls, just over 4,000 live on campus. Further, a typical graduating class is composed of 60% transfer students, the majority of whom work off campus. For these students, there were no inherent incentives for spending additional time on campus taking standardized tests. For the teaching faculty, the tests provided little information they could use to change the way they taught or what they taught.[3] One of the primary reasons these tests did not serve as an impetus for examining the curriculum is that the faculty had no role in conceptualizing or creating the tests (although they were reviewers) and were

---

[1] It should be noted that all assessment at George Mason takes place in the curriculum; students are not tested outside of the classroom. In some cases, questions are included in final exams that are used for broader assessment purposes (scientific and quantitative reasoning); in others, computer-based modules are completed as part of course requirements (information technology). Groups of faculty using collaboratively agreed-upon rubrics review both written and oral work in critical thinking, oral communication, and written communication.

[2] Both the Academic Profile and the MFAT are products of the Educational Testing Service (ETS). The Academic Profile was replaced in 2005 by the Measure of Academic Proficiency and Progress (MAPP).

[3] The MFAT, which is discipline-specific, was more meaningful for department faculty, but for the most part, it tended to reinforce shared beliefs about student ability rather than serve as a spotlight on the curriculum. (The one exception to this was the poor showing on one area of an MFAT that encouraged a department to continue offering a course in a subfield they had been considering eliminating.)

passive receivers of the results. Further, these tests were "assessment" tests, something perceived as being outside the realm of faculty responsibility.

Philosophically, there were and remain many reasons for the course-embedded commitment. As we explained earlier, the point of conducting an assessment is to improve teaching and learning. This happens when faculty own the assessment process, with both the process and the results contributing to their understanding of the effectiveness of the curriculum, and, for the purposes of this article, the effectiveness of writing instruction in and across courses in the curriculum. Further, when faculty have a stake in the results, they are more inclined to use the information generated by the assessment to make changes both in the curriculum and in their own courses. Thus, faculty must be involved, at some level, in developing and participating in the process, and, whatever their role, they must be vested in knowing the results of the assessment. These are the principles that Karen, as director of Institutional Assessment since 1988, has long endorsed and that made her enthusiastic about the writing assessment plan proposed to the State Council, which entails a holistic scoring process using student papers collected from an upper-division writing-intensive (WI) course in the major and assessed by faculty teaching in that major.

Given a strong culture of writing in the disciplines at Mason, which is described later, we were well poised to respond to the 2001 mandate when it came to assessing students' writing competence. As director of our nationally recognized Writing Across the Curriculum (WAC) program, Terry was eager to lead an assessment effort that would focus not only on student writing in the majors but would also allow for a wider discussion of teachers' expectations for student writers and how these are conveyed to students through assignments, comments on papers, grades, and grading criteria. Because all of our students must fulfill a writing-intensive requirement, the plan also made practical sense in that we would be able to include our transfer students among those whose writing was being assessed. We also had practicality in mind when we decided to assess randomly selected papers written in response to only one representative assignment in the course rather than for several different assignments or even course portfolios. While portfolios may have given us a fuller picture of students' competence at writing in multiple genres, we knew that most faculty would be unlikely to accept an invitation to spend a day or more reading and assessing stacks of portfolios, particularly when the papers included in the portfolio would likely require discussion of the different assignment purposes and contexts. Our choice of a single sample of writing has limitations, of course: students might respond differently to different stimuli; the writing from any given student could be less than that student's best effort. Nonetheless, our methods mitigate against many other sources of error, such as a general lack of student motivation (students are typically motivated when papers are part of the course grade); an unrepresentative sample (papers were randomly selected); and rater bias (raters were trained and papers were rated anonymously).

Writing Across the Curriculum (WAC) at George Mason

Before we describe the specifics of the assessment plan we designed, with the assistance of the Provost-convened Writing Assessment Group, we want to give some background on WAC at Mason and the genesis of the plan, which was developed a year prior to the state mandate. Along the way, we'll also provide a theoretical context, based in composition studies, for our approach. Mason's WAC program dates back to 1978, when the first teaching-with-writing workshops were offered to faculty across disciplines with funding support from the deans of several colleges; in 1980, interested faculty attended a summer institute, sponsored by a grant from the state's Funds for Excellence in Higher Education program. The Faculty Senate convened the WAC committee in 1990 and in 1993 voted to require one upper-division writing-intensive course for all majors, in addition to an advanced composition course focused on writing in disciplines (e.g., writing in humanities, social sciences, natural sciences, business, and technology). While these courses, along with first year composition, constitute the curricular requirements for the WAC program (http://wac.gmu.edu/), our goals are realized through a variety of "writing-infused" majors and courses and through our extensive and ongoing faculty development efforts. The writing assessment workshops we planned would be, in many ways, a continuation of these efforts, with the required writing-intensive (WI) course(s) in the major offering a context-appropriate venue for assessing students' competence as college writers.

The year before we received the 2001 mandate to assess writing, we already had begun to set in place a process for determining the effectiveness of the WI requirement. We were motivated, in part, by a new general education program that specifically called for the assessment of written communication. With the support of the Provost's Office, Terry and Karen convened the Writing Assessment Group (WAG that included representatives from each of the colleges, appointed by the respective deans. The group decided that our first step should be to find out what writing tasks faculty typically assign and their satisfaction with students' ability to achieve those tasks; to that end, we designed and circulated a survey to all undergraduate faculty (see http://wac.gmu.edu/assessing/assessing_student_writing.php#part1). WAG then developed a proposal in response to the state mandate in which we defined student writing competence very generally as the ability to use writing to discover, to learn, and to express knowledge. We explained that, while there are some shared criteria for good writing across disciplines, we recognized that different disciplines have distinct goals and priorities for student writers. Thus, we proposed to embed the assessment in required WI courses using papers selected by faculty in the major and a rubric developed by faculty through participation in a holistic scoring workshop.

Institutions in Virginia may chose a variety of ways to comply with the state requirement to assess writing competence; the approach taken by George Mason fits with and reflects our strong WAC culture, which is built on the premise that, because genres and conventions reflect disciplinary exigencies for writing, faculty in the discipline are most suited to help students become competent writers in their majors. Further, they are the most qualified to evaluate their students' writing competence; thus, our belief that assessment should be embedded in ongoing curricular activities, not conducted apart from the curriculum.[4] (See Figure 1 for an overview of the complete process for assessing and reporting writing competence.)

**George Mason University
Writing Assessment Process**

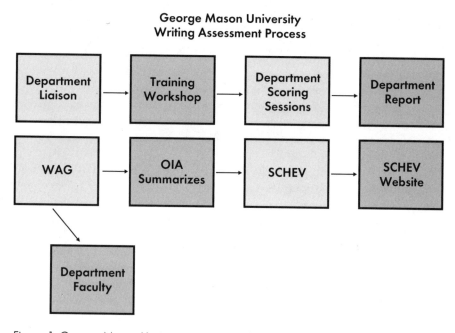

Figure 1. George Mason University writing assessment process.

Writing Assessment and Writing in the Disciplines, Theory and Practice

Our choice to embed assessment in the upper-division WI course with responsibility for the process given to faculty in the major is also supported by theory and research on writing assessment and writing in the disciplines (WID). Charles Cooper and Lee Odell's 1977 collection, *Evaluating Writing: Describing, Measuring, Judging,* continues to be useful for developing writing assessment plans and procedures, particularly Cooper's chapter on the "Holistic Evaluation of Writing." Cooper uses the term "holistic" to describe any procedure that seeks to qualify rather than quantify the features of a piece of writing. A holistic scoring process entails comparing papers against others in the group to develop a basis for making judgments about quality. The comparison often results in a list of features—primary traits—that may be used to develop a scoring rubric. Although some do not consider

---

[4] Given time and resources, our preference would be to begin the assessment process by meeting with disciplinary faculty to articulate writing outcomes for students and then using these outcome statements to guide and inform the assessment process. The work being done by Michael Carter and colleagues at North Carolina State offers one of the best models we know for this approach. For a description of the process and the results thus far, see http://www2.chass.ncsu.edu/CWSP/outcomes.html

primary trait scoring as a holistic process, Cooper is more inclusive in suggesting that this kind of scoring still requires attention to "the special blend of audience, speaker role, purpose, and subject required by that kind of discourse and by the particular writing task." Furthermore, the scoring rubrics are "constructed for a particular writing task set in a full rhetorical context," as is the case in our departmental scoring workshops. This kind of scoring, Cooper suggests, will "very likely have an indirect impact on the way teachers give writing tasks and respond to them," which makes it "potentially the most useful" of all the evaluation processes he describes (p. 11). Besides being useful for informing pedagogical change, Cooper argues emphatically that raters from similar backgrounds who devise their own scoring guides "on the spot" through conversations about student writing samples can achieve very high scoring reliability (p. 19).

More recently, we also turn to the guiding principles Brian Huot (2002) lays out in (Re)Articulating Writing Assessment for Teaching and Learning, which reiterates many of the values we described in our introduction: the assessment should be site-based and locally controlled, with questions and assessment measures developed by those in the community; writing professionals should lead these efforts; and, finally, our practices should be theoretically grounded, practical, and carried out with a conscious awareness of and reflection on the beliefs and assumptions underlying our actions.[5] Huot argues for a view of writing assessment as "social action" in that it can help shape instruction and promote literacy for all students, not just carry out the political agendas of others. Huot's purposeful use of the key term "social action" echoes Carolyn Miller's (1984) formulation of genres as social actions rather than static forms; as such, they arise from and adapt to the shared motives and goals of discourse communities and, in turn, also help to shape those motives and goals. Yet, Miller also argues, discourse communities, because they are made up of many different members, are also "fundamentally heterogeneous and contentious" (1994, p. 74). Miller's conception of genres and disciplines as fluid and dynamic has been especially important to writing-in-the-disciplines (WID) theorists and, by extension, to those of us assessing writing in disciplines, as we cannot assume that there is agreement about what constitutes a correct way of writing across or even within the same disciplines.[6]

These points were borne out in the cross-disciplinary training workshops we describe next and in departmental assessment workshops; in both, faculty initially

---

[5] See also the important body of work on writing assessment produced by Edward White, e.g., *Teaching and Assessing Writing: Recent Advances in Understanding, Evaluating, and Improving Student Performance* (1994), and Richard Haswell, e.g., *Gaining Ground in College Writing* (1991) and his edited collection *Beyond Outcomes: Assessment and Instruction Within a University Writing Program* (2001). For university practices focused on writing-in-the-disciplines, see Barbara Walvoord's *Assessment Clear and Simple: A Practical Guide for Institutions, Departments, and General Education* (2004), in which she makes a strong case for course-embedded procedures.

[6] For fuller explanations of these theories, see, also, the work of Amy Devitt (2004) on genres and Charles Bazerman and David Russell (2002) on activity theory.

used the same general terminology to describe the features of good writing but discovered, as they elaborated on the terms in discussing the student samples, that they often disagreed about the specifics. The scoring rubrics reflect these differences across disciplines, as we'll explain, and they also reflect, in the way the criteria were ordered on the page, the different disciplinary values faculty placed on some features in relationship to others.

Training workshops. Once the WAG proposal was accepted by SCHEV, our assessment efforts began with a series of training workshops for a cross-curricular group of faculty members who had been appointed by their chairs to lead departmental writing assessment efforts with assistance from WAG members. The first training workshops were led by Terry and two WAG members from the English department: Ruth Fischer, former director of Composition, and Chris Thaiss, the creator and former director of the WAC program. In these training workshops, the leaders used sample papers collected from students in the advanced composition course we mentioned earlier, which is focused on writing from research. Students across all summer sections of the course, regardless of their major, were given the same "review of the literature" assignment and were asked to submit a second copy of their paper with no name attached to be used for assessment purposes. This assignment was chosen for the training workshops because most upper-division students are assigned research papers of one kind or another in their major and most faculty are familiar with the genre even though many may not do the kind of experimental research that is typically reported in a research review.

In the training workshops, the leaders modeled the holistic process described earlier by having faculty participants (a) read four of the sample literature review papers against each other, (b) describe the traits for "good" writing that were demonstrated (or not) in the papers, (c) group these traits into larger, more general categories, and, (d) finally, arrive at a set of criteria to be included on the scoring rubric. (For a detailed explanation of the holistic scoring rationale and process, see documents available at http://wac.gmu.edu/assessing/rationale.pdf and http://wac.gmu.edu/assessing/holistic.pdf) The sample papers for the training workshops had been selected carefully to represent different majors and a range of writing abilities. While the workshop leaders hoped that the literature review assignment and the papers that had been selected would lead to interesting cross-disciplinary discussions of expectations for writing, all of us were surprised by the disagreements that emerged and the valuable insights both we and the faculty in attendance gained from the conversations that ensued. We expected, for example, that faculty might have different views regarding the construction and placement of a thesis, appropriate evidence, and the seriousness of certain kinds of errors. However, faculty from different disciplines also differed significantly in their definitions of concise prose, the kind of research information that must be cited, and the appropriate voice and style for academic writing. In one workshop, for example, several faculty members from the humanities were strongly at odds with others from the sciences about the long and "exceedingly dull" opening paragraphs of the literature review that introduced the writer's hypothesis for a psychology lab report. They preferred the "fresh voice" of the autobiographical introduction for a review of the research on body image and female athletes, which the science faculty dismissed as irrelevant and inappropriate.

It is not difficult to understand why faculty from different disciplines might disagree about the features of good writing nor why they might be surprised to discover that their disagreements extend to features they assume to be characteristic of good academic writing across disciplines. While faculty certainly understand that there are significant epistemological differences among disciplines, they often do not see the ways in which these differences influence prose styles and other written conventions, believing instead that good writing is good writing across the curriculum. David Russell (1997) calls this the "myth of transparency," by which he means that, because the written conventions in a discipline are learned very gradually by its apprentices as an integral part of the discourse, the process of writing becomes transparent with both genres and conventions appearing to be "unproblematic renderings of the fruits of research" (pp. 16–17). That helps to explain why many of the workshop faculty marked the psychology paper down for its "tedious" writing style and lack of transitions between sections, while others criticized the "flowery" prose and overly complex sentences in a humanities paper. One valuable outcome of this training workshop, then, was the realization on the part of the cross-disciplinary faculty that they did not necessarily share the same values for acceptable student writing nor even assign the same meanings to the terms they were using on the rubric.

Departmental rubrics and scoring. These differences can be seen most clearly in a comparison of the departmental rubrics faculty subsequently developed when they met to assess papers from the writing-intensive (WI) course in their own majors. To illustrate, we'll compare the first two criteria on the scoring rubrics for WI courses in government and international affairs, biology/ecology, and business. Because all government courses above the 300-level are designated writing-intensive and so fulfill the requirement, the papers to be assessed were drawn from political theory courses across several concentrations for which all students were given the same assignment prompt (though the prompt differed in the material to be discussed). After reading and discussing four sample papers to derive the traits to be included on the rubric, the government and international affairs faculty decided that the first criterion on the list should address the content of the argument itself and whether it was "clear, complex, original; showed knowledge of the material, conceptual sophistication and engagement with the topic; and demonstrated the ability to recognize multiple perspectives." The second criterion addressed the form of the argument, including a "well-stated thesis," logical evidence, balanced paragraphs, and relevant conclusion.

Although the biology faculty assessing papers from the writing-intensive ecology lab course used considerably different language to describe their top criterion, like the government and international affairs faculty, they also wanted papers to demonstrate a conceptual understanding of the discipline. Their rubric begins with this criterion, which also addresses the formal structure of an experimental report: "Demonstrates understanding of scientific writing: Abstract summarizes key points and sections; understands what needs to be cited; each section has content appropriate to the section; graphics integrated into and integral to the paper; discussion section synthesizes results with literature; evidence of analytical thinking." The second criterion on the rubric assessed the content, i.e., how well the student used research data ("relevant information," "correct and accurate paraphrasing") and employed technical terminology, among other features.

In sharp contrast, business faculty who participated in scoring papers from the gateway business models WI course and from several other writing-infused core courses decided that the ability to follow formatting instructions and write error-free prose was critical to a student's success in the major. Further, they agreed that a student's failure to perform satisfactorily on this criterion would mean that the paper overall could not be considered competent. This insistence on adhering to format guidelines for prescribed genres (e.g., memo, executive summary) and writing correct prose reveals the importance placed on writing appropriately for the workplaces that students will encounter. Tellingly, the second criterion on the rubric—audience, tone, and style—is also focused on a reader's reception of the text and, by extension, of the writer him/herself. Content features move to third place on their rubric. It's interesting to note that, while biology faculty ordered the criteria on their rubric much differently than business faculty and placed much less emphasis on audience, they decided that papers receiving an "unacceptable," as compared to a "less than satisfactory," rating on any one criterion must be deemed unacceptable in overall writing competence. This decision reflects their strongly held belief that reasoning scientifically and the ability to report information accurately in scientific formats are foundational criteria for students of the discipline. Interestingly, government and international affairs, biology, and business faculty were all concerned about many students' practice of quoting excessively and/or inappropriately from sources.

While faculty in their own departmental workshops may have agreed upon the criteria to be included on the rubrics and the weight to be given to each item, this is not to say that they were in complete agreement about whether and how papers satisfactorily fulfilled these criteria. Government and international affairs faculty, for example, discovered, to their surprise, that many of them were teaching students to write thesis statements in a form that was unsatisfactory to others. After some discussion about each other's preferences for a thesis, they decided to include the following elaboration in parenthesis after the "Form of Argument" criterion: "(Note: Some would like a thesis paragraph to lay out a framework for the argument to follow; others noted that the "conclusion" should not come in the first paragraph.)." In a workshop assessing the writing in portfolios[7] from the capstone nursing course, faculty were similarly surprised when they realized that almost a third of them had given an unsatisfactory score on "Style and Mastery of Mechanics and Grammar" to a portfolio that the others had ranked satisfactory or more than satisfactory. When Terry probed with faculty the reasons for the disparity in scores, those giving unsatisfactory scores explained that the long, complex sentences (termed "run-ons")

---

[7] Nursing faculty chose to assess portfolios rather than single papers to fulfill both the SCHEV mandate and the requirements of the Commission on Collegiate Nursing Education (CCNE).

were not appropriate in a field where precise, concise communication to audiences of doctors, patients, administrators, and/or the public was the chief goal. Others argued, however, that two of the portfolio papers—a reflection paper and the "paradigm case" assignment (a personal narrative about a nursing experience)—lent themselves to a more complex writing style, which this particular portfolio demonstrated with great success. To give another example, in almost a replay of the run-on discussion in the nursing workshop, faculty from the health/recreation major used the term "run-on" to describe "elaborate sentences, i.e., those containing more than three clauses," which, they conceded, after hearing the differing opinions of colleagues, might be acceptable for certain concentrations and/or genres in the major. Disagreements like those in nursing and health/recreation reveal how important it is to assess writing not just in the context of the discipline but also in the context of a particular course with the learning and writing goals for any given assignment being taken in consideration.[8]

But how does one explain disagreements among faculty, like those in government and international affairs in regard to thesis statements, where faculty are assessing papers in the same genre, in this case position papers, a genre that is central to political discourse? Faculty expectations for student writers and their standards for good writing derive from a complex mix of variables, not just the discipline, Terry and co-author Chris Thaiss (2006) suggest in *Engaged Writers and Dynamic Disciplines: Research on the Academic Writing Life*. Their conclusions are based on interviews with faculty from 14 different disciplines and data from departmental assessment workshops and student focus groups. Variables include faculty's often-opaque understanding of general standards for academic writing; conventions of disciplines and also sub-disciplines; institutional and departmental cultures; and faculty's personal writing goals for students and idiosyncratic likes and dislikes (pp. 60, 95). While evidence of these variables can be seen in teachers' assignments and responses to student writing—by students, certainly, and by writing researchers—faculty are often unaware of their own preferences and how these might differ from others in the same field, and so they rarely explain them to students.[9] Far from being a negative aspect of the assessment process, the disagreements that surface among faculty in the departmental workshops prove to be good opportunities for faculty development, as they result in a better understanding of each other's expectations and a clearer articulation of the agreed-upon scoring criteria, as the thesis discussion described above illustrates. Further, the conversations that occur around the merits of the sample papers and the features to be included on the rubrics also lead to wider discussions about the appropriateness of particular assignments for achieving learning outcomes, and, even more broadly, the appropriateness of the designated WI course itself for helping students to achieve the writing and learning outcomes for the curriculum.

---

[8] An overarching goal for the paradigm case assignment, for example, is to help nursing students gain confidence in their own authority and intuitions about patients by telling and sharing their own care-giving stories.

[9] In turn, as Terry and Chris Thaiss learned from the student focus groups they conducted as part of their research, students across disciplines generally considered teachers to be idiosyncratic and unpredictable in their comments and grades on papers (Thais & Zawacki, 2006, pp. 108–110).

Using Assessment for Faculty, Course, Curricular Change

In addition to giving faculty a clearer understanding of their own expectations for student writers and how these may differ from the expectations of others in the same discipline and across disciplines, the workshops also help faculty acquire a more precise language for expressing their expectations to students. While the scoring rubrics are posted on many department websites as a guideline for evaluating student writing, faculty are always encouraged to adapt the rubrics to reflect the specific writing goals of their assignments as well as their own stylistic preferences. The recognition that they do have stylistic preferences—whether embedded in the discipline, as the nursing example illustrates, or derived from other contexts, e.g., "rules" they learned in school—has been enlightening for many faculty, especially those who have been annoyed at their colleague's seeming ability to overlook the errors that they find so distracting. In the workshops, these annoyances are aired and some agreement is reached about which errors can be tolerated and which must result in an overall unsatisfactory score. Interestingly, while faculty are often most vocal in their complaints about the number of errors students commit in their writing, in workshop discussions of sample papers other features of the written text, e.g., "an understanding of scientific reasoning," emerge as top priorities in scoring students' writing competence. Discussions like these extend from the papers at hand to the ways teachers grade papers and whether they are spending too much of their time correcting errors and not enough time explaining higher order concerns related to the quality and structure of the students' arguments.

In workshops where faculty find that they are dissatisfied with students' scores on a number of the criteria on the rubric they've devised, the discussion often turns to the assignment itself and/or the course from which the assignment came. Sometimes the assignment is pinpointed as a possible cause of the students' problems if it isn't clearly worded or hasn't required students to demonstrate the thinking and writing skills faculty think are important to assess. Occasionally, the content of the WI course and its place in the curriculum is scrutinized as a possible reason for students' inability to fulfill expectations articulated on the rubric. This was the case, for example, with the WI course for information technology, where an initial attempt to assess student writing was unsuccessful because faculty determined the assignment for which the papers were written did not elicit the skills they considered critical to students' success as writers in their majors. Nor did the designated WI course give students the opportunity to learn those skills in an appropriate context. This discovery led to a change in the course to be designated WI and, subsequently, a second assessment workshop focused on papers from that course. A similar discovery was made by dance faculty who are looking at the overall curriculum to determine which course(s) might be most appropriate for the WI designation depending upon their students' professional goals, which, for dance, might range from dancing professionally, choreographing dance, or writing about dance.

The Mason business school has also used the assessment process for their own ends as a way to improve student writing in courses throughout the curriculum as well as to gather data to report to their accrediting body, the Association to Advance

Collegiate Schools of Business (AACSB). After meeting to read sample papers to develop a rubric, a business faculty task force exchanged electronic versions of the rubric to produce a more nuanced articulation of each of the criteria (see http://wac.gmu.edu/assessing/rubrics/SOM_Rubric_07.pdf). In a subsequent scoring session, the task force evaluated 51 papers from a range of core courses in the major. According to their report, they achieved an 82% inter-rater reliability on what had initially seemed to many of them to be a very subjective process. The task force also reported its pleasure in seeing the higher-than-expected number of satisfactory scores for overall competence. But they also recognized the challenges they faced in determining how the student writers of papers deemed "not competent" overall managed to have passed successfully both the advanced composition course and the business gateway WI course.

From the perspective of a composition professional, one possible response to the business task force is to point out that all writers may struggle and have trouble formulating their ideas clearly in writing when writing about unfamiliar content, for unfamiliar audiences, and in contexts that are likewise unfamiliar. Over time, and with practice, most writers become proficient in meeting the rhetorical and discursive demands of a given writing situation, even though these are rarely spelled out explicitly. Students, then, do not learn how to write in college once and for all in, say, a required composition course. Rather, to gain proficiency, rhetorical flexibility, and confidence, they need sustained practice in writing in their majors, across courses, and for different teachers. This is not a one-way process; when teachers explain to students, and to themselves, their expectations for student writing and the multiple contexts from which they may derive, students will be better equipped to fulfill those expectations. The rubrics that faculty develop in the assessment workshops are a step in this direction.

How Assessment Results Are Reported and Utilized

As a further commitment to faculty development and course and curricular change, the WAG, with Karen's endorsement, decided not to report each department's assessment results to the state as individual units, so that no department would be embarrassed if their assessment results did not meet their expectations. Rather, each unit analyzed their own data and reported to WAG in a standard format in which evaluations were summarized as percentages in categories of *high competence*, *competence*, and *needs improvement*. In some cases, units used slightly different terminology, e.g., *more than satisfactory*, *satisfactory*, *unsatisfactory*, but all scales were grouped into three categories. As part of the internal report, departmental assessment leaders, with WAG assistance, also analyzed and summarized as percentages the scores on each of the criterion on the rubric, which were rated with the same three-part scale. All of this information was given back to the department in a report that also included recommendations for faculty to help students improve their writing and, in some cases, for faculty to change aspects of particular courses and/or the curriculum. For purposes of reporting to SCHEV, the Office of

Institutional Assessment utilized the common criteria across rubrics and aggregated the data from all departments that had conducted the assessment, thus preserving the confidentiality of all units. At the same time, the state was provided with sufficient information to judge the compliance of George Mason with the assessment mandate (details of the George Mason writing assessment reports are available at https://assessment.gmu.edu/StudentLearningCompetencies/Written/written.html).

A few years into our assessment process, WAG members interviewed the liaisons from each unit who had participated in the training workshops to identify changes that had been made as a result of participating in the writing assessment. We found that the most common improvements included the sharing of the departmental writing rubrics among faculty, particularly with new and adjunct faculty, and posting the rubrics on department websites for students and others to view. Some departments had developed training workshops for teaching assistants focused on how to use the rubrics and the scoring process to calibrate their evaluations of and responses to students' writing; others added additional writing requirements to existing courses in order to give students more opportunities to engage in writing. Harder to determine is the impact on faculty teaching. Did those who participated in the assessment process make changes in their writing assignments to better elicit the kind of writing they had identified as important? Did faculty share the rubrics in their classes with students so they would have a standard to work towards? This information was harder to capture, but as we will soon begin the second cycle of writing assessment, we intend to examine not only changes in student outcomes, but in faculty practices in the classroom.

One of the ways we plan to continue focusing on the centrality of faculty development in the assessment of writing is to utilize wiki web pages as we revisit existing rubrics and create new ones for units who have not yet been through the process. By doing so, we should be able to encourage more faculty to participate in the development and final approval of any given rubric. Talks are also underway about how to incorporate the assessment of critical thinking, one of our required state competencies, with the assessment of writing. To date, we have assessed critical thinking through oral presentations, but we feel we can expand our writing assessment workshops so that critical thinking becomes a part of rubric-development, allowing each unit to assess both student writing and critical thinking using the same sample of papers.

We also plan to continue a tradition started a few years ago when we held a Celebration of Writing reception after being recognized by *US News and World Report* for our exemplary WAC program. All faculty who regularly teach WI courses and/or who participated in the assessment process were invited to the reception where they were thanked by the President of the university and the Provost for their commitment to improving student writing. The celebration began with the creation of posters representing the work of each unit that had assessed writing. At the request of the President, the posters were next displayed in the atrium of the central administration building for a meeting of the Board of Visitors. Individual departments and the bookstore also displayed posters

What's Next?

While the U.S. Department of Education continues to try to expand No-Child-Left-Behind legislation to include students in higher education, state higher education authorities can and do feel the need to be at the forefront of this political pressure, which has resulted in requirements and proposed legislation to further ensure "accountability" from state institutions. In Virginia, this has taken the form of additional reporting requirements by colleges and universities to include the "value added" that institutions are providing their students. "Competence" in the previously identified six core areas will no longer be sufficient to demonstrate accountability. Institutions must now report change in student attainment from a given point, presumably at matriculation, to some later date in the students' college career. What this means for the assessment of writing in the state is that students will likely either be tested or will provide a sample of student work that will be compared to a later test or sample of work. While the final guidelines have not been adopted as of this writing, there is no doubt that some kind of pre/post comparison will become central to future assessment in Virginia. Will faculty continue their commitment to assessing writing as well as other important areas? At George Mason, we are committed to the course-embedded, faculty-driven approach we have described in this article. But the strain on faculty will be evident as we move to this next stage.

Meanwhile, regional accrediting agencies, as well as specialized accrediting bodies such as AACSB and the Commission on Collegiate Nursing Education (CCNE) also continue to examine and revise their requirements so that the assessment of student learning is now a critical focal point of the self-studies done in preparation for reaccreditation. The Southern Association of Colleges and Schools (SACS), for example, requires institutions to identify the "student learning outcomes for educational programs," including general education, and assess "whether it achieves these outcomes" (see http://sacscoc.org). Written communication, along with critical thinking, are nearly always identified as basic competencies within general education, as well as the major. Thus, the importance of developing effective strategies for assessing writing is nearly universal. No institution can ignore the need to focus on effective methods for assessing and improving writing among its students.

The opportune circumstance of the beginning of the Mason writing assessment program, i.e., the prior decision by the Faculty Senate to require all students to take designated intensive-writing courses in the major, gave us the foundation to develop a faculty-owned, discipline-specific writing assessment program. The culture of writing that took root and provided political support for institutionalizing WI courses began many years prior to the WI policy decision. The relentless effort of many individuals, but particularly Chris Thaiss, mentioned earlier, and Terry Zawacki, nurtured a sense of common responsibility across disciplines to develop and support student writing. The compatibility of this culture of writing with a culture of assessment in which we routinely use information to reflect on where we are, where we want to be, and how to get there has resulted in a thriving, sustainable program of writing assessment. Improved student writing should be the reward we will document as we begin a second cycle of assessing writing.

REFERENCES

Bazerman, C., & Russell, D. R. (2002). Writing selves/writing societies: Research from activity perspectives. *Perspectives on Writing*. Retrieved July 30, 2009, from the WAC Clearinghouse at http://wac.colostate.edu/books/selves_societies/

Cooper, C. (1977). Holistic evaluation of writing. In C. Cooper, & L. Odell (Eds.), *Evaluating writing: Describing, measuring, judging* (pp. 3–32). Urbana, IL: National Council of Teachers of English.

Devitt, A. (2004). *Writing genres*. Carbondale, IL: Southern Illinois University Press.

Haswell, R. (1991). *Gaining ground in college writing: Tales of development and interpretation*. Dallas, TX: Southern Methodist University Press.

Haswell, R. (Ed.). (2001). *Beyond outcomes: Assessment and instruction within a university writing program*. Westport, CT: Ablex.

Haswell, R., & McLeod, S. (1997). WAC assessment and internal audiences: A dialogue. In K. Yancey, & B. Huot (Eds.), *Assessing writing across the curriculum: Diverse approaches and practices* (pp. 217–236). Greenwich, CT: Ablex.

Huot, B. (2002). *(Re)Articulating writing assessment for teaching and learning*. Logan, UT: Utah State University Press.

Miller, C. (1984). Genre as social action. *Quarterly Journal of Speech, 70,* (151–167).

Miller, C. (1994). Rhetorical community: The cultural basis of genre. In A. Freedman, & P. Medway (Eds.), *Genre and the new rhetoric*. Bristol, PA: Taylor and Francis.

Russell, D. (1997). Rethinking genre in school and society: An activity theory analysis. *Written Communication, 14*(4).

Thaiss, C., & Zawacki, T. M. (2006). *Engaged writers and dynamic disciplines: Research on the academic writing life*. Portsmouth, NH: Heinemann.

Walvoord, B. (2004). *Assessment clear and simple: A practical guide for institutions, departments, and general education*. San Francisco: Jossey-Bass.

White, E. (1994). *Teaching and assessing writing: Understanding, evaluating, and improving student performance*. San Francisco: Jossey-Bass.

Yancey, K., & Huot, B. (Eds.). (1997). *Assessing writing across the curriculum: Diverse approaches and practices*. Greenwich, CT: Ablex.

CHAPTER 5

GUIDING PRINCIPLES IN ENGINEERING WRITING ASSESSMENT:

CONTEXT, COLLABORATION, AND OWNERSHIP

Jen Schneider, Jon A. Leydens, Barbara M. Olds, Ronald Miller
Colorado School of Mines

Several years ago, one of the authors of this chapter was privy to details of a large-scale writing assessment of junior high students. The students had been given a brief prompt asking them to think through how watching television affects people's thinking styles. One of the students involved in the assessment had approached the task creatively, beginning his essay as one would a television commercial and echoing that tone, complete with channel changes and other fragmenting interruptions. He began his essay this way: "Hi there! Television has not affected my mind..." and then proceeded to show, in a sophisticated demonstration of self-satire, how television had indeed fragmented his mind. Most of the evaluators participating in the assessment were impressed at the level of thinking, awareness, and creativity that went into the student's writing sample.

However, one of the evaluators—a prominent state politician—was not at all impressed. This evaluator read the student's essay, shook his head, and tsk-tsked. "That's too bad," he said, putting the essay down. The same essay that earned accolades from most of the English teachers and faculty evaluators was, in his mind, a disaster. Instead, he had found the essay's unconventional approach and sentence fragments distracting and inappropriate.

This vignette illustrates what might be called a "paradigm clash." In her book on the history and theories of writing assessment, Patricia Lynne (referring to the work of Thomas Kuhn) defines a paradigm as a concept "indicating a set of common models, values, commitments, and symbolic exchanges that unite disciplinary communities" (Lynne, 2004, p. 5). Paradigms are important because they allow disciplinary communities to have a common set of assumptions, a "knowledge base" that is shared. A paradigm clash, therefore, occurs when two communities operating under different paradigms meet on the terrain of ideas, definitions, or approaches. The vignette exemplifies a paradigm clash in that the politician held certain assumptions about what "good writing" looks like—formal in tone, grammatically clean, organized in a linear fashion—while the educators valued writing in terms of unique expression of thought, risk-taking, the ability to mock conventions appropriately, and an awareness of multiple forms or rhetorical strategies. The paradigms each group operated under reflected different sets of assumptions and values. Such clashes often have very real-world consequences: this mixed group had to reach some sort of consensus about the student's performance, and about the message he would receive that day defining "good writing."

Lynne is particularly interested in the clash that occurs between composition instructors and theorists—those who teach writing, and analyze the teaching of writing—and measurement specialists—those tasked with the challenge of assessing student performance in writing. Composition instructors and theorists, argues Lynne, are often trained to see writing as contextual, constructed by the social relationships and/or events that give rise to the writing act itself—a paradigm often referred to as "social constructionism." For this group, good assessments measure writing within the context that produced it (i.e., at the programmatic or departmental level). Measurement experts, on the other hand, are more guided by concerns of "validity" and "reliability" in their efforts to make assessments fair and consistent, often because they are performing larger-scale assessments and may be responsible to stakeholders at institutional or governmental levels. Lynne recognizes that such characterizations oversimplify these two disciplinary communities, but suggests that they can nonetheless help us to understand how these two groups speak, or do not speak, effectively to one another.

This chapter represents our effort to reveal our own assumptions about writing assessment in an effort to reach out across groups concerned with assessment—both to those who teach writing and assess it at the local level and to researchers charged with assessing writing within an institutional context. We are keenly aware, as is Lynne, of the need for effective and appropriate writing assessment. Furthermore, we understand that there are occasions when objectivist data and analyses are necessary in the institutional settings of higher education. Our goal, therefore, is to think through how we, as composition instructors and theorists, can guide good, appropriate assessments of writing while still providing useful information and data for institutional decision makers. Below, we present a series of five guiding principles for writing assessment, which have developed out of what has worked (and not worked) at our own institution. To put it another way, we want to offer suggestions for how different stakeholders—like the English teachers and the state politician in our opening example—talk to one another about and value writing. We take this localized approach, in part, because we believe the most effective writing assessments meaningfully integrate, among other stakeholders, local actors.

Background

Measurement specialists, composition instructors, and theorists alike can agree that understanding context is key to developing appropriate assessment tools. Specific measurements used at a state-sponsored, research-intensive university enrolling 25,000 students may not necessarily work at a private liberal arts college enrolling 700. We realize that the experiences we write about below may be unique to our institution: the Colorado School of Mines (CSM) is a public university with "enterprise" status, which provides certain freedoms within the constraints of the publicly mandated university; its focus is on science and engineering education; and it is home to approximately 3,500 undergraduate and 1,000 graduate students. In other words, the kinds of writing assessments we perform are going to be specific to the needs of our particular student and faculty populations and informed by employer, taxpayer, and other stakeholder expectations. That said, we believe that while our specific stories are unique, the guiding principles below are judiciously generalizable and can be used to guide writing assessment at any institution. The examples we use may provide special insights to measurement specialists working with science and engineering populations, but the principles themselves are supported by research from multiple contexts and experiences.

Engineering and science universities operate within a specific assessment context that to some extent, defines who our stakeholders are and sometimes mandates or drives the kinds of assessment we do. In a chapter for an AIR volume on assessment practices in engineering and science universities in general, Olds describes this context in detail (Olds, 2008). For the purposes of this chapter on writing assessment, however, it is perhaps most important to understand that CSM has been grappling with outcomes-based assessment for 20 years, as a result first of a state mandate and then a shift in Accreditation Board of Engineering and Technology (ABET) assessment guidelines. As a result, some outcomes-based assessment practices at CSM are well established, others have been tried and revised or even abandoned, and still others are nascent. Engineering educators are still grappling with how to develop effective, sustainable assessment strategies given this developing context (Leydens & Santi, 2006; Olds & Miller, 1998; Shuman et al., 2000).

One significant constraint that affects writing instruction and assessment in engineering and science education has to do with credit hours. According to the 2004 National Academy of Engineering report, *The Engineer of 2020: Visions of Engineering in the New Century*, the average engineering student already takes on 10% more coursework than undergraduates in other fields and takes 4.8 years to complete the degree. In practical terms, this means that those of us who work in humanities and social sciences (including composition) face fierce competition for credit hours. The credit-hour difficulty has significance for those who organize required writing courses, writing- or communication-across-the-curriculum initiatives, and the assessment practices that accompany all writing activities. In some areas, we see possibilities for innovation; in others, difficult constraints.

All of this is to say that we know there is no "ideal" environment in which writing assessment occurs. Every context will have its opportunities and limitations. However, this fact makes it even more important to be guided by a series of principles for assessment, principles supported by theory and practice. Because the stakeholders in assessments are numerous and varied, because the pressures and the stakes are high, as evaluators of student writing, it is imperative that we keep some sort of North Star above us, to give us direction when we get distracted, hijacked, or lost. Our North Star(s), or guiding principles, are described in the next section. Although there is necessarily some overlap among them, together they constitute a theory of writing assessment that we hope will find common points of departure across the composition and measurement paradigms.

Setting the Compass: Guiding Principles for Writing Assessment

In planning this chapter, we carefully considered our local practices of writing instruction and assessment. We wanted our writing on this subject to reflect our experiences, not merely dictate some abstract theory. Our first exercise together was, in fact, to construct the list of guiding principles below based on our experiences. It is worth noting, however, that many of our guiding principles echo those developed by groups such as the International Reading Association and the National Council of Teachers of English (*Standards for the Assessment of Reading and Writing*, 1994), the American Association for Higher Education (*Nine Principles of Good Practice for Assessing Student Learning*, 1996), and the Conference on College Composition and Communication (*Writing Assessment: A Position Statement*, 2006). They are also supported by recent research in composition and rhetoric studies. While we present and describe these guidelines individually, it's also important to bear in mind that they are not distinct, but instead overlap and support one another, particularly in their emphasis on the localized nature of writing assessment.

Guiding Principle 1: People most support what they help to create.

We are all familiar with failed educational initiatives or assessments that were developed with the best of intentions but that failed to work "on the ground." Perhaps the developers of those initiatives did not have a good sense of local realities; perhaps political or personal values clashed and stakeholders withdrew; perhaps funding or other resources were inadequate to appropriately carry out the tasks required for the initiative to be successful. Guiding Principle 1 suggests that assessments that begin "on the ground" have a better chance of success than those that do not begin there; effective, appropriate, sustainable writing assessments are most frequently supported by "buy-in," commitment to success from those most directly affected by the assessment: students and writing instructors and theorists.

In his book *What We Really Value: Beyond Rubrics in Teaching and Assessing Writing* (2003), Bob Broad describes one method for developing assessment at the ground level. Broad studied a portfolio assessment process at "City University," a process that, surprisingly, was not informed by the use of rubrics. Broad, in fact, takes issue with most writing assessment rubrics in use today, arguing that "traditional rubrics and scoring guides prevent us from telling the truth about what we believe, what we teach, and what we value in composition courses and programs" (Broad, 2003, p. 2). This is because rubrics are often developed by administrators and are effectively "normative" and "formative," but are not adequately "descriptive" or "informative" (p. 2). Broad argues that, instead of using rubrics, writing programs might adopt a process that he calls "Dynamic Criteria Mapping" (DCM) to identify what they "really value" in student writing.

DCM is a process wherein an outside observer studies the evaluative language and criteria that an assessment group uses as they evaluate student writing. Mapping this language—employed in the absence of a rubric—reveals important details about what writing assessors really value in student writing. The observer analyzes the transcripts of assessment sessions in order to develop this "map," which may reveal assessment strategies or values that are not adequately represented or explicitly

68

defined in programmatic objectives or mission statements. For example, at City University, DCM revealed that writing instructors penalized students for writing about an implicit list of "Terrible Topics," topics that instructors saw repeatedly and found boring or amateurish. Broad writes,

> The gravity and complexity of Terrible Topics in the evaluative dynamics of this writing program call for open discussion of the issue among instructor-evaluators in an attempt to set program policy and, at the very least, for instructors to inform students of the Top Ten Terrible Topics so they can choose topics knowing the relative risks associated with them. (p. 69)

DCM is most effective, in other words, because it emanates from actual assessment practice and provides students with a clearer picture of how their work is actually evaluated. Programs and departments can use DCM results to then revise stated objectives, mission statements, assignments, or assessment practices.

Unlike Broad, we find that one positive outcome of the DCM process is rubrics that have been developed collaboratively by key stakeholders and informed by their explicit and implicit values. We have included in our appendices examples of locally developed and supported rubrics that have worked well in our institutional context. But we are excited by the potential of DCM to reveal assessment values, and we support the development of DCM at the local level.

Guiding Principle 1 and the practice of DCM are driving forces behind a new Portfolio Project initiative at CSM. Co-author Schneider coordinates a first-year required writing course entitled Nature and Human Values (NHV). To better assess student learning and writing improvement over time, the NHV faculty, with input from stakeholders such as technical CSM faculty, students, and administrators, will be developing a portfolio assessment tool. Substantial research exists on the use of portfolios (Broad, 2003; Elbow, 2006; White, 1994, 2005; Yancey & Huot, 1997), and it would have been possible for the course coordinator to develop a portfolio assessment system, introduce that system to the faculty as a *fait accompli*, and have seemingly acceptable levels of reliability and validity. But the process would suffer from little faculty buy-in (the faculty did not, after all, have input throughout the process), and there might be even less student buy-in (we might not tell them what we value in the assessment, how we determine those values, or what we do with the assessment). In short, the project could have a short life-span or, in the final analysis, be inappropriate to what it is we are truly trying to measure.

In engineering education, the shift to outcomes assessment has been shaped by the revision in ABET criteria; however, it is possible to use this external, or top-down, impetus as a means of propelling bottom-up assessment design. In NHV, we will work together as a team to identify key stakeholders and to determine what levels of expertise and commitment those stakeholders have in the design of the portfolio system. Looking at course objectives and other key institutional and program documents (mission and vision statements, for example), the key stakeholder group will design an assessment that incorporates multiple stakeholder perspectives and that makes sense given the context and objectives of the course, testing and revising the assessment over several years. Our hope is that in developing the assessment this way, our work will look something like Broad's DCM process, in which the stakeholders take ownership of the assessment, modifying it where appropriate, gaining value from the design process and the outcome, and using the outcome to gain understanding about student writing, the course, teaching and learning, and their own standards of evaluation. Initially, this investment in bottom-up assessment design will be more time- and resource-intensive than a top-down initiative, but we are convinced the rewards will be greater in the long run. Top-down initiatives may be appropriately valid and reliable, but if there is no "buy-in," the "meaningfulness" of the assessment, to use Lynne's term, will be compromised, and the assessment will probably not be appropriate or sustainable in the long run (Huot, 2002; Lynne, 2004). By contrast, a bottom-up process more readily lends itself to the meaningful integration of assessment findings that inform teaching and learning.

Implementing Guiding Principle 1

Identify key stakeholders in the assessment process and work with them to develop meaningful assessments. Strive for a win-win outcome.

Guiding Principle 2: We assess most effectively what we value most.

When people have a stake in the outcome of assessment, they are more likely to value the assessment results. In an important assessment text, Huot (2002) argues that what matters most to writing faculty generally is assessment results that foster better teaching and learning, which is a primary value (if not *the* primary value) among composition faculty. He calls assessment "a direct representation of what we value and how we assign that value," adding that "it says much about our identities as teachers, researchers, and theorists" (p. 11).

Occasionally, we are not sure what we *do* value, or find that our values work implicitly, rather than explicitly, to shape our assessment strategies. As was the case in Broad's study of City University, our tacit values may contradict our explicitly stated goals and objectives. Often, figuring out "what we really value" is a key first step in designing or revising assessments that work. Assessments occur at multiple levels—institutional, programmatic, classroom, and others—and one classroom example can help illustrate the process of discovering what learning objectives and corresponding assessments one values most (Leydens & Santi, 2006). A CSM colleague participated in a Writing Across the Curriculum (WAC) workshop to more effectively integrate writing into a geological engineering course for upper division undergraduates and graduate students. Having taught the course several times already, he began the revision process by more explicitly connecting students' learning difficulties with his course objectives and assignments, so the assignments directly addressed their struggles and thus helped them meet key course objectives. For him, the act of writing out his students' learning difficulties led to a discovery of what he valued most in those assignments; he was also assisted in this regard by two other acts: writing assignment rubrics and creating write-to-learn prompts.

70

The act of articulating performance criteria in assignment rubrics helped render explicit not only how students would be evaluated but also the (previously more tacit) criteria the instructor held of highest value. In other words, this instructor's review of his own instructional practices led him to develop rubrics that explicitly stated what he "really valued." Although Broad cautions against the use of rubrics, we believe this is an example in which the instructor used the rubrics to identify and more effectively communicate his assessment values to his students, which led to improved student performance.

Perhaps the most helpful assessment tool was—paradoxically, for some—an assignment he never formally graded. Write-to-learn prompts are informal, generally ungraded writing assignments that serve to help students write to discover rather than write to communicate what they already know. Our colleague carefully examined what conceptual difficulties students typically encountered and turned these into in-class writing prompts. For instance, in a structural geology report, students typically depended excessively on maps, so he asked them to write for three minutes on what lab and drilling data suggested that cannot be construed from mapping alone. Thus, he began the process of composing write-to-learn activities by reviewing student misconceptions or incomplete understandings and creating focused write-to-learn prompts to address these; he then evaluated the learning success as students translated such insights into their geology reports. Initial data suggest important improvements in student performance when comparing students who did and did not use write-to-learn prompts. To summarize, what learning outcomes our colleague most valued came more fully into view by examining assignments in light of course objectives and common student difficulties, articulating assignment criteria in written rubrics, and aligning both ungraded and formal assignments to address student learning struggles (Leydens & Santi, 2006).

We realize these examples occur at the classroom and programmatic level rather than at the institutional level, which is perhaps of most concern for readers of this chapter. We would argue, however, that the best assessments at any level are localized to particular contexts. Barlow, Liparulo, and Reynolds (2007), writing about an assessment process at the University of Houston, provide three "lessons learned" from their efforts: "stakeholders must be included, design must emerge (rather than being pre-defined), and the study must be formative rather than summative" (p. 52). The authors of the assessment note that they were very invested in involving local stakeholders in the assessment process, because it is important for establishing validity, but also "it makes good political sense if you want your findings to lead to change" (p. 46). The success of locally grown, program-level assessment is supported by research and theory (Anson, 2006; Huot, 2002; Lynne, 2004; Olds & Miller, 1998).

Implementing Guiding Principle 2

With your assessment team, first work to define what you value and then develop methods that will assess those values.

Guiding Principle 3: Assessment is not something done to us, but something we do to deepen our own knowledge and practice.

The value of assessment findings lies in their ability to transform practice. Assessment should be used not only to assess student learning, but to facilitate it. Portfolios, for example, can be as useful for students in assessing their own learning as they are for instructors or administrators. In "The Scoring of Writing Portfolios: Phase 2," Edward M. White (2005) argues that the self-reflective cover letters students draft for inclusion with their portfolios should function as *both* an assessment and a learning tool: "When a student introduces a portfolio with serious reflection about it, the student is taking responsibility for the quality of the work, the choices that were involved in the writing, and the learning that occurred—or not occurred. It is a powerful metacognitive act..." (White, 2005, p. 583). The portfolio, then, becomes not simply a way to evaluate student writing, but to propel student learning.

The idea behind Guiding Principle 3 is, in fact, also a driving force behind Brian Huot's *(Re)Articulating Writing Assessment for Teaching and Learning* (2002). Huot argues that writing assessment is an opportunity for "progressive social action" that should not reinforce or hold up accepted power relations and class systems, but seek to question them via teaching and learning practices. Huot's implicit argument is that practice and assessment are ideally mutually shaping factors—practice should shape assessment and assessment should shape practice. Assessments that are driven by teaching and learning and that, in turn, inform teaching and learning are going to be most valuable.

An example from CSM's Chemical Engineering department illustrates this Guiding Principle. At CSM, each undergraduate engineering program includes a three- to six-week summer field session to help students acquire more hands-on practice in their chosen discipline. In chemical engineering, the junior-level field session is used to teach unit operations laboratory, a traditional lab experience involving large-scale (at least for academic institutions) process equipment that students are likely to encounter in chemical process plants when they graduate.

Since the chemical engineering program's inception in the 1950s, the unit operations laboratory has been viewed by the faculty as an ideal context for helping students become better engineering practitioners. This goal is achieved by enhancing students' higher-order thinking skills and familiarity with many aspects of chemical engineering professional practice, including data collection and experimental design; statistical analysis of experimental data; data evaluation and interpretation of results; identification and analysis of accepted empirical models and of potential hazardous equipment operations; and effective oral, written, and graphic communications.

In its original format, the course required students to present their results for half of the experiments orally and half using written reports. No formal communications instruction and little feedback was provided to students during the six-week term. Not surprisingly, growth in writing quality was minimal. Based on feedback from constituents, the chemical engineering faculty in 1989 decided the laboratory course had to be revamped with explicit instruction and practice in oral and written communications so that students' skills would be adequate upon graduation. After rich deliberations with a campus technical communications expert in the process of course revisions, several course improvements emerged that focused on writing instruction and practice:

- Inclusion of two 3-hour writing workshops to review writing fundamentals and report requirements;
- Conversion of report preparation to a process involving submission of drafts, review sessions with both chemical engineering and technical communication faculty members, and submission of revised reports for grading; and
- More emphasis on developing communication skills throughout the course, including lab notebook preparation, a pre-lab oral exam prior to entering the lab to ensure adequate preparation before experiments, and professionally-prepared graphics for both oral and written reports.

In addition to these course improvements, new ABET program-level assessment expectations in the mid-1990s resulted in use of the unit operations laboratory course as a primary location for assessing several student outcomes including:

- An ability to identify, formulate, and solve chemical engineering problems (addressing ABET outcomes 3a and 3e);
- An ability to design and conduct experiments and analyze and interpret data (addressing ABET outcome 3b); and
- An ability to communicate effectively (addressing ABET outcome 3g).

These outcomes are now successfully assessed using the rubric shown in Appendix A, which was originally developed for program-level assessment activities but is now also used to guide grading of individual student work in the course. The use of the rubric in this program is a good example of the ways in which assessment both drives and is driven by the need to improve teaching and learning.

Implementing Guiding Principle 3

Develop assessment methods and instruments that you and other stakeholders can learn from, via both the process of designing them and implementing findings.

Guiding Principle 4: Contextualized, bottom-up, not top-down, approaches work best.
Local knowledge about genres, rhetorical situations, assignment emphases, time constraints, and so on, should all play roles in the assessment process, so the best assessment procedures are ones *grown* by primary stakeholders and *informed* by institutional researchers. This key principle is clearly linked to Guiding Principle 1, but here we emphasize the importance of encouraging stakeholders to develop ownership of assessments—even when they are mandated from above—because they (the stakeholders) most clearly understand the particular practices and constraints of specific writing practices. Similarly, we encourage institutional researchers to offer

their expertise where it makes sense to do so, to offer their skills as facilitators of assessment rather than enforcers of it.

This principle is closely correlated to the "social constructionist" paradigm of composition instructors and theorists, explained at the beginning of this chapter. Composition instructors and theorists "more readily accept the notion that knowledge—and by extension, writing—is socially constructed," writes Patricia Lynne (2004), "than that knowledge resides in material reality apart from human and linguistic perception or that knowledge is the property of the autonomous individual" (p. 120). Successful writers learn to write in different ways, using different voices and vocabularies, for different situations. How, what, and why we write is always dictated by a particular set of social, contextual circumstances.

This is a salient guiding principle for those teaching writing in engineering programs because so many of the writing practices students are engaged in are shaped by disciplinary conventions, many of which are often kept implicit rather than being made explicit or transparent to novice or apprentice writers. Nonetheless, engineering students must develop a solid understanding of audience expectations, of how to translate technical material for a variety of readers and purposes, and of the conventions of particular disciplines (a metallurgist, for example, will present his or her results differently than a geologist). This principle is also a central tenet of the WAC movement (Young & Fulwiler, 1986) and is supported by research in institutional assessment practices (Anson, 2006; Barlow et al., 2007; Hillocks, 2003).

Following this principle may mean that both composition instructors and theorists *and* measurement specialists occupy an advisory role in writing assessment as opposed to a leadership role. Another example from our university's chemical engineering program illustrates how WAC administrators can *support* assessment that is organically developed and appropriate to the local context.

Traditionally, undergraduate engineering programs culminate in a senior-level design experience of one or two semesters. In the Chemical Engineering Department at CSM, this experience is encompassed in a one-semester course focused on designing large-scale chemical processes. The course has evolved over the last 10 years to include a heavy emphasis on the use of powerful simulation software (ASPEN Plus) with a corresponding decrease in hand calculations to estimate process operating conditions and equipment sizing. Software is also available to complete economic analyses of process profitability. As a result, student design teams now spend less time on routine, repetitive calculations and more time generating design alternatives and analyzing each in more detail (a key to identifying good engineering design choices).

However, with this increased power to analyze complex process alternatives comes the need for better written documentation throughout the design process. Design instructors recognized this need and, with input from campus writing faculty, included several new writing tools in the course. These included write-to-learn exercises and other assignments, including increased opportunities for feedback and revision.

In addition, the instructors soon realized that better assessment of summative documentation (i.e., a comprehensive final written report) was required both to assess students learning outcomes and to provide guidance to student teams about faculty expectations. Faculty from the design course and the Chemical Engineering Department Assessment Committee (formed in the late 1990s to respond to accreditation expectations for program-level outcomes assessment) met over a two-year period to iteratively develop a scoring rubric for use at the course level (student formative feedback and summative evaluation) and program level (outcomes assessment). The version now in use encompasses six outcomes and is shown in Appendix B.

A key revision to the rubric occurred after the assessment tool was first implemented. The version in Appendix B is modified from the original in that the first outcome involving engineering design has been subdivided into four sub-outcomes. This modification was made when both design faculty and assessment committee members realized that a single design outcome did not allow them to adequately assess each critical step in the engineering design process. The rubric, in other words, was not the assessment endpoint; faculty used their own expertise and actual student learning outcomes to revise the rubric over time, making it fit "what they really valued," as opposed to allowing it to dictate their values to them.

Overall, we estimate that approximately 250 person-hours of time were required to develop this rubric, but the effort was worthwhile given the rich discussions about department expectations for students. Since it helps assess changes over time in student learning, the rubric is now used as one of several key assessment tools for ongoing program assessment efforts in addition to its use in the process design class each academic year. It should be underscored that the rubric's effectiveness stems in part from its bottom-up creation, as it originated with course instructors and spread to the faculty within the department assessment committee.

Important corollary to Guiding Principle 4: Sometimes assessment, even specific assessments, are mandated.

The challenge, therefore, involves making what may be a top-down initiative (for example, an assessment mandated by an accrediting agency) develop into a bottom-up initiative, wherein local stakeholders, especially those most directly affected, play vital roles in the assessment design and implementation (White, 2005).

Implementing Guiding Principle 4

Welcome, value, and encourage involvement at the grassroots level.

Guiding Principle 5: Writing is a uniquely complex cognitive and social activity and presents unique assessment challenges.

Several years ago, one of our students submitted a paper for NHV (our first-year composition course firmly rooted in the humanities) that she had completed earlier for an introductory engineering design course. She deservedly received an "A" on the paper in the design course and a "C" for the paper in Nature and Human

Values, also deservedly. This student clearly felt that writing was a "one-size-fits-all affair," and she is likely not alone in assuming that good writing is good writing, not recognizing the rhetorically situated nature of effective communication. All of us have seen analogous assessment practices, wherein an assessment tool developed in one context to assess one set of criteria is, for reasons of expedience, applied to another context. The consequences of such a mis-application are often unfortunate.

If good writing depends on an understanding of audience, purpose, topic, and context, good writing assessment should measure that understanding. According to Lynne (2004),

> ...contextual literacy attaches meaning in writing to the location and purpose of that writing, so contextual assessment would involve evaluating writing for its ability to respond to rhetorical situations. The paradigm also claims an integrated view of writing and consequently would encourage the assessment of whole writing tasks which treat literate ability as a situated act rather than as discrete skills or pieces of information, as would be preferred in a technocratic paradigm. (p. 127)

To understand the contextually situated nature of writing, it is vital to recognize that writing skills and rhetorical abilities develop slowly over time yet can atrophy rapidly through disuse (Lindemann, 1995). Furthermore, academic writing requires a level of sophistication and daring that must be tried on and wrestled with, and such daring will entail some amount of failure. As David Bartholomae (1985) puts it:

> To speak with authority [students] have to speak not only in another's voice but through another's code; and they not only have to do this, they have to speak in the voice and through the codes of those of us with power and wisdom; and they not only have to do this, they have to do it before they know what they are doing, before they have a project to participate in, and before, at least in terms of our disciplines, they have anything to say. (p. 156)

Students, Bartholomae continues, "cannot sit through lectures and read textbooks and, as a consequence, write as sociologists or write literary criticism. There must be steps along the way" (p. 157). In other words, writing is something that must be practiced, practiced, and practiced some more, across a variety of contexts, for a variety of audiences and purposes, and at multiple junctures in a student's process of learning. This practice, furthermore, must be sustained, or it will quickly atrophy. This fact could have particular significance for those working in science and engineering education, where the gaps in time between students' writing or writing-intensive classes may be substantial as they pursue technical classes that do not incorporate communications instruction.

Given this reality—that writing ability develops in fits and starts over time, and is shaped by context—the assessment of writing can be challenging. This principle will require composition instructors and theorists and institutional researchers as assessment specialists to think creatively about writing assessment practices. As the vignette at the beginning of this chapter illustrated, writing skills and abilities are contextually defined. An assessment tool that looks only at grammar or mechanics, for example, provides a very limited angle of view; broader, more holistic approaches to assessment, on the other hand, help us to see writing ability as multi-faceted and complex (Moskal & Leydens, 2000; White, 1994).

Over the past several years, writing portfolios have deservedly become an accepted method of gathering and assessing student writing (and program goals, as we see in the case of Broad's DCM), presumably because they allow for this more holistic view. Composition instructors and theorists are still thinking through best practices in portfolio assessment, but most agree that the concept itself, which works to assess "whole writing tasks," is a step in the right direction (Lynne, 2004, p. 127). CSM's own experiences with writing portfolios are illustrative of both the potential successes and drawbacks of such assessments.

In response to state-mandated requirements for assessment, CSM implemented its first portfolio program in 1989. The program took a statistically based random sampling of incoming first-year students each year, and as background gathered data such as SAT and ACT scores and GPAs. An institution-wide Assessment Committee then collected selective materials for the students' first and second years; departments did their own assessments of junior- and senior-level work. The portfolios did not focus exclusively on writing, although writing assessment was a part of the program. The Assessment Committee, made up of faculty from across the disciplines at CSM, used the institution's mission and Profile of the Future Graduate to develop a number of educational goals that the portfolios would help to assess. Using these goals as guidelines, the Committee established a matrix for assessing portfolio materials. For more specific information on what materials were included and on how they were assessed, see Olds and Pavelich (1996).

In many ways, this portfolio assessment, which ended several years ago, was successful. Although mandated, the specific assessment practices developed organically, with involvement from many faculty members (Guiding Principle 1). In accordance with Guiding Principle 3 above, it was used to provide feedback to departments and faculty members, who used the assessment to shape and revise teaching. For example, one department made changes in the types of writing it required of its students when it saw that students were only completing short, surface-level writing assignments. Another department revised the content of its test questions. Furthermore, the portfolio assessments allowed for complex analyses of student performance over time, and though their focus was not simply on writing assessment, they did lead to significant changes in the writing program at CSM, including the hiring of a Writing Program Administrator in 1997. Finally, analyses of students' thinking abilities demonstrated growth in student learning as a result of curricular changes.

The shaping of the educational goals and the matrices for completing the assessment were in keeping with the ideal of an assessment that takes into account the situated performance of all student work, and allowed student work to emerge from within the contexts that gave rise to it, a practice supported by Guiding Principle 4.

But the assessment also faced some challenges, primarily dealing with the logistics of such an ambitious assessment project, and with the need to respond primarily to outside forces—in this case, the state agency that mandated the assessment in the first place. If we had this portfolio project to do over, we would have access to and take advantage of two main knowledge sources: what we learned from orchestrating the project and from new research on technology that facilitates portfolio assessment.

Important corollary to Guiding Principle 5: There is an inverse ratio between ease of assessment and value of result.

If writing is a complex activity, and if appropriate writing assessments allow for that complexity, it stands to reason that "easy" assessments—such as multiple-choice tests or measurements focusing only on grammar, for example—are not effective. Writing assessment, when done correctly, requires resources: financial, professional, and institutional. In the case of the CSM portfolio project discussed earlier, we underestimated the need for all three, and the project eventually collapsed under its own weight. Although the school's administration was supportive of the portfolio project, very few financial resources were available to support it. In addition, with limited assessment expertise on the campus at that time, there was no plan for succession and thus, when the program developers left to assume other duties, enthusiasm for the process left with them. Finally, the Assessment Committee, which was responsible for the portfolio project, never gained status as an official university committee and, therefore, had no real power to enforce compliance.

Implementing Guiding Principle 5

Recognize that writing is a complex, situated activity, and design your assessment accordingly.

Conclusion

We believe that these five principles suggest important guidelines for developing successful, meaningful, and ethical writing assessments:

1. People most support what they help to create.
2. We assess most effectively what we value most.
3. Assessment is not something done to us, but something we do to deepen our own knowledge and practice.
4. Contextualized, bottom-up, not top-down, approaches work best.
5. Writing is a uniquely complex cognitive and social activity and presents unique assessment challenges.

We understand that it may often be easier to develop top-down strategies for assessment that rely on easy-to-evaluate criteria or testing mechanisms; our own experiences and research in composition practice and theory, however, suggests that the best assessment practices are developed organically, with buy-in from local stakeholders. They are appropriately complex—just as the act of writing is—and as a result often require time and resources to complete properly. But the outcomes for all involved when assessment is done well are sure to be positive. We believe that composition instructors and institutional researchers alike are most interested in understanding and improving student and faculty learning, and the principles listed above suggest how we might achieve this shared goal. On this common ground, we stand to address potential paradigm tensions and work toward meaningful assessments for a multitude of stakeholders.

REFERENCES

American Association for Higher Education. (1996). *Nine principles of good practice for assessing student learning.* Washington, DC: Author.

Anson, C. M. (2006). Assessing writing in cross-curricular programs: Determining the locus of activity. *Assessing Writing, 11,* 100–112.

Barlow, L., Liparulo, S. P., & Reynolds, D. W. (2007). Keeping assessment local: The case for accountability through formative assessment. *Assessing Writing, 12,* 44–59.

Bartholomae, D. (1985). Inventing the university. In M. Rose (Ed.), *When a writer can't write: Studies in writer's block and other composing process problems* (pp. 134–166). New York: Guilford Press.

Broad, B. (2003). *What we really value: Beyond rubrics in teaching and assessing writing.* Logan, UT: Utah State University Press.

Conference on College Composition and Communication, Committee on Assessment. (2006). *Writing assessment: A position statement.* Retrieved July 30, 2009, from http://www.ncte.org/cccc/resources/positions/writingassessment

Elbow, P. (2006). Do we need a single standard of value for institutional assessment? An essay response to Asao Inoue's "community-based assessment pedagogy." *Assessing Writing, 11,* 81–99.

Hillocks, G., Jr. (2003). Fighting back: Assessing the assessments. *English Journal, 92*(4), 63–70.

Huot, B. (2002). *(Re)Articulating writing assessment for teaching and learning.* Logan, UT: Utah State University Press.

International Reading Association and National Council of Teachers of English. (1994). *Standards for the assessment of reading and writing.* Newark, DE: Author.

Leydens, J. A., & Santi, P. (2006). Optimizing faculty use of writing as a learning tool in geoscience writing. *Journal of Geoscience Education, 54*(4), 491–502.

Lindemann, E. (1995). *A rhetoric for writing teachers* (3rd ed.). New York: Oxford University Press.

Lynne, P. (2004). *Coming to terms: A theory of writing assessment.* Logan, UT: Utah State University Press.

Moskal, B., & Leydens, J. A. (2000). Scoring rubric development: Validity and reliability. *Practical Assessment, Research, and Evaluation, 7*(10).

National Academy of Engineering. (2004) *The Engineer of 2020: Visions of engineering in the new century.* Washington, DC: National Academies Press.

Olds, B. (2008). Twenty years of assessment: A retrospective case study. In W. Kelly (Ed.), *Assessment in engineering programs: Evolving best practices* (pp. 159–172). Tallahassee, FL: Association for Institutional Research.

Olds, B. M., & Miller, R. L. (1998). An assessment matrix for evaluating engineering programs. *Journal of Engineering Education, 87*(2), 173–178.

Olds, B. M., & Pavelich, M. J. (1996, June). *A portfolio-based assessment program.* Paper presented at the American Society for Engineering Education Annual Conference, Washington, DC.

Shuman L. J., Besterfield-Sacre, M., Wolfe, H., Atman, C. J., McGourty, J., & Miller, R. (2000, June). *Matching assessment methods to outcomes: Definitions and research questions.* Paper presented at the American Society for Engineering Education Annual Conference, St. Louis, MO.

White, E. M. (1994). *Teaching and assessing writing: Recent advances in understanding, evaluating, and improving student performance* (2nd ed.). San Francisco: Jossey-Bass.

White, E. M. (2005). The scoring of writing portfolios: Phase 2. *College Composition and Communication, 56*(4), 581–600.

Yancey, K. B., & Huot, B. (1997). *Assessing writing across the curriculum* (Vol. 1). Greenwich, CT: Ablex.

Young, A. R., & Fulwiler, T. (Eds.). (1986). *Writing across the disciplines: Research into practice.* Upper Montclair, NJ: Boynton/Cook.

APPENDIX A: ChE Department
Scoring Rubric for Unit Operations Laboratory Reports

Group members: _____ Lab Session: _____ Experiment: _____

Outcome	4 Exemplary	3 Proficient	2 Apprentice	1 Novice	Score
1.3) ChE graduates will be able to apply knowledge of unit operations to the identification, formulation, and solution of chemical engineering problems.	Student groups apply knowledge with virtually no conceptual or procedural errors affecting the quality of the experimental results.	Student groups apply knowledge with no significant conceptual errors and only minor procedural errors.	Student groups apply knowledge with occasional conceptual errors and only minor procedural errors.	Student groups make significant conceptual and/or procedural errors affecting the quality of the experimental results.	
2.1 & 2.2) ChE graduates will be able to design and conduct experiments of chemical engineering processes or systems and they will be able to analyze and interpret data from chemical engineering experiments.	Student groups design and conduct unit operations experiments with virtually no errors; analysis and interpretation of results exceed requirements of experiment and demonstrate significant higher-order thinking ability.	Student groups design and conduct experiments with virtually no errors; analysis and interpretation of results meet requirements of experiment and demonstrate some higher-order thinking ability.	Student groups design and conduct experiments with no significant errors; results are analyzed but not interpreted; very limited evidence of higher-order thinking ability.	Student groups design and conduct experiments with major conceptual and/or procedural errors; no evidence of significant analysis and interpretation of results; fail to meet requirements of the experiment; demonstrate only lower-level thinking ability.	
3.2) ChE graduates will demonstrate an ability to communicate effectively in writing.	Written report is virtually error-free, presents results and analysis logically, is well organized and easy to read, contains high quality graphics, and articulates interpretation of results beyond requirements of the experiment.	Written report presents results and analysis logically, is well organized and easy to read, contains high quality graphics, contains few minor grammatical and rhetorical errors, and articulates interpretation of results which meets requirements of the experiment.	Written report is generally well written but contains some grammatical, rhetorical and/or organizational errors; analysis of results is mentioned but not fully developed.	Written report does not present results clearly, is poorly organized, and/or contains major grammatical and rhetorical errors; fails to articulate analysis of results meeting requirements of the experiment.	

Evaluator: _____ Date: _____

82

APPENDIX B: ChE Department
Scoring Rubric for Senior Design Projects

Outcome	4 Exemplary	3 Proficient	2 Apprentice	1 Novice	Score
2.3) ChE graduates will be able to design chemical engineering processes or systems which meet specified project requirements by:					
a. identifying specific project objectives based on general project and client requirements	All important project objectives are identified.	Important objectives are identified but 1 or 2 minor ones are missing.	Most objectives are identified but at least 1 or 2 important ones are missing.	Most or all important objectives are not identified.	
b. gathering and using relevant background information	All relevant information is obtained and used to support design recommendations.	Sufficient information is obtained and used to support design recommendations.	Some information is obtained but more is needed to support design recommendations.	No significant background information is gathered.	
c. generating and analyzing alternative solutions by synthesizing and applying appropriate chemical engineering knowledge	Three or more alternative solutions are considered; each is correctly analyzed for technical feasibility.	At least 3 alternative solutions are considered; analysis is complete but contains minor procedural errors.	At least 2 alternative solutions are considered; analysis contains minor conceptual and/or procedural errors.	Only one solution is recommended; analysis does not apply all relevant chemical engineering knowledge.	
d. choosing the optimal solution based on evaluation of technical and economic criteria.	Best solution is recommended based on stated criteria.	Reasonable solution is recommended; other alternatives should have been developed and analyzed.	Satisfactory solution is recommended; better solutions were available and should have been considered.	Only one solution considered; no optimization included; better solutions were available.	
1.5) ChE graduates will be able to analyze the economic profitability of chemical engineering projects or systems.	Economic analysis is complete and correct; all relevant economic factors are considered.	Economic analysis omits 1 or 2 minor economic factors but computations are correct.	Economic analysis omits 1 or more major economic factors but computations are correct.	Economic analysis contains major computational errors and/or omits more than 1 major economic factor.	
3.2) ChE graduates will demonstrate an ability to communicate effectively in writing.	Written report is virtually error-free, logically presents design recommendations and analysis, is well organized and easy to read, and contains high quality graphics.	Written report presents design recommendations and analysis logically, is well organized and easy to read, contains high quality graphics, and contains few minor grammatical and/or rhetorical errors.	Written report is generally well written but contains some grammatical, rhetorical and/or organizational errors; design recommendations and analysis are mentioned but not fully discussed.	Written report does not present design recommendations or analysis clearly, is poorly organized, and/or contains major grammatical and/or rhetorical errors.	

CHAPTER 6

THE SCHOLARSHIP OF ASSESSMENT: INCREASING AGENCY AND COLLABORATION THROUGH THE SCHOLARSHIP OF TEACHING AND LEARNING

Cassandra Phillips and Greg Ahrenhoerster
University of Wisconsin Waukesha

In the current assessment climate, it is not unusual for academic departments to balk at the idea of a mandated state- or national-level assessment protocol. In Composition, instructors can feel particularly imposed upon as the majority of standardized testing and rubrics endorsed by many administrations and institutions can conflict with a discipline that places high value on the writing process. With the Spellings Commission concluding that national standardized testing is the best way to study how students learn at the college level (American Association of Colleges and Universities, 2006), there does not seem to be a near end to such ideological conflict. As Schneider, Leydens, Olds, and Miller articulate in Chapter 5 of this volume, "Guiding Principles in Engineering Writing Assessment: Context, Collaboration, and Ownership," there is a "paradigm clash" in effect as instructors and measurement experts often view assessment through differing ideological lenses.

These ideological lenses, while different, do not have to be combative or mutually exclusive, however. Instructors and researchers have begun to find new and innovative ways to expand on Huot's suggestion to increase agency in the assessment process (see Huot, 2002). Some have combined elements of differing methodologies (Beyer & Gillmore, 2007) while others like Zawacki & Gentemann have localized the process by embedding assessment within their courses (see Chapter 4). What's more, Zawacki and Gentemann have shown how assessment at the state level can work to benefit both parties. At the University of Wisconsin Colleges (UW Colleges),[1] the English department has also found a way to conduct meaningful state-level assessment through the merging of the principles of the Scholarship of Teaching and Learning (SoTL) with the principles of assessment. By keeping the overall mission of SoTL in mind, we were able to produce meaningful data that focused on the learning processes and outcomes of our courses.

In 2003, the Higher Learning Commission (HLC) mandated a more streamlined, documented approach to both institutional and department assessment at the University of Wisconsin Colleges.[2] While the English Department at the UW Colleges

---

[1] The University of Wisconsin Colleges consists of thirteen freshman/sophomore campuses across the state of Wisconsin.

[2] The Higher Learning Commission (HLC) of the North Central Association of Colleges and Schools is an independent corporation that provides institutional accreditation to degree-granting institutions in the North Central United States.

was readily able to meet the goals of the HLC, the assessment process seemed, at times, to lack a connection to the teaching and research interests of the department. In particular, the requested evidentiary support, which (in order to complete institutionally mandated assessment reports) required us to look for results that could be categorized as exceeding, meeting, or failing to meet institutional or departmental expectations, promoted an assessment protocol that might be considered isolated and impractical from the tenets of our discipline. It also severely limited the types of questions about teaching and learning that we could ask. This disparity led to noticeable departmental apathy about the assessment process as well as the results it produced.

After becoming co-Departmental Assessment Coordinators in 2005, we piloted the merging of assessment with a SoTL project. Initially, our primary hope was simply to increase agency by researching an issue of interest (of our own choosing) within our department, and to do so by using methodology more appropriate to our discipline. However, by the end of the two-year cycle, we were pleased to discover that not only had we met our project goals, but we had also conducted a thorough research study that supported several important goals about student learning. While we do detail some of the key components of the research project, the focus of this chapter is the way in which departments can re-envision assessment through SoTL, even when in a mandated form.

Background

The HLC's assessment policy requires institutions to provide specific evidence indicating student learning. Upon a first reading of HLC policy, it might appear that assessment protocols more theoretically compatible with these guidelines would demand a more quantitative approach. For example, consider the following section on evidence in HLC policy:

> Core Component C. The organization's ongoing evaluation and assessment processes provide reliable evidence of institutional effectiveness that clearly informs strategies for continuous improvement.
>
> Examples of Evidence:
> - The organization demonstrates that its evaluation processes provide evidence that its performance meets its stated expectations for institutional effectiveness.
> - The organization maintains effective systems for collecting, analyzing, and using organizational information.
> - Appropriate data and feedback loops are available and used throughout the organization to support continuous improvement.
> - Periodic reviews of academic and administrative sub-units contribute to improvement of the organization.
> - The organization provides adequate support for its evaluation and assessment processes. (HLC, 2008, p. 17)

In addition to its emphasis on the collection and organization of data, the methodology assumes a specific outcome—evidence of "effectiveness." As a result, the UW Colleges as a whole developed an assessment program that consisted of a series of institutional "proficiencies" and rubrics for measuring whether students exceeded, met, or failed to meet expectations for demonstrating proficiency of desired skills. There are a total of 17 institutional proficiencies, from four different skill categories: Analytical skills, Quantitative skills, Communication skills, and Aesthetic skills. Figure 1 provides a typical example.

Exceeds Expectations	• Synthesizes information and ideas (i.e., evidence, statements, graphics, questions) very well • Interprets the information and ideas accurately
Meets Expectations	• Synthesizes information and ideas (i.e., evidence, statements, graphics, questions) adequately • Interprets most of the information and ideas accurately
Fails to Meet Expectations	• Fails to synthesize information and ideas (i.e., evidence, statements, graphics, questions) • Fails to interpret information and ideas accurately

Figure 1. Analytical skill 1: Interpret and synthesize information and ideas.

While individual academic departments were encouraged to create similar proficiencies and rubrics specific to their courses and to assess students, it is clearly assumed that the assessment of those proficiencies will take place in the exceeds, meets, or fails to meet categories. That assumption is what caused our department's feeling of limitation in regards to assessment.

The English department conducted assessment in this way for a few years and did gain some insight about student learning; however, it became apparent that the department was resistant to this approach for two reasons. The first reason was that all of the results came in the form of numerical data. Almost all of the members of the department are trained as literature and/or composition scholars and, thus, are generally more comfortable analyzing textual data than numbers. And second, we found ourselves asking questions about our teaching that did not always lend themselves to rubrics. However, we knew that assessment was important for a number of reasons, so we participated sincerely, assuming that the current protocol was the way that it needed to be done to satisfy the HLC.

After a couple of years, however, and upon closer reading and discussion of HLC policy, we began to see that there was room to maneuver within policy rhetoric. We then began to envision an assessment project that focused on student learning using a combination of qualitative and quantitative approaches. The first step toward such a project was to get an idea as to what our department was interested in assessing. After preliminary research of department interest, the Assessment Committee chose the topic of peer review. At department meetings and other venues, we noticed that our faculty frequently discussed the quantity and quality of student learning during peer review sessions. Like Freedman (1987a, 1987b) found in her 1987 survey, our faculty seemed to be generally divided as to the effectiveness of peer review. While many of our faculty recognized the potential of peer review for student learning, we seemed to spend most of our time discussing the more negative aspects, to the point of asking ourselves whether or not it was an effective tool for both teaching and student learning. Generally, then, we wondered, "What do our students learn from peer review?"

We formulated a seven-member assessment committee and began to design a study. Our official research question (at that point) became: How do students perceive peer review? Certainly, we were not intending to make broad statements about why students respond to peer suggestions the way they do. In her study of college-level response groups, Berkenkotter (1984) has shown the complexities of student response (p. 319), and we knew that our data would come with a number of complex variables. Rather, we were attempting to provide a snapshot as to what our students did after, not necessarily because of, peer review. And because so many of our faculty used peer review in some form in the classroom, we believed it to be a valid way of assessing department performance.

Thus, while our research question was one that did not easily lend itself to rubrics, we were confident that it was still within the realm of assessment. There is established research in Composition and Rhetoric by Bruffee (1984, 1993), Elbow (1997), Gere and Abbott (1985) and others that shows successful peer review sessions significantly improve student writing. Therefore, any information that we could gather about how students perceive and use peer review could help us understand how well they are learning to write, which, in turn, could give us useful information about how best to teach them. We realized that this information would clearly answer the HLC's charge that we find "appropriate data" that would allow is to "support continuous improvement."

It was also our hope that such a project would not only provide meaningful data for our teaching, but it would also help us understand assessment and how it can be used for faculty development. Ultimately, we hoped we could inspire other departments to consider using SoTL projects as assessment tools.

Methodology

In order to produce multiple sources of data, we conceptualized a research process that would involve an extended data collection period (Yin, 1993, p. 35) that would take place over two assessment cycles, or two years. In the first year of research, we employed surveys and reflective logs to paint a broad picture of peer review and student learning at the UW Colleges. Miles and Huberman (1994) have acknowledged that a great deal of qualitative research can be between a tight, prestructured design and a loose, emergent one (p. 17), and while we were deliberate in our data collection, we were also flexible in our analysis. That is, we used our initial data to design a more focused research methodology for the second year of research. For example, after considering our first year of data, which we will discuss in more detail later, our research question became more specific in the second year, *What do students learn from a peer review session, and how do they apply that knowledge to their writing?* For the second year of research, then, we relied on a more postmodern methodology that utilized a variety of research methods from several different academic traditions (Daniel, 1999, p. 403).

For the first year of the study, however, we designed faculty and student surveys that were distributed department-wide (see Appendices A and B). Through these surveys we received preliminary data concerning perceptions of peer review at the UW Colleges. We wanted to see not only how faculty were using peer review in the classroom, but also how their perceptions of student learning might relate to the students' responses. This information was not only important in terms of establishing a learning environment, but it was crucial in demonstrating to the HLC how our research could assist in continuous improvement.

In the student survey, we asked students to rate the quality and quantity of peer review they received under different categories. The goal of this survey was to assess the kinds of advice students perceived from their peers, as well as to begin to identify factors that contributed to their positive and negative perceptions of peer review. The variety of questions that we asked allowed us to address a wide range of student subsets based on such things as what class they were in, how many semesters they had been in school, how much training in peer review the instructor provided, how much class time was spent on peer review, whether the students received points for participating in peer review, and how the peer review groups were formed. By comparing the students in the various subsets, we could begin to identify many factors that affected the students' peer review experience.

To get a more detailed picture of what students learned from peer review sessions, we created more detailed student logs (completed by students immediately after a peer review session) and reflective responses (completed by students after revising the essay) that were distributed to the committee members' students (see Appendices C and D). Through these logs and responses, we hoped to triangulate the data we received from the faculty and student surveys.

Through the data gathered from the students and faculty surveys, we were able to learn a great deal about the factors that caused students to view peer review more positively or negatively. For example, students felt more positively about peer review if they could choose their own groups and then could stay in them all semester. In addition, student perceptions of peer review improve if more class time is devoted to it (and students are much more likely to complain that not enough time was spent on peer review than that too much time was spent). However, we also learned that giving students points for participating in peer review did not significantly affect their perception of it. These sorts of findings proved helpful to faculty who were looking for practical advice on improving the quality of peer review in their classes. Other findings were a bit more abstract, but still proved interesting to the department. For instance, we learned that students in their second or third semester of college have a more positive attitude towards peer review than students in their first or fourth semester. Obviously this factor is largely out of our hands, but the finding does contribute to our understanding of how our students are learning.

Furthermore, close reading of the student logs and responses helped us understand the mindset of the students more completely. Among the things that we learned from the logs and reflective statements were that while students initially valued peer review because of the positive support they received from classmates, as the semester moved along the need for positive support declined, and, in fact, they begin to grow frustrated with classmates who offered only positive feedback. This development might demonstrate that the students were learning to be more discerning about the feedback that they received (and also that their needs changed throughout the semester). Another development over the course of the semester was that the peer reviews shifted focus away from mechanics and sentence-level issues and more towards issues concerning content and organization. This change was, again, seen as a positive development, as it suggests that the students understand that the revision process needs to focus on these more global concerns first. One less encouraging finding that we learned from the logs and reflective statements is that, while immediately after peer review students report that they will use the feedback they received to improve the content of their paper, in fact, after revising, they admit that most of their attention was on mechanics.

In the second year of the study, we found that our changed methodology both supported and challenged some of our findings from the first year. In that second year, we randomly selected 10 classrooms on which to focus. For each classroom, we had students complete a two-part questionnaire that asked more specific questions about the feedback they received (see Appendix E). We asked students to consider the advice they received specifically in terms of content, organization, mechanics, and "other" (these were the categories they considered in the first-year, multiple-choice questionnaire). The first part was completed immediately after peer review had taken place, and the second part was to be completed after they revised their essay. The goal of the second part was to have the student identify what they actually changed in their essay from the previous draft.

For the coding process, we looked to several studies for guidance. To process the student surveys and questionnaires, we looked to research using reader/response theory such as Connors and Lunsford's "Teachers' Rhetorical Comments on Student Papers" (1993), especially when considering the quality of the advice given. We also looked to studies like Perl's "The Composing Processes of Unskilled College Writers" (1979) to develop a research methodology that would help us process "observable and scorable" learning moments in peer review (p. 418). We coded each response with a "C" for content, "O" for organization, "M" for mechanics, and "A" for miscellaneous and/or other types of comments. We then assigned a number level to each comment. A "1" would mean the student response was blank or not relevant, a "2" would mean the student made a brief, general observation about the draft, a "3" would indicate the student made a specific observation about the draft, and a "4" would mean the student made a concrete suggestion for revision. For example, a comment such as "expand" next to an example would warrant a C2, while a comment such as "expand, there isn't enough here about your experience" would warrant a C3. A C4 would indicate a comment such as "You should expand here...why don't you tell more about how you felt when you returned from your trip?"

By using such a protocol, we were able to see not only the quantity of varying comments by peers (which we believed would help satisfy the needs of the HLC), but we would also see the quality of those comments, which would help satisfy the needs and questions of our department.[3]

General Findings

Nelson argued in 1995 that students are "highly literate about how classrooms work" (p. 411). Likewise, we concluded that our students were highly literate in the peer review process at some level as well as at the revision process—a lot more so than we thought at our faculty meetings. Just as Nelson's goal in her research was to "complicate" our understanding of student writers at the time (p. 426), so, too, do our results complicate the idea of what students learn from peer review. We found that student learning from peer review was not as simple as whether or not they followed the peer reviewer's suggestion—even though that was a big part. It was also about learning from the social network of student writers, and it was also about learning to take, process, and evaluate revision suggestions.

To begin, we found that students are taking away more than just proofreading (mechanics) suggestions from peer-review sessions. For example, consider the breakdown of responses from the student surveys in Figure 2 below.

Question 4: In general, what did you learn from your peer review session? (The session includes reviewing other students' essays, discussing them, reviewing your own essay, and discussing it.)

Nothing	4.5%
Mechanics	18.0%
Content	24.5%
General improvement	39.4%
Organization	10.3%
Something related to social aspects	6.5%
Seeing how others approach the writing assignment or the writing process	34.2%
Positive reinforcement from peers	2.6%

Figure 2. Breakdown of responses from a student survey related to peer review.

---

[3] We coded the data ourselves, along with one other Assessment Committee member. For the first set of data, we worked collaboratively to make sure we had the same idea of what kinds of answers/writing would fall into each category. Once we felt confident we had a similar understanding of each category, we coded data individually.

In support of our first year of data, our statistics also revealed that students become more critical as peer reviewers as they progress through their education. The survey data shows that students feel steadily more confident about their own skills as a peer reviewer (from 3.34 on a 5-point scale in semester one, up to 3.83 for students beyond the fourth semester, with an increase each semester). However, their trust in their peers declines slightly (from 3.68 to 3.48), perhaps suggesting that they no longer accept everything the peer reviewer says, again implying their own level of confidence has grown. Yet, these experienced students are still more likely to find peer review "very useful" than less experienced students (37% for students with four or more semesters of experience, compared to 29% of first-semester students), which suggests that they may have learned to make effective use of the feedback they are given, even if they recognize they do not always agree with it. Furthermore, the fact that the more experienced students report that they focus more on content (4.19) than mechanics (3.81) during their own revision is encouraging news, as peer review is designed to help with these higher-order changes. Our analysis of student revisions supports this assertion—by examining copies of students' final revisions, we were able to see that most students did revise their texts after the peer review process. In each class where we examined student revisions, there were never more than two students (in classes capped at 22) who made no revisions to their final draft. One could even argue through the change in those revisions that students were able to critique and change certain suggestions made by their peers, which supports even further the claim that students become more proficient at peer review and analysis over the course of the semester.

Another major conclusion we reached is that learning to be a peer reader is almost equally important to students (34%) as the suggestions they receive from peers (39%). This knowledge is not usually documented in peer review, and it shows the value of the social element of the process. Nystrand (1986) found that students working in groups produced higher quality revisions and were more aware of writing as "reconceptualization" and recursive (p. 4). Our student logs often reflected this social awareness from a basic level about topic interest, "I learned that this seemed to be an interesting topic for others to read about. At first when I started this paper, I wasn't sure if people would be interested," to a more sophisticated awareness of audience, "You learn more about how people react to your paper, and it may not be the reaction you wanted to show." As students might articulate that they are concerned about audience awareness, their revisions in their final drafts show that they do, on many levels, care about what their peers say about their drafts and their revisions reflect that awareness accordingly.

Our data also corroborated some earlier, more negative findings about peer review as well. For example, Newkirk (1984) has explored the problems that can arise when students try to read like their teachers. For instance, he found that students would "indulge their own opinions and idiosyncrasies," therefore, changing and/or rejecting text rather than helping their peer find a way to express it more clearly (p. 309). We found, particularly through the textual analysis and student reflections, that students were less likely to take peer suggestions seriously when they thought their peers weren't credible and/or knowledgeable about the subject being discussed. One student remarked, "I will not follow through on the revision because all she offered were her opinions about my topic rather than my writing," while another added, "He clearly knows nothing about politics, so I won't follow any of his suggestions."

Our most conclusive finding, however, was that the more focus and guidance the instructor provided the better, or more "successful," peer review. This finding was also the most helpful to our faculty, many of whom were looking for specific advice as to how to improve peer review in the classroom.

Finally, peer review is, at least at the UW Colleges, taking place in the majority of our classrooms (97%). What's more, its influence on student revisions is considerable. Consider student responses on the surveys as shown in Figure 3.

Question 5: (After student revised) How did the peer review experience actually influence the way you revised your paper?

Note: student responses often covered more than one of these areas.

	No Changes (4.2%)	Made changes, but not related to peer review (6.9%)	Made some changes (31.3%)	Made most/ all changes suggested in peer review (57.6%)
Nothing	4.2%			
Mechanics		2.1%		19.4%
Content		1.4%	12.5%	35.4%
General Improvement		5.5%	9.7%	24.3%
Organization				4.9%
Social aspects			0.7%	1.4%
Seeing how others approached the assignment			4.9%	2.8%
Positive reinforcement from peers helped			0.7%	

Figure 3. Breakdown of responses from a student survey related to peer review.

As the data show, almost all students are revising their essays on some level after the peer review session. While a small number of students (6.9%) report making changes not related to peer review, the vast majority have made changes to their writing as a direct result of their peers' comments.

Our experience as assessment coordinators has helped us to see that, though it is true that faculty members can be apathetic or even disgruntled with assessment, there are many ways for departments to take ownership of the process. By viewing assessment as a research opportunity, it becomes an opportunity to help student learning. In particular, the SoTL guidelines (see Hutchings, 2000) not only help departments design their assessment research projects, but they help legitimize research and answer questions about whether these projects really qualify as formal assessment. By focusing on such guidelines, we have also discovered how learning, particularly student learning, opens a window to explore department goals and teaching effectiveness.   The key is to remember that assessment is not just about reporting progress to another party, but also about refocusing and sharpening that lens toward research and methodology that improves our teaching.

REFERENCES

American Association of Colleges and Universities. (2006). *AAC&U statement on Spellings Commission draft report.* Retrieved July 31, 2009, from http://www.aacu.org/About/statements/SpellingsFinalDraft.cfm

Berkenkotter, C. (1984). Student writers and their sense of authority over texts. *College Composition and Communication, 35,* 312–319.

Beyer, C. H., & Gillmore, G. M. (2007). Longitudinal assessment of student learning: Simplistic measures aren't enough. *Change, 39*(3), 44–47.

Bruffee, K. (1984). Peer tutoring and the conversation of mankind. In G. A. Olson (Ed.), *Writing centers: Theory and administration.* Urbana, IL: National Council of Teachers of English. (ERIC Document Reproduction Service No. ED 246483)

Bruffee, K. (1993). *Collaborative learning: Higher education, interdependence, and the authority of knowledge.* Baltimore, MD: Johns Hopkins University Press.

Connors, R. J., & Lunsford, A. (1993). Teachers' rhetorical comments on student papers. *College Composition and Communication, 44*(2), 200–224.

Daniel, B. (1999). Narratives of literacy: Connecting composition to culture. *College Composition and Communication, 50*(3), 393–410.

Elbow, P. (1997). Some guidelines for writing-response groups. In C. B. Olson (Ed.), *Practical ideas for teaching writing as a process at the high school and college level* (Rev. ed.). Sacramento, CA: Bureau of Publications, California Department of Education.

Freedman, S. W. (1987a). *Peer response in two ninth-grade classrooms.* (Technical Report No. 12). Berkeley, CA: Center for the Study of Writing.

Freedman, S. W. (1987b). *Response to student writing.* (Research Report No. 23). Urbana, IL: National Council of Teachers of English.

Gere, A. R., & Abbott, R. D. (1985). Talking about writing: The language of writing groups. *Research in the Teaching of English, 19,* 362–385.

Higher Learning Commission. (2008). *Higher Learning Commission policy book.* Retrieved July 31, 2009, from http://www.ncahlc.org/index.php?option=com_content&task=view&id=101&Itemid=117

Huot, B. (2002). *(Re)Articulating writing assessment for teaching and learning.* Logan, UT: Utah State University Press.

Hutchings, P. (2000). Approaching the scholarship of teaching and learning. In P. Hutchings, (Ed.), *Opening lines: Approaches to the scholarship of teaching and learning* (pp. 1–10). Menlo Park, CA: Carnegie Foundation for Teaching and Learning. (ERIC Document Reproduction Service No. ED449157)

Miles, M. B., & Huberman, M. A. (1994). *Qualitative data analysis: An expanded sourcebook.* Thousand Oaks, CA: Sage.

Nelson, J. (1995). Reading classrooms as text: Exploring student writers' interpretive practices. *College Composition and Communication, 46,* 411–429.

Newkirk, T. (1984). Direction and misdirection in peer response. *College Composition and Communication, 35*(3), 301–311.

Nystrand, M. (1986). Learning to write by talking about writing: A summary of research on intensive peer review in expository writing instruction at the University of Wisconsin-Madison. In M. Nystrand (Ed.), *The structure of written communication* (pp. 179–211). Orlando, FL: Academic Press.

Perl, S. (1979). The composing processes of unskilled college writers. *Research in the Teaching of English, 13*(4), 317–336.

Yin, R. K. (1993). *Applications of case study research.* London: Sage Publications.

APPENDIX A

Faculty Survey

1. How do you employ peer review in your classroom? (If your answer is "a" skip to question 8)
   a.   I do not use peer review.
   b.   I use a guided peer review (i.e., I provide the students with a specific set of questions to answer or prompts to respond to for each essay they read).
   c.   I use a more general peer review (i.e., the students are asked to respond however they see fit).

2. How is peer review structured in your classroom?
   a.   Students work in pairs.
   b.   Students work in groups of more than two.

3. What kind of training or instruction do you provide for students conducting peer review in a typical semester?
   a.   I provide no (or almost no) training and/or instruction.
   b.   I provide written instruction (i.e., a handout) only.
   c.   I provide verbal training/instruction (i.e., lecturing, modeling a peer group in front of the class, showing a video, etc) only.
   d.   I provide a combination of written and verbal training.

4. How much class time (for each class in a typical semester) do you devote to training (see question 3) your students to conduct peer review?
   a.   I spend no (or almost no) class time training students.
   b.   I spend less than 30 minutes training students.
   c.   I spend between 30 and 75 minutes training students.
   d.   I spend more than 75 minutes training students.

5. How do you assess student performance during peer review?
   a.   Students are not graded or given points/credit for peer review performance.
   b.   Students are graded for the quality of their peer review performance.
   c.   Students receive points/credit for participating in peer review, but quality is not assessed.

6. How much class time do you spend on peer review for each essay assignment?
   a.   Less than an hour (less than one class period)
   b.   An hour (one class period)
   c.   Around two hours (two class periods)
   d.   More than two hours (two class periods)

7. **Do you encourage your students to look for global concerns (*content, arguments, development, effectiveness, structure, logical arrangement*), local concerns (*grammar, spelling, diction, punctuation, clarity of sentences/ phrases*), or both?**
   a. global concerns
   b. local concerns
   c. both

8. **How valuable do you think peer review is?**
   a. It is one of the most important things we do in a composition class.
   b. It is useful but limited.
   c. It doesn't help students very much.

APPENDIX B

Student survey

1. What English class are you currently in (e.g. ENG 101, ENG 102)?

2. How many semesters have you been in college (here or elsewhere):
   a. This is my 1st semester.
   b. This is my 2nd semester.
   c. This is my 3rd semester.
   d. This is my 4th semester.
   e. I have been in college for more than 4 semesters.

3. Thinking about your experience in previous classes (before the one you are currently in), either in high school or college, how would you describe the experience you had using peer review?
   a. mostly positive
   b. mixture of positive and negative
   c. mostly negative
   d. I never used peer review in any previous class.

NOTE: All of the remaining questions are about the class you are currently sitting in.

4. How often did you participate in peer review in this class? (Note, if your answer to question 4 is "d" skip to question 18.)
   a. on every paper
   b. on most papers
   c. on a few papers
   d. not at all

5. When revising your paper, how useful do you find the feedback given by your peers during peer review?
   a. extremely helpful
   b. somewhat helpful
   c. not very helpful

6. **On a scale from 1–5, five being very qualified and comfortable, how qualified/comfortable do you feel when giving feedback on other students' essays?**

Very Comfortable   *Moderately Comfortable*   *Not at all Comfortable*

   5   4   3   2   1

7. **How much class time in the entire semester did the instructor of this class devote to training the students how to do peer review (this could include handouts, lecture, showing a video, modeling a peer review in front of the class)?**
   a. none
   b. less than 30 minutes
   c. between 30 and 75 minutes
   d. more than 75 minutes

8. **In your opinion, the amount of training the students received on how to do peer review was**
   a. not enough
   b. about right
   c. too much

9. **In this course, peer review was conducted**
   a. entirely in class
   b. outside of class, online
   c. outside of class, face-to-face
   d. using a combination of these types.

10. **In this course, how was peer review graded or assessed by the instructor**
    a. The quality of the students' peer review comments was graded (either the instructor read the comments later and graded them or listened in on the sessions and added or reduced points based on the quality of the comments).
    b. Students received points for participating in peer review, but the quality of the comments was not graded.
    c. The students received no points or grade for participating in peer review.
    d. I am not sure how peer review is graded or assessed in this class.

11. **Typically, how much class time were peer-review groups/pairs given to complete peer review for the group/pair?**
    a. less than one hour (less than one class period)
    b. about an hour (one class period)
    c. about two hours (two class periods)
    d. more than two hours (two class periods)
    e. the time varied greatly from assignment to assignment
    f. peer review was completed entirely outside of class

12. **In your opinion, the amount of class time that students were given to complete peer review was**
    a. not enough
    b. about right
    c. too much

13. **How were the peer review groups/pairs formed in the class?**
    a. The instructor assigned students to different groups/pairs each time.
    b. The students were allowed to form their own groups/pairs each time.
    c. The instructor assigned groups/pairs at the beginning of the semester, and students were required to stay in them all semester.
    d. Students chose groups/pairs at the beginning of the semester and stayed in the same groups all semester.
    e. It varied from paper to paper.

14. **On a scale from 1–5 (5 being *very strongly* and 1 being *not at all*), how much did the peer reviewers typically focus on the following aspects of your essays?**

    Content (developing the argument, providing more evidence or explanation)

Very Strongly		Moderately		Not at all
5	4	3	2	1

    Organization (having a clear thesis, logical development of ideas, paragraph unity)

Very Strongly		Moderately		Not at all
5	4	3	2	1

    Diction and Mechanics (grammar, spelling, word choice, punctuation, documentation)

Very Strongly		Moderately		Not at all
5	4	3	2	1

15. **When you were revising drafts of essays this semester, how strongly, on a scale from 1–5, did you focus on the following aspects of your essays?**

> **Content** (developing the argument, providing more evidence or explanation)
>
> | Very Strongly | | Moderately | | Not at all |
> |---|---|---|---|---|
> | 5 | 4 | 3 | 2 | 1 |

> **Organization** (having a clear thesis, logical development of ideas, paragraph unity)
>
> | Very Strongly | | Moderately | | Not at all |
> |---|---|---|---|---|
> | 5 | 4 | 3 | 2 | 1 |

> **Diction and Mechanics** (grammar, spelling, word choice, punctuation, documentation)
>
> | Very Strongly | | Moderately | | Not at all |
> |---|---|---|---|---|
> | 5 | 4 | 3 | 2 | 1 |

16. **Thinking about the peer review comments that other students made on your essays, how strongly do you think the student reader's comments reflect what your instructor is looking for when he or she grades your essays?**

Very Strongly		Moderately		Not at all
5	4	3	2	1

17. **Circle the response that best indicates your level of agreement or disagreement with the following statements:**

> a. I find it useful to read the drafts my peers wrote to see how they approached the assignment.
> Agree strongly   Agree   Neutral   Disagree   Disagree strongly

> b. I trust my peers to read my draft carefully and give me useful feedback
> Agree strongly   Agree   Neutral   Disagree   Disagree strongly

> c. When I revised my essay, I made changes specifically based on the feedback I got from my peers.
> Agree strongly   Agree   Neutral   Disagree   Disagree strongly

> d. I enjoy peer review because it lets me get to know my classmates better as people, which makes me feel more comfortable in the class.
> Agree strongly   Agree   Neutral   Disagree   Disagree strongly

18. **Thinking in terms of how much these things improved your writing, how useful did you find the following things?**

   Punctuation and Grammar exercises (worksheets, editing journals, etc.)
   a.   extremely helpful
   b.   somewhat helpful
   c.   not very helpful
   d.   I did not do these for this class.

   Conference(s) with the instructor
   a.   extremely helpful
   b.   somewhat helpful
   c.   not very helpful
   d.   I did not do this for this class.

   Working with a tutor or writing specialist
   a.   extremely helpful
   b.   somewhat helpful
   c.   not very helpful
   d.   I did not do this for this class.

   Looking, as a class, at past student papers on the same assignment
   a.   extremely helpful
   b.   somewhat helpful
   c.   not very helpful
   d.   I did not do this for this class.

APPENDIX C

Student Logs

Fall Assessment 2005
Course:
Instructor:

1. In general, what was valuable from today's peer review session?

2. What specific feedback from your peers will you apply to your revision?

3. Thinking about the essays you read, as well as your own, what similarities and/or differences did you notice about how the writers structured the essays or responded to the assignment?

APPENDIX D

Reflective Statement

Fall Assessment 2005

Course:

Instructor:

How did you revise your final paper based on your peer review? What useful feedback did your peers offer? What useless feedback, if any, did they offer? Provide examples of your peers' comments as evidence.

APPENDIX E

Peer Review Record

Part A: To be answered immediately after peer review

1. What general advice did you receive in regards to *your paper* in each of the following categories?

    Content:
    Organization:
    Mechanics:
    Other:

2. What specific examples from the critique of *your draft* do you think best reflect the advice?

    Suggestions about content:
    Suggestions about organization:
    Suggestions about mechanics:
    Other suggestions:

3. Do you think you will follow the suggestions you received? Why or why not?

4. In general, what did you learn from your peer review session? (The session includes reviewing other students' essays, discussing them, reviewing your own essay, and discussing it.)

Part B: To be answered after completing revision

How did the peer review experience actually influence the way you revised your paper?

What advice from peer reviewers did you end up not following and why?

CHAPTER 7

ASSESSING FROM WITHIN: ONE PROGRAM'S ROAD TO PROGRAMMATIC ASSESSMENT

Anthony Edgington
University of Toledo

As Ed White (1994), Brian Huot (2002), Bob Broad (2003) and others have pointed out, composition teachers, researchers, and especially administrators need to have an understanding of program assessment. As White points out, "assessment is too important and its implications too far-reaching to be left to assessors and other specialists in measurement" (1994, p. 135). However, when composition scholars and teachers avoid assessment, White's well-know dictum often becomes apparent: either assess yourself or someone will do the assessment for you. Often, those outside the program doing the assessment will have limited knowledge of your program, your courses, your teachers, and your students, leading to results and suggestions that offer little value to you—and also possibly leading to critical actions from those in upper administration. Huot (2002) concurs with White's views, arguing that writing assessment needs to be seen as both a field of study and as a form of research that helps to contextualize the arguments and decisions writing program administrators make in their programs. All too often, assessment occurs in response to a local "crisis...cobbled together at the last minute in response to an outside call that somehow puts a program at risk" (Huot, 2002, p. 150). However, if program administrators take the first step by conducting continuous assessment and use this assessment as research for making program decisions, many of these crises can be adverted or, at the very least, can be more easily handled.

In this chapter, I discuss how the composition program at the University of Toledo (UT) has developed various methods for program assessment, which may serve as a model for other programs. At times, additional assessment was spurred by administrative demands. Often, however, our striving to include more assessment originated in a more pro-active stance, resulting from our agreement with Huot's belief that assessment is an important form of research. As a program that consists mainly of full-time lecturers (with only one tenured and one tenure-track professor), we consistently believe in the need for evidence to support our claim that our program has the ability to teach writing to over 20,000 students. Like other composition programs across the country, our program is continuously approached about various program changes, ranging from increased caps to higher course loads to involving new technology or projects in our classrooms. Having assessment data helps us to either resist or consider these changes.

Specifically, I discuss here three recent events affecting program assessment. The first, a composition course assessment survey, has produced extensive feedback from students and instructors and has already provided us with research that will help in revising program goals and curriculum in the future. The second, a move to electronic portfolios, holds the most promise for longitudinal program assessment. Yet, it is a move that has not been without pitfalls and problems, and one that will need consistent review over the next several years. The final method, a move to online submission of placement essays, has encountered many obstacles and has taught our program lessons about creating a university-wide assessment method and about how to navigate internal politics.

In discussing each of these assessment methods, I offer our reflections on the experience and suggest ways that other programs can use these methods or similar ones for their own assessment. Specifically, I want to draw attention to:

- The importance of understanding student perceptions about their writing and their time in writing courses. While composition's assessment methods do incorporate significant time in collecting, analyzing, and reflecting on student writing, developing a broader understanding of one's composition program must also include some collection and analysis of how students think and talk about writing and writing classes at a specific university. After collecting these perceptions, composition programs should study and consider how these beliefs and assumptions can strengthen specific courses and the composition sequence. And, while administrators should develop methods for finding out about student perceptions from across the disciplines and from different student populations, the beginning focus needs to be on first-year writers and first-year writing courses, since these make up the majority of writing course offerings and are, arguably, the most vital writing-related courses at a university.

- While one-time and/or short-term assessment, through surveys, interviews, and other research methods will help administrators strengthen their curriculum and courses, upper administrators may not consider this information valuable for larger assessment and accreditation. Thus, composition programs and administrators would be wise to develop some type of longitudinal assessment, which can be done though the repeated use of surveys, portfolio assessment, pre- and post-writing samples, and focused interviews with students over the course of their college careers. This information will be most important when attempting to show individual writing growth and the long-range effects of composition programs.

- Finally, this chapter will stress the need for locally designed and administered writing assessments. Our revision of current student placement procedures, moving from an on-site, 45-minute timed writing sample to an online, two-hour writing sample including reading, highlights issues that need to be considered in creating local assessments. Two stories intertwine in this narrative. First, our story highlights problems that can occur when programs are pressured by administration to accept nationally standardized assessment tests, such as the recent ACT writing sample. As Anne Herrington and Charles Moran point out in Chapter 9 of this volume, computer-based

108

feedback and scoring programs are limited because of the inauthentic writing situation imposed and due to the lack of feedback offered to the student writer (feedback, they note, is often vague, misleading, and dead wrong). I would add a further variable; not only is the feedback not valuable for the writer, but it is often not valuable or is downright confusing for those attempting to use that score to make an official decision (such as placement). It is for this reason that I agree with Herrington and Moran when they argue that assessment should be with a locally designed prompt, one that is created and used by those with the most experience with and knowledge of that specific community. And, second, our story highlights that while locally designed assessments should be the norm, these are often the most difficult assessments to create. Bringing together different members of a campus community (some with power, some without, some with knowledge of assessment, and some with limited knowledge even of the university) can cause obstacles and headaches for those attempting to create an assessment. My program's story is one such tale.

Our Program

The University of Toledo is one of the last remaining open access schools in the state of Ohio. As such, the first-year composition sequence is organized to best help the wide range of writers and writing abilities that enter our classrooms. Incoming first-year students are currently placed based on ACT scores and, if necessary, an on-site timed writing sample (which will soon change to an online writing sample). Students with ACT scores of 20 or higher or who display average to above-average writing skills in the timed writing sample are placed into ENGL 1110, the three-credit traditional course designed to help student writers in the areas of purpose, development, organization, reading, researching, and grammar. Students who score below 20 on the ACT are required to take the on-site timed writing sample and, if they display below-average writing skills, they are placed into ENGL 1100, a five-credit workshop course. The curriculum for ENGL 1100 and ENGL 1110 are the same (textbook, assignments, focus areas); the difference is that ENGL 1100 is capped at a lower class size (16 students compared to 23 in ENGL 1110) and offers additional workshop time, which is often used for peer reviews, work-shopping, or student-teacher conferences. A small number of students (who display significant weaknesses in their writing and/or grammar) are placed into a non-credit skills course, which students must pass before moving on to ENGL 1110.

Reaction to Prioritization: The Composition Program Satisfaction Survey

I begin here with the composition program satisfaction survey, the first assessment measure designed by our program and the one that has gathered the most feedback at this point. At our university, the word *prioritization* will cause most faculty members to shiver. In 2003, the university administration created a Prioritization Task Force with the goal of developing and implementing a system that would measure and rank departments and programs in relation to the university's overall Strategic Plan and in reaction to decreased funding at the state level. The criteria of department and program productivity, centrality, demand, and quality were to be used in making these decisions. The end goal, and the reason most faculty members experienced a strong negative reaction to the initiative, was the objective to eliminate programs low on the university's priority list. In addition, certain high priority programs would be strengthened (apparently through additional funding and tenure lines). In essence, the task force appeared to have been created to eliminate some programs while providing additional support to others. There was a strong belief that these decisions would create a binary between the humanities and social sciences against natural sciences and technical programs, leading to both verbal and written protest throughout the university faculty.

In the midst of the prioritization discussion, another major development occurred at the university. In 2005, the University of Toledo completed a merger with the Medical University of Ohio (MUO), as MUO became the University of Toledo Health Science Campus. The merger increased UT's student body and, more importantly, the university's position within the Ohio state university system (with the merger, UT became the third largest state university in Ohio). While the merger became the focus of all administrative activity, placing the prioritization process on the backburner for a period of time, it would be unwise to think that the cry for prioritization and program elimination has been completely forgotten. If anything, the merger and increased visibility of the university may lead to an increased interest in "cutting" and "purging" across both the main and health science campuses, with several support services, offices, and programs seeing staff and teaching positions, along with funding, cut further in the future.

As composition administrators, I (as Associate Director) and the director of the program both knew that our program could be a target of future cutbacks. Over the past five years, the composition director has made great progress in moving towards a full-time teaching faculty, converting over two dozen part-time lines into full-time lecturer positions, complete with higher pay, health benefits, and continued employment based on review. However, while composition courses have long been seen as a "cash cow" for the university (it is the only required course for all students), there is still a belief among some faculty and administrators that composition courses could be taught just as effectively by part-time, adjunct faculty and graduate students at a cheaper rate of pay. As administrators, we recognized the possibility of seeing our full-time teaching positions depleted, along with challenges to our course caps and funding, if we cannot show continued success and improvement within our writing courses.

The call for prioritization, along with a rising interest at our university in the technological and scientific programs, heightened our concerns about the future makeup of UT composition courses. Our decision was to make a more concerted effort to put program assessment methods into place. Unlike several of our fellow programs and faculty—who appear to have taken the "let's see what happens with this prioritization idea first" approach—we believed it was better to enact these methods proactively in order to provide us with relevant data while also offering us a chance to conduct real research on our classes and students so we can build upon our already strong program. We began to contemplate ways to validate the instruction in our classrooms and, in essence, strengthen the view of our program across the campus. However, we were also cognizant of recent work in educational and writing assessment that argues for a more robust view of validity when creating assessments while also striving to incorporate Huot's view of assessment as a form of research. Current validity theory (Huot, 2002; Messick, 1989; Moss, 1994) argues that those creating assessment methods must take into consideration effects on those conducting and completing the assessment. Unlike previous notions of validity, which focused mainly the how the method was constructed, new views on validity ask assessors to consider whether the assessment is appropriate given the desired outcomes, what effect the assessment has upon various stakeholders involved, and what decisions and actions will be taken based upon the assessment results. This view of validity moves beyond the test and argues for additional empirical data in order to support the assessment that is taking place.

In designing assessment tools that would help us study the impact our composition courses have on student writing development, we carefully considered these views on assessment. Creating a way for students to offer us continuous feedback about their perceptions on their writing and on the courses they were taking was the first step. Our first assessment tool was a composition course assessment survey that would be distributed to students in all first- and second-semester composition courses. There had been a paper survey, created by a previous composition administrator, distributed during past semesters, and we began the creation of our new survey using the previous questions. Working with a small group of experienced composition instructors, we designed a 15-question survey that we felt gave students the opportunity to provide feedback on their experiences in our composition courses. Unlike the more general, university-wide teacher evaluations, this survey asked students to respond to specific questions related to our program's goals and objectives (which focus on assisting students in the areas of purpose, development, organization, grammar, reading, and research). In addition, while the university-wide evaluations offered limited space for open-ended feedback, our survey offered students the chance to offer more extensive feedback throughout the survey in the form of multiple comment sections.

This is not to say that we did not face some problems when creating and, subsequently, distributing the survey. Some members of the group disagreed with the number of questions, encouraging the rest to consider a smaller survey that asked more general questions. Instructors throughout the program also expressed some trepidation, mainly in two specific areas. First, in our program, students have several options when taking a second-semester course, including one course on scientific and technical writing (usually taken by science and engineering majors) and another course on organizational report writing (usually taken by business majors). Instructors in our program who regularly taught these courses worried that the survey questions did not adequately represent the objectives and goals of those classes and may not offer students in these courses a chance to express their concerns. The second area of concern focused on who would have access to the survey results and whether this information could be used in faculty assessment. While most faculty voiced little concern about whether administrators would be able to access results for individual teachers or sections, others were greatly troubled by this and, in resistance, raised issues related to the university's teaching and union contracts. Finally, there was the issue of disbursement: what would be the best way of getting the survey out to students? The previously used composition survey was paper-based, which meant that a large number of students would have access to it, but also meant an increased amount of time administering the survey and later calculating and analyzing the results (which was major pitfall, given that the two administrators are the only permanent, tenure-track faculty in the program).

Concerns like these are a normal and, in fact, healthy part of assessment. As Cronbach (1988), Messick (1989), and others point out, assessments should be designed with the concerns and beliefs of the most affected stakeholders in mind. Rather than overlooking or ignoring these concerns, a program would be wise to consider them, bringing various voices into the process of creating the assessment. In our program, we have been fortunate to receive continued funding through the Center for Teaching and Learning, allowing us to send teachers for conferences and pay teachers for summer work projects. In addition, this funding provides for our Composition Colloquium, a series of monthly meetings with composition instructors where we talk about current issues and problems and address possible solutions. The Colloquium became the site for discussion about the survey, providing instructors the opportunity to voice their concerns and for administrators to address these issues. For example, we were able to address the issue of teacher confidentiality, deciding that while students would still place a checkmark beside the course and section number in which they were currently enrolled, information on the section number would be kept confidential and only accessible to the college assessment officer overseeing the survey. Teachers in the Colloquium also assisted us in revising the questions and validating the need for specific questions (even if this meant maintaining the longer survey).

To resolve the problem concerning distribution, we needed to include another important constituent: the research office for the College of Arts and Sciences, our governing body at the university. Fortunately, we developed a good relationship with one of the research analysts in the college, who assisted in developing the survey (see Appendix A) and has since provided us with strong support in collecting and analyzing the data we have received. I spoke with him about the potential problems of a paper-based survey, and he suggested moving to an online format, where students would be emailed a link to the survey and asked to fill it out over the last three weeks of the semester. While he cautioned that not all students use their university email accounts, he remarked that other campus programs using this method for their surveys still received a 15–20% return rate. He also suggested that the online method would allow for quicker and more detailed analysis and would be more cost effective than a paper-based survey. It would not cost the program or English department money for the time needed to distribute, collect, tabulate, and analyze the survey responses. We have used this online method for the past two years and have consistently received responses from 18–20% of the first-year writing population. And, as the university places more emphasis on students using their university email accounts and as the survey becomes a more noticeable tool in composition classrooms, we feel that the response rate could rise over the next few years.

While the current version of the survey has only been used for a few semesters, we are already beginning to see some trends in students' answers. First, students have been consistently happy with their growth as writers in the composition courses. For four consecutive semesters, over 80% of survey respondents remarked that they either agreed or strongly agreed that their writing has improved after taking a respective composition course. Another area of strength has been in students' views on their ability to write for different purposes and for different genres, with four semesters of 70% or higher responses in the strongly agree and agree categories. In addition, most respondents believe that the skills they are learning in composition courses will be valuable to them in future classrooms and employment opportunities, and a few have already pointed to specific ways they have used these skills in their discursive statements. Finally, the survey has shown that our current placement practices are also succeeding, since a high number of respondents agreed that the course they were in was appropriate to their current writing level. These findings, along with more detailed discursive comments, provide us with valuable information to take to upper administration, in case the call for prioritization is heard again.

Yet, a good assessment tool should not only acknowledge a program's strengths, but should also help in identifying where the program is currently lacking or needs improvement. The survey has provided us with information to help strengthen some problem areas in our classrooms. For example, from the survey data and written comments, we have discovered that composition students feel a low level of comfort with technology and do not believe that our composition courses are doing enough to help them better understand how to critically reflect on and use new technology, especially writing-related software, or how to write in online environments and for virtual audiences. Since technology has been a component of our program's goals and objectives, this trend has been a disturbing one (and has helped further fuel the move to electronic portfolios, as detailed below). Another area of concern has been with critical thinking skills, as students' responses are mixed on how much these skills are being developed in composition courses (finding that only slightly more than 60% of students believe they have developed better critical thinking skills in our classrooms). Finally, while about 70% of students believe they have developed the skills necessary to work with their peers, the percentages within classes vary, with more second-semester students responding favorably to peer work than first-semester students. Over the past few years, more emphasis has been placed on creating pedagogically oriented resource materials—including a program-wide faculty handbook and handbooks for teaching our first- and second-semester courses. Using data from our survey, we plan to continually revise these current resources and create new ones that will help to strengthen these weaker areas.

Creating an in-house assessment tool like the composition course assessment survey assists a program in strengthening its goals, objectives, and curriculum. The process of creating our survey has been mostly a positive one, and we have learned some important points during the process. First, all programs should strive to create some type of assessment that will gauge overall student reactions to their courses, not waiting until someone from upper administration mandates the assessment. In addition to a survey like the one we developed, focus-group interviews or student-written reflective texts can provide productive feedback. Second, when creating the assessment, it is important to involve as many connected individuals as possible, including students, teachers, and administrators. And, finally, the assessment should include opportunities for both quantitative (i.e., Likert questions) and qualitative (i.e., open-ended questions) research, offering programs a more robust view of their courses and pedagogies. While the process of creating a survey was a time-consuming one, the results and subsequent changes that will be made based on its findings have convinced us that the composition course assessment survey is a tool that will remain part of our program assessment for years to come.

Longitudinal Assessment and Electronic Portfolios

While the composition course assessment survey offers us informative student feedback and allows us to locate potential problems in our courses, the survey does not tell us whether students' writing becomes more developed over their college careers. To obtain some of this information, we needed to think about a longitudinal system for assessment that would allow us to collect and analyze student texts over several semesters. For us, portfolios offered the best method for longitudinal assessment and have long been promoted as a possible program assessment tool in composition literature (Condon & Hamp-Lyons, 1994; Huot, 1994; Larson, 1991). While the two administrators of the composition program had already been thinking about the need for an electronic portfolio system (including hosting visits from experts on formative assessment and open-source portfolio systems), it was an invitation from the university to participate in discussions about the Epsilen portfolio system that opened the door to consider moving to an online portfolio system for both classroom and program assessment. Epsilen is an online service that offers students a place for both social networking and e-portfolios (electronic portfolios). Students who create an account receive a website where they can store various documents (print, image, sound, etc.), maintain wikis and blogs, join academic discussion groups, and participate in online courses. As the creators of the system explain, "users describe Epsilen as an academic 'MySpace' and 'FaceBook', connecting peers to share knowledge and exchange objects" (http://www.epsilen.com/Epsilen/Public/Home.aspx). Our university invited a professor from a regional campus already using the Epsilen system to discuss the process of incorporating Epsilen into our courses, along with some limited information on how his program was using the portfolios for programmatic assessment. While the two composition administrators were still interested in the possibility of an open-source portfolio system, which could be provided free of cost and did not present possible ownership dilemmas, the university argued that it could not provide technical support for an open-source portfolio system (Epsilen could provide this as part of the licensing fee to be paid by the university). Thus, we offered our support to a pilot study of the Epsilen system in various classes, including several composition courses.

Regardless of the system chosen, we were excited and saw great potential with the introduction of an online portfolio system. Over the past several years, many classes in our program had moved to a web-assisted, WebCT class site, and it could be estimated that in any given semester, 30–40% of composition courses utilize WebCT. The class sites often become the home for important class documents, like the syllabus, assignment sheets, and reading selections. WebCT also offers teachers a place for assignment submission; for some instructors, this helped to make the act of responding to and grading writing more manageable. Finally, several communications functions, including chat rooms and discussion boards, are available with a WebCT class site. Epsilen offers similar tools, through both individual student sites and sites generated for classroom use; however, we feel that Epsilen offers even more possibilities. For one, Epsilen offers students the chance to collect and select class writings into an online portfolio, a feature not yet available with WebCT. Epsilen sites remain active throughout the students' time at the university, thus allowing students the opportunity to create portfolios of texts from multiple semesters and multiple disciplines (WebCT sites are taken down at the end of each semester). Unlike WebCT, Epsilen users can communicate with students outside of their class and even outside of their university. And, the hope is that these portfolios will remain active after graduation, offering students at place for maintaining job employment showcase portfolios. Thus, as a classroom tool, Epsilen offers teachers and students the chance to maintain an ever-increasing showcase of their work, a showcase that can be made available to others both within and outside our university, while also supplying teachers with many of the course management tools to which they have grown accustomed (such as online submission of assignments, response and grading mechanisms, and online communication options). As administrators, the move to an online portfolio system offers us the chance to follow students longitudinally, investigating the level and range of student growth from first-year students to seniors. We also believe that an online portfolio system will assist us in better understanding the level of writing development both within our own composition courses and also in writing-across-the-curriculum classes. Finally, this information provides strong data to present to upper administration in case a new round of prioritization dialogues takes place on our campus.

Thus, when departments and programs were offered a chance to pilot Epsilen with our students, we quickly volunteered and asked four full-time lecturers to incorporate the online program into their writing classes. One of the four lecturers already had extensive experience with the Epsilen system, so he took on a leadership role with the pilot study lecturers. All four had experience using paper-based portfolios and were thus able to use that knowledge to make the shift to e-portfolios. Portfolios can take different forms, including working portfolios (that ask students to include all drafts and final papers from a course), showcase portfolios (where students select certain texts to include in the final portfolio), and, as discussed here, e-portfolios, which are published online for multiple readers and could include links to outside sites and sources. Portfolios have long been seen as a more progressive assessment tool, offering instructors a chance to view student progress over several drafts and over a range of papers. They also provide students a way of reading and assessing student work outside of the traditional grade-oriented lens, as portfolios allow teachers to defer grading until later in the course. The move to e-portfolios offers the additional variable of longitudinal assessment of student writing across specific courses, disciplines, and the university.

Over the course of two semesters, the four instructors worked on different ways of incorporating both e-portfolios and the Epsilen system into their courses. In some classes, students used the Epsilen site to upload only a final portfolio; in others, peers and teachers responded to rough drafts using the Review It folder within the Epsilen system. Two of the instructors experimented with the course software components of the system and created course sites. Student-generated blogs became a new and exciting addition to many of these classes (a blog function is provided with each individual website). And, instructors with extensive Epsilen experience set up communications with other Epsilen users outside of the university, leading to cross-class dialogue among students and the creation of shared projects among classes. There was general agreement among the pilot teachers that the Epsilen system was a strong pedagogical tool, with each remarking that students appeared to enjoy not only the academic use of the site, but also the social networking and communication functions that Epsilen offered. Each hoped that the program (and the university) would invest in the system long-term.

During the summer of 2007, we received word that the university would, in fact, renew its membership with the Epsilen system. During this same time, two of the original four lecturers working on the pilot project created a handbook that could be used by teachers and students in creating and using either an individual Epsilen e-portfolio site or a course management site. One significant part of this handbook was the creation of an assessment matrix to be uploaded to student portfolio sites, where students would be able to upload course texts that showcased their work across their academic careers and highlighted how they had satisfied program goals (see Appendix B). In the left column, composition program goals and objectives are listed along with questions to consider when choosing a document(s) to upload that satisfies those objectives. Under the proposed assessment, students submit documents at various intervals during their college careers (as outlined at the top of the matrix). We then hope to bring together instructors from both within and outside of the composition program to review a percentage of these matrix portfolios, using this knowledge to create a picture of writing within our composition classes and at our university.

The matrix is the first step in developing a programmatic assessment tool; it is our hope that over the next few years, students will use the matrix to enter papers from first- and second-semester writing courses that support the learning objectives defined. Later, we hope to encourage faculty from across the disciplines to have students

116

in their writing-across-the-curriculum classes enter course texts into the matrix. The eventual goal is to be able to look at student writing from across semesters, disciplines, and genres in order to gauge the level of student writing development. Of course, this is not to say that the move to e-portfolios will be easy. We expect resistance from faculty both within and outside of our department, who see Epsilen as another time-consuming tool or who still do not see the value of moving to an e-portfolio assessment system. We worry about possible funding and whether the administration will continue to support the Epsilen system. Some of those working in our distance learning program, who have invested a great deal of time and money into the WebCT system, view the move to Epsilen as a threat to their software and program. These problems are of an internal nature; we will most likely experience problems with the system itself. For example, as I write this chapter, we are experiencing problems with the Epsilen course management software, as many teachers are complaining that they do not have access to course sites. But, while the move to online portfolios has been and may continue to be somewhat rocky, we believe that the need for a consistent assessment tool, the benefits electronic portfolios offer to students, and the ability to gather data for longitudinal assessment offer strong arguments for moving to the online portfolio system.

Online Placement and Outside Influences

While the composition survey and the move to electronic portfolios were influenced by outside factors but largely created within the composition program, recent moves toward an online placement system were mainly directed by outside forces, with little initial direction supplied by the composition administrators. For the past several years, placement of incoming students at our university has consisted of a two-step process. First, students who achieve a 20 or higher ACT English score (or 480 SAT critical reading score) are placed directly into ENGL 1110, the first course in the composition sequence. Those who score below those marks take a 45-minute single sample writing test, based on prompts designed by instructors in our composition program and overseen by members of the on-campus testing services. These exams are then read by experienced instructors in our program using the direct course placement system developed by William Smith, writing teacher and researcher from the University of Pittsburgh. Using Smith's system, instructors read exams and place students into one of our four composition courses based upon the curriculum for those courses, not on an independent rating system. The courses include Skills 0990, a non-credit remedial course for our most inexperienced writers; ENGL 1100, a five-credit workshop course for novice writers; the more traditional three-credit ENGL 1110 course; or a second-semester course, receiving advanced placement and credit for ENGL 1110. Two instructors read each exam and enter a course placement based upon their readings. If the two placements differ, a third reader reads the exam and enters a course placement. If there are still differences (i.e., all three readers enter a different course placement), the three readers are instructed to talk about their reactions and placements until a consensus is reached.

117

As mentioned earlier, students responding to the composition survey most often agreed that they were correctly placed into their respective courses, and most of the instructors supported the placement system in informal surveys and conversations. Nevertheless, in the summer of 2004, our program was asked by the university administration to consider a move to using the ACT writing sample and scores as a method of placement. Resisting any move that would take placement out of the hands of the composition program, the composition director eventually agreed to a pilot study that would compare placement via the ACT writing exam to our current, in-house placement system. We asked students currently enrolled in composition courses to complete the test under the same circumstances that incoming students would. These exams were then sent to ACT for scoring,[1] and later read and scored by our own placement readers using the direct-course placement method. Our findings from the two-year study were similar to what others have found in studies of the ACT and SAT writing samples: while there was some agreement among ACT and UT readers on placing "upper-end" students (i.e., students receiving a high score from ACT and a high-course placement from UT readers), there was considerable difference in relation to less experienced writers. While UT readers more often placed these students into the ENGL 1100 workshop course (the five-credit workshop course from which students would be able to gain three credits, upon successful completion), the ACT scores placed a much higher number of students into the non-credit-bearing Skills 0990 course. Later correlations with final grades found that many of these possible Skills 0990 students successfully completed either ENGL 1100 or ENGL 1110, justifying our belief that sole use of the ACT score would have led to a harmful amount of misplacement for incoming writers, especially among our novice, inexperienced writers.

While the findings of this study did allow us to momentarily slow down the administration's call for using the ACT writing samples, it also initiated a dialogue within our program about the possible need for a new placement method. Asking students to write for a set time-period on an unfamiliar prompt is not indicative of common writing situations. Several researchers and administrators in composition have called for new placement methods that are either more representative of the writing process (such as portfolio submission), involve students more in the placement decision (such as directed self-placement), or eschew placement altogether through a system of mainstreaming. One additional method that has recently gained popularity is online writing placement, where students are given a prompt, reading, and/or writing situation in advance and then a longer period of time (anywhere from 24 hours to one week) to write a response via an online submission system. Mainstreaming and online placement were two methods we were already considering, and when the administration later approached us, prior to the summer

---

[1] We created the following placement guide to use for the ACT scores: scores of 11 and 12 would receive advanced placement; scores of 7, 8, 9, and 10 would receive placement into ENGL 1110; scores of 4, 5, and 6 received placement into ENGL 1100; and scores of 0, 2, and 3 received placement into Skills 0990.

2007 terms, about considering an online placement system, we were equally interested in exploring this option, although a bit leery about the administration's sudden interest in the method. The first obstacle we faced was a time constraint, since the administration wanted an online system in place prior to the first on-campus orientation sessions, set to begin in early June. While we only had a few weeks to prepare, we felt that it could be possible to have a system up and running before the start of summer orientation (arguing that we would still need the opportunity to make more substantial changes to it before the summer 2008 terms). The director explored different online placement methods and talked to composition administrators at regional schools who were already using this form of placement. We eventually decided to make use of the existing WebCT technology, hoping to create a system where students would be directed to log in to a placement section of WebCT and receive a prompt that asked them to consider a current social or cultural situation. We had explored the idea of offering students an article to read and later write about—an option we are more invested in—but felt that this would be difficult given the short time we had to create the system. Students would then have up to 24 hours to write a response to the prompt, allowing them time to reflect on the writing task, pre-write, draft and, if necessary, revise the answer before final submission. While we were not entirely comfortable with the system and already were recognizing ways to improve it, we did feel it was more valid than our current timed writing sample and that the system could be strengthened over future summers.

However, our excitement waned considerably after the first meeting with other programs and services involved with placement. First, we discovered from the distance learning program that the time needed to create IDs and passwords for incoming students so they could access the WebCT site may extend past the first few orientation sessions, leading to several students not being able to take the placement essay before they enrolled in classes. The bigger issue, however, was contacting students to make them aware of the new placement method. Orientation materials had already been sent out to incoming students with information about the on-campus single sample test, and those at the meeting worried about the method and timing of delivering the new placement information to incoming students. Adding to these concerns was the fact that no one from orientation was at the meeting, and thus many of our questions could not be immediately answered.

Given these constraints, we were approached again about the possibility of using the ACT writing sample as a short-term solution for our online method (we later discovered that the pressure of using some form of online placement came about because the acting provost had prematurely told the university president and board of directors that we would be using the method this year). As mentioned earlier, our program had decided against using the ACT writing sample based on our findings from an earlier study. In addition, several of our placement readers were concerned about the prompts used for the ACT exam, which they found to be very general and unchallenging, discouraging the use of any critical thinking skills. However, with pressure mounting, we offered a compromise. We would consider using the ACT writing samples, but would not use ACT's scoring of those samples as the basis for our placement decision. Instead, we wanted our placement readers to read the samples and score them based on the direct-course placement system we had used in the past. This compromise allowed the administration to continue to sell the idea of online placement, but ensured that placement decisions remained in the hands of our program. We also argued that the method should be a short-term, one summer stopgap, and that we should be able to further pursue online placement the next summer. After receiving assurance from the administration, we began to plan for this new system.

Once again, insurmountable problems emerged. First, we discovered that while the ACT writing sample was required for all incoming students, this did not apply to transfer students. Thus, any transfer student who had not yet completed the first-year composition requirement would still have to take the on-campus timed exam. The second, and more significant, problem was that the composition administrators and placement readers were unable to access many of the online samples. We discovered that students were asked to designate which schools would receive the sample at the time of testing; for many students who made a late decision to attend UT, our university was not listed as one that could receive their sample. We were told by ACT that these samples could be made available, but only after (a) we contacted the students to ask for permission, (b) the students contacted ACT to verify their permission, and (c) the students paid a fee to have the samples released. So, we were once again faced with similar problems—contacting students in a short period of time and, additionally, convincing them to quickly pay a fee—in addition to the fee they had already paid to ACT—to release writing samples to us before their orientation date. With all of these problems confronting us, the program administrators made the decision to end our pursuit of an online placement system. At the next campus meeting, the director made this known to the rest of those programs involved, leading to a heated confrontation with the acting provost. However, most everyone agreed that the obstacles facing us would be extremely difficult to overcome; in the end, we agreed to go back to our original on-campus timed writing sample.

Should this experience with online placement be considered a failure? Yes and no. On the one hand, the project failed because of the various unexpected problems related to technical and access issues. But the project also failed because the administrators in the composition program were not fully prepared for how quickly and vigorously the upper administration would want to move to this new method. While we had begun preliminary talks about a new placement system, we learned that a program needs to be continually researching and preparing itself for any possible initiative, because time may be a factor. We also learned how difficult it can be to develop a system with multiple stakeholders involved, because not all stakeholders saw the move to a new system as one worthy of an investment of significant time and energy, leading to many unanswered questions and endless email conversations.

On the other hand, there were some positive developments that occurred because of this experience. For one, we in the composition program now understand that there is interest in an online placement system; the door has been opened for us.

Second, our time researching national and online placement systems has increased our knowledge about the method, and we already have new ideas for how we can approach the process during the next orientation period. Most importantly, we realized how important it is for the composition program to have a main, even the main, voice in this process. When discussing our goals for next summer, the director of the program asked the new provost both for a guarantee that the university was committed to creating this placement system and that the composition program would make the major decisions in the process (in effect, giving composition sole control over development of the system). She received assurances in both regards. Thus, not only do we now feel confident that an online placement system will happen, we now know that we will be able to create a system that best aligns with our current theories and practices.[2]

Conclusion

Our situation may not be typical of yours. But, more often than not, I have met and talked with other administrators who share similar stories of assessment calls from above and last-minute decisions. We present our path toward programmatic assessment as one more voice in this dialogue, stressing the following points:

- Administrators in writing programs need to take the first step when it comes to program assessment (because, as we have learned, someone in upper administration is probably already thinking about it).
- When designing program assessment, it is best to start local. Talk with students, teachers, other administrators, composition researchers, even local employers and public officials, relying on their knowledge and expertise to help guide your development.
- When talking with administration about your assessment, get guarantees that the assessment will be your own and that decisions about how to implement it will start with you. Avoid having too many hands in the cookie jar.
- And, finally, view assessment not as a necessary evil that needs to be completed, but as a chance to further your knowledge of your program, curriculum, and faculty. Assessment can and should be envisioned as a form of research; thus, do not just let data from your assessment pile up, but find ways to use it to strengthen your writing program.

---

[2] During the fall 2007 semester, discussion of an online placement system (under the direction of the composition director) restarted, and a system was created over two and a half months. As of this writing, no orientation dates had occurred and, thus, no feedback is available on the success or failure of the system.

REFERENCES

Broad, B. (2003). *What we really value: Beyond rubrics in teaching and assessing writing*. Logan, UT: Utah State University Press.

Condon, W., & Hamp-Lyons, L. (1994). Maintaining a portfolio-based writing assessment: Research that informs program development. In L. Black, D. A. Daiker, J. Sommers, & G. Stygall (Eds.), *New directions in portfolio assessment: Reflective practice, critical theory, and large-scale scoring*. Portsmouth, NH: Boynton/Cook.

Cronbach, L. J. (1988). Five perspectives on validity argument. In H. Wainer (Ed.), *Test validity*. Hillside, NJ: Lawrence Erlbaum.

Huot, B. (1994). Beyond the classroom: Using portfolios to assess writing. In L. Black, D. A. Daiker, J. Sommers, & G. Stygall (Eds.), *New directions in portfolio assessment: Reflective practice, critical theory, and large-scale scoring*. Portsmouth, NH: Boynton/Cook.

Huot, B. (2002). *(Re)Articulating writing assessment for teaching and learning*. Logan, UT: Utah State University Press.

Larson, R. L. (1991). Using portfolios in the assessment of writing in the academic disciplines. In P. Belanoff, & M. Dickson (Eds.), *Portfolios: Process and product*. Portsmouth, NH: Boynton/Cook.

Messick, S. (1989). Meaning and values in test validation: The science and ethics of assessment. *Educational Research, 18*, 5–11.

Moss, P. (1994). Validity in high stakes writing assessment: Problems and possibilities. *Assessing Writing, 1*, 109–28.

White, E. (1994). *Teaching and assessing writing* (2nd ed.). San Francisco: Jossey-Bass Publishers.

APPENDIX A

Composition Program Satisfaction Survey

In an effort to assess how effective our composition courses are and to identify areas of concern, we are asking you to take a few minutes to respond to the following questions. Your name will not be asked for at any time during the survey. The survey should take approximately 10–15 minutes to complete.

Please check the composition course in which you are currently enrolled.

ENGL 1100 Composition I with Workshop_____

ENGL 1110 Composition I_____

ENGL 1130 Composition II: Academic Discourses and Disciplines_____

ENGL 1140 Composition II: Writing in the Community_____

ENGL 1150 Composition II: Language and Identity_____

ENGL 1930 Technical Writing for Engineers_____

ENGL 2950 Scientific and Technical Report Writing_____

ENGL 2960 Organizational Report Writing_____

Please select the college you are currently enrolled in:

Arts and Sciences_____

Business_____

Education_____

Engineering_____

Health and Human Services_____

Pharmacy_____

Student Success Center_____

University College_____

Use the following scale when answering:

5 = *Strongly Agree*

4 = *Agree*

3 = *Not Sure or Not Applicable*

2 = *Disagree*

1 = *Strongly Disagree*

1. This course helped me improve my writing skills.

2. I am a more effective writer because of this course.

3. I am more confident in my writing ability because of this course.

Please suggest any comments that helps explain your answers above:

4. Through what I have learned in this course, I am better able to incorporate the results of research, including citing other writers' work and/or my own research, in my writing.

5. This course helped me to write more effectively in different genres (such as commentaries, letters, reports, narratives, and other genres).

6. My writing is more focused and organized because of this course.

Please suggest any comments that helps explain your answers above:

7. I feel more comfortable working with technologies (word processing, email, website analysis and design, WebCT) because of this course.

8. I have learned to analyze an audience and write more effectively for different audiences in this course.

9. This course helped me to become a more critical reader.

Please suggest any comments that helps explain your answers above:

10. Because of this course, I am better able to write in appropriate ways for different purposes.

11. This course helped me to critique my own and others' writing more effectively.

12. I learned to work more effectively with my peers in this course.

Please suggest any comments that helps explain your answers above:

13. I feel this writing course was appropriate for my writing ability.

14. My instructor's comments helped me become a better writer.

15. I believe I will use what I have learned in this course in my future courses.

Please suggest any comments that helps explain your answers above:

APPENDIX B

Composition Program Matrix
(to be used as part of longitudinal assessment with Epsilen portfolios)

	Composition I	Composition II	WAC course	WAC course	Senior Capstone	Reflection
Reflective Essay Write a 500-word explanation of the items you have placed in your ELM for the current course and describe your learning experiences in the course.						
Purpose and Focus Provide an example to show how you were able to vary the purpose of your writings to create texts that adequately and effectively consider audience and genre.						
Organization/Arrangement Provide an example to show how you were able to use effective patterns or arrangements to organize ideas, sentences, paragraphs, or supporting examples.						
Development/Evidence Provide an example that appropriately and strongly supports its main argument. Show that the development of evidence is complex and sophisticated. Describe the method of development: e.g., exemplification, extended definition, summary, illustration, comparison/contrast, synthesis, causation, etc.						
Language and Style Provide an example that illustrates your tone and style. Explain how vocabulary and syntax are adapted to the audience and occasion.						
Secondary Research Provide an example that incorporates library research. Explain how this example illustrates careful choices in published sources. Demonstrate knowledge of the appropriate documentation system (MLA, APA, CSE, Chicago Manual of Style, etc.)						
Reading Response/ Argumentation Provide an example that illustrates your critical reading response to an assigned course reading, a controversial course topic, or another student's document (e.g. peer review or reaction)						
Media Literacy Provide an example that illustrates proficiency in composing text in an alternative medium, such as a webpage, PowerPoint, media clip, oral presentation, formal business letter, workplace document template, graphic aids, etc.						

CHAPTER 8

ASSESSING ENGINEERING COMMUNICATION IN THE TECHNICAL CLASSROOM: THE CASE OF ROSE-HULMAN INSTITUTE OF TECHNOLOGY

Richard House, Jessica Livingston, Mark Minster,
Corey Taylor, Anneliese Watt, and Julia Williams
Rose-Hulman Institute of Technology

Introduction

Within engineering education circles, there has perhaps been no single more transformative event than the move in the 1990s to outcomes assessment for the purpose of engineering program accreditation (a process overseen by ABET, Inc.). George Peterson, ABET, Inc.'s Executive Director, writing in IEEE's *The Interface* newsletter in 2006, noted the impact of the transition to outcomes assessment:

> The move to outcomes-based accreditation criteria was a direct result of challenges to the conventional criteria and, at times, to the organization [ABET, Inc.] itself. Since EC [Engineering Criteria] 2000 was created, the organization has adapted rapidly to the new paradigm for which it calls: Know what you do, do it well, and prove it. (Peterson, 2006, p. 1)

The outcomes approach has necessitated that all engineering programs (and engineering technology, as well as computer science programs too) "know/do/ prove," or, in other words, examine their curricula to determine where students are given the opportunity to develop their skills in eleven student learning outcomes areas, referred to in the shorthand as "ABET a–k," then demonstrate student achievement based on authentic evidence, rather than final course grades (ABET, 2007). Communication is one of the outcomes for which programs must provide evidence.

Analyzing the curriculum and determining opportunities has been one dimension of the focus on communication we see among our engineering colleagues at Rose-Hulman Institute of Technology. But, as a recent survey of our colleagues indicated, ABET, Inc. and program accreditation does not drive the engineering faculty at Rose-Hulman to incorporate written and oral communication into their courses. In a survey of all faculty members conducted during October 2007, we asked respondents to identify the primary reasons why they incorporate written and oral communication into their courses. We were surprised to learn that ABET, Inc. and program accreditation are not the primary motives for such inclusion. Faculty who participated in the survey responded that their primary motivations to include communication in their technical courses were to assess student learning and to prepare students for professional practice. The need to fulfill accreditation requirements was, for these faculty members, the least important reason to include communication (House, Watt, & Williams, 2007). Even so, program accreditation requirements must be fulfilled and evidence of student learning outcomes achievement must be submitted in the Self Study Report that forms part of the documentation for ABET program accreditation. The question may be, how do we align the pedagogical interests of faculty members to the accreditation needs of the engineering programs and the institution?

As the survey results indicate, our engineering colleagues believe that they must contribute to the development of the communication skills of their students who enroll in their technical courses, rather than expecting that the two required writing courses in our curriculum (Rhetoric and Expression in the first year, and Technical Communication in the third year) will be sufficient. They recognize that as practitioners in the field of engineering, they provide students with important models of how to write and speak like an engineer. As faculty without a background in communication pedagogy, however, they sometimes feel less ready to bring writing and speaking assignments into their classrooms. As a result, we often find ourselves consulting with members of the engineering faculty when they decide to incorporate communication into their courses. Fortunately, our work at the class level has been complemented by an institute-wide student learning outcomes assessment effort.

At the institute level, we have defined a set of student learning outcomes that students should demonstrate by the time of graduation. One of these institute learning outcomes is communication. Through a process of curriculum mapping, evidence collection in an electronic portfolio, evaluation of the evidence, and final reporting, we have constructed an assessment process that meets the needs of faculty while still providing important evidence that can be used for program accreditation and improvement. This case study discusses the work we are doing at the class level and the institute level to align the teaching and assessment of communication for students, faculty, and programs.

Institutional Background

Rose-Hulman Institute of Technology (http://www.rose-hulman.edu/) is a private, undergraduate college of approximately 1,900 students located in Terre Haute, Indiana. Its emphasis is on educating undergraduates to pursue careers in the fields of science, engineering, and mathematics. We have a strong track record of creatively developing and rigorously assessing pedagogies for teaching in these fields. For example, we were innovators of the Integrated First Year Curriculum for Science, Engineering, and Mathematics, a curriculum designed to help students understand unifying ideas across seemingly disparate technical disciplines; our experience with the Integrated First Year Curriculum led to our invited participation in the National Science Foundation-sponsored "Foundation Coalition," a nationwide coalition of schools applying current learning theories to revitalize fundamental engineering courses.

In addition to our curricular innovations, we have led the field of science, engineering, and mathematics education in the use of technology in the classroom. We were among the first colleges to require the use of laptop computers (beginning in 1995), and we were one of the first campuses to use Maple (a computer algebra system) in all first-year calculus classes. We continue to produce new technology-enabled "studio" courses (in, for example, physics and electrical engineering) that link hands-on learning in laboratory sessions with theories and concepts from traditional lectures. In addition, we have implemented tablet PCs in the technical classroom with a focus on collaboration and visualization. For these and other education innovations, Rose-Hulman Institute of Technology has been ranked first by engineering educators as the nation's best college or university that offers the bachelor's or master's degree as its highest degree in engineering for the ninth straight year. This ranking is published in the 2008 edition of "America's Best Colleges" guidebook by *U.S. News & World Report*.

Our move to outcomes assessment came early in the implementation of the ABET Engineering Criteria 2000 (now referred to only as the Engineering Criteria). We were one of the early adopters of the criteria, and our accreditation site visit in 2000 was conducted using the Engineering Criteria. By combining our tradition of innovative curricular development with our dedication to the use of technology to enhance education, we began in 1997 to develop an Institute-wide assessment process. The centerpiece of the project included developing a defined set of Institutional learning outcomes and the Rose-Hulman electronic portfolio project, the RosE Portfolio System (REPS), recipient of the 2007 Council for Higher Education Accreditation (CHEA) Award for Institutional Progress in Student Learning Outcomes. We initiated the process by developing a set of Institute-wide student learning outcomes, outcomes that would constitute the set of skills all Rose-Hulman students develop by the time of graduation. These outcomes were designed based on input from a wide variety of constituents: faculty, alumni, industry (those who hire our graduates), graduate schools, and other sources. By the end of the 1997–1998 academic year, we had a set of 10 Institute Student Learning Outcomes. These 10 learning outcomes were adopted by the faculty of the Institute and subsequently published in Rose-Hulman official documents, like our course catalogue and web pages. These outcomes covered communication, as well as ethics, contemporary issues, global issues, culture, teams, problem solving, interpreting data, experiments, and design. The outcomes were recently revised based on our 2006 ABET site visit; the six Institutional outcomes still retain an outcome for communication.

Leveraging Buy-in for the Institute-level Student Learning Outcomes Assessment Plan

The faculty approval of the Institute outcomes reflects an important dimension of our assessment process design. All the engineering programs at Rose-Hulman, as well as the computer science program, are accredited by ABET, Inc., and one component of maintaining accreditation is to publish, assess, and report on achievement of student learning outcomes in each program. In addition, we are accredited as an institution by the Higher Learning Commission (HLC) of the North Central Association of Colleges and Schools; HLC also requires that we demonstrate achievement in student learning. We believed we could leverage the demands for both program and institutional accreditation if we designed Institutional outcomes in a way that could map efficiently to program outcomes. ABET-accredited programs must show that students can demonstrate communication skills (only one of the 11 outcomes specified by ABET). By defining a communication outcome for the Institute, we gained cooperation from all of our programs; they agreed to use the data collection method (the RosE Portfolio System or REPS) and the portfolio rating results in their own self-study reports to submit to their accrediting boards. The evaluation results are produced for each department, which in turn uses the data to measure the learning of their own students and to plan curricular improvements.

We began the process of establishing an assessment process for the purposes of program and institutional accreditation by defining student learning outcomes. We also needed to develop an effective and efficient data collection method. At that time, there were no electronic portfolios available commercially that reflected our assessment model. We therefore began to construct our own portfolio. Our decision to develop an electronic portfolio was based on the fact that we had initiated an Institutional laptop computer requirement for all students in 1995 (one of the first colleges to do so). Thus, all students used an Institute-specified laptop computer with a pre-installed software suite. We believed we could make the portfolio assessment process both effective and efficient if all dimensions of the process—from student submission to portfolio evaluation—occurred within an electronic system. REPS was first used during the summer of 1998 to evaluate a set of student submissions for a pilot project. Every year since then, we have used REPS to collect, evaluate, and report out achievement in student learning outcomes to students, faculty, employers, graduate schools, and various accrediting agencies. Currently, we have developed the REPS system within the course management software we use on campus, Angel Learning Management Software (LMS).

Institutional Learning Outcomes, Performance Criteria, and Evaluation Rubrics

The Institutional Student Learning Outcomes that were developed early in 1997 are the foundation for the assessment process. They were subsequently revised in 2006–07. The challenge of the outcomes, however, is that they are not measurable: in other words, while we expect each student to demonstrate skills in communication, the broad outcome does not provide measurable behaviors we could observe and then evaluate to determine if the student has met the outcome. For that reason, we developed a set of performance criteria and evaluation rubrics to both define the required behaviors and to quantify the levels of performance that we expect. The complete set of outcomes, performance criteria, and rubrics is available at the RosE Portfolio System (REPS) Help Zone website (http://www.rose-hulman.edu/REPS/).

For example, each Rose-Hulman student is expected to demonstrate communication skills defined at the Institute level as follows: "Communication, regardless of the media, requires unique skills whether communicating with individuals or with groups." This statement alone, however, is not measurable, meaning that the statement does not describe what the student should actually be able to do or the skills that he/she should possess. For this level of measurable behavior, we developed a set of performance criteria (specific statements that explain exactly what "communication" means) and evaluation rubrics (descriptions of what successful performance means for each criterion) for this particular context. For instance, one performance criterion for communication is as follows: "Criterion B3: Adapt technical information for a non-specialized audience." In order to evaluate a student's achievement of the outcome, evaluators of the document determine if the student work meets the primary traits of the evaluation rubric:

Criterion B3: Adapt technical information for a non-specialized audience.

Primary traits: A passing submission for this criterion must:
1. Be derived from a field of mathematics, science, or engineering.
2. Be free of unexplained technical jargon and acronyms.
3. Be presented in a manner that is appropriate for the educational level of the intended audience (appropriate vocabulary levels, images, activities, etc.).

Potential documents: Documents appropriate for this criterion include (but are not limited to):
o   An outreach presentation/activity teaching science, mathematics, or engineering content to K-12 students.
o   A description of current research in science, mathematics, or engineering written as if for submission to a "popular press" magazine or newspaper.
o   An oral presentation to individuals skilled in disciplines other than the technical discipline of the subject matter.

An explanation of the assessment methodology that underlies the portfolio system, as well as a discussion of the work of portfolio raters, is provided in Appendix A.

Curriculum Mapping

Defining outcomes at the institute level was a significant first step in our effort to establish an effective and efficient assessment process. In order to ensure that the process is valid, however, we needed to understand where in the curricula of our programs students received the opportunities to develop their skills for each outcome. As a result, the assessment process begins with faculty identifying the outcomes that are addressed in their courses. Each program (not just the engineering programs) submits a Curriculum Map to the Dean of the Faculty annually. These Curriculum Maps show where students receive the opportunity to develop their skills in the Institutional learning outcomes in specific courses. By creating the Curriculum Map, the program and the faculty members teaching the mapped courses agree to require that all students in the courses submit evidence of their learning in the specific outcome to the REPS.

In order to provide the best evidence of student learning, faculty members determine which assignments in their courses are most appropriate to the performance criteria and rubrics of the outcome. Faculty members teaching courses in technical communication, for instance, identify specific assignments in their courses that can show evidence of improvement in their students' communication skills. Once the assignments have been identified, faculty members direct students to submit those assignments to the REPS in the Angel LMS.

Mapping and Assessing the Communication Outcome at the Program Level

So far we have focused on the development of mapping and assessment at the Institute level. The success of the institute-level process depends, however, on a concomitant process developed at the program level. In other words, individual courses provide students the opportunities to develop their skills in communication and to work on assignments that will be submitted to the REPS for evaluation. The process of completing the Curriculum Map demonstrated early on, however, that students were not being given adequate opportunities to develop their skills.

In the early stages of assessment process development, we encountered an interesting paradox. The ABET Engineering Criteria require that evidence of student achievement in the communication outcome be collected. In addition, faculty members of the engineering departments on our campus voiced their belief that communication skills are important for the future success of their program graduates. The task of completing the Curriculum Map demonstrated, however, that students were not provided with adequate opportunities to develop their skills. In other words, everyone believed that students should acquire effective communication skills, but few faculty members were including communication tasks in their courses or offering students feedback on their work.

As a result (and also because of accreditation demands), each department created program-specific maps for student learning outcomes. In the civil engineering department, for instance, faculty members created a department Curriculum Map for the communication outcome as shown in Figure 1.

Several features of the department-level map are important to note. First, the course in Technical Communication (shaded in black on the map) and required of all civil engineering students during their third year) is the only site within the curriculum where evidence of student learning is collected in the portfolio and evaluated at the Institute level. The faculty members of the department do not, however, look on the single course as adequate to develop communication skills in their students. Instead, the department Curriculum Map for communication identifies courses at each level (first through fourth year) where students are given the opportunity to develop and reinforce their skills. Communication assignments are made in each of these courses,

	1st Year			2nd Year			3rd Year			4th Year		
F A L L	MA 111	Calc I	5	MA 221	Diff. Equations & Matrix Alg I	4	CE 321	Structures I Prob. Solving	4	CE 489	CE Design & Synthesis	2
	PH 111	Physics I	4	EM 202	Dynamics	4	CE 371	Hydraulic Engineering	4	CE 450	Codes & Regs Contemp Iss.	4
	EM 104	Graph Comm	2	CHEM 201	Engr Chem I	4	CE 336	Soil Mechs Experiments	4	CE Elect	CE Electric	4
	RH 131	Freshman Comp	4	HSS	HSS Elective	4	ECE 206 or	Elements of EE I OR	4	HSS Elect	HSS Elective	4
	CLSK 100	College & Life Skills	1	CE 201	Engineering Surveying II	2	CHE 201	Conservation Prin. & Bal.		HSS Elect	HSS Elective Global	4
W I N T E R	MA 112	Calc II	5	MA 222	Diff. Equations & Matric Alg II	4	CE 432	Concrete I	3	CE 489	CE D & S Teams	4
	PH 112	Physics II	4	EM 203	Mechanics of Materials	4	CE 471	Water Res. Engineering	4	CE 303	Engineering Economy	4
	CE 110	Comp Apps & GIS	4	CHEM 202	Engr Chem II	4	Sci Elect	Science Elec.	4	Tech Elect	Technical Elective	4
	HSS Elect	HSS Elective	4	HSS	HSS Elective	4	CE 441	Construction Engineering	2	Tech Elect	Technical Elective	4
							me201 ch202	Thermo. I OR Chem Proc.	4			
S P R I N G	MA 113	Calc III	5	MA 223	Engineering Statistics I	4	CE 431	Steel Design I Prob. Solving	3	CE 489	CE D & S Design/Ethic	2
	Sci Elect	Science Elective	4	EM 301	Fluid Mechanics	4	CE 460	Environ. Engineering	4	CE 400	Career Prep. Seminar	0
	EM 103	Intro to Design	2	CE 320	CE Material Science	4	CE 461	Environ. Lab Interpret Data	2	HSS Elect	HSS Elective	4
	EM 120	Engineering Statics	4	CE 310	CE Computer Applications I	2	CE 311	CE Computer Applications II	2	Tech Elect	Technical Elective	4
	CE 101	Engineering Surveying I	2				RH 330	Tech Com. Communicat.	4	HSS Elect	HSS Elective Culture	4

Class that produces the deliverable for the Communications outcome (RH 330 - Tech. Com.)
Classes that train students explicitly in the Communications outcome

Figure 1. Civil Engineering Curriculum Map for the communications outcome.

and they are evaluated by the course instructor. The evaluation is one component of the course grade, and the evaluation data are also used in the program's ABET Self Study Report. Providing students with multiple opportunities to develop their skills is an important dimension of a successful communication program, as long as faculty members are provided with support and expertise from communication and assessment specialists within the institution. The following sections provide detailed case studies of these in-course communication assignments and evaluation methods.

Communication in the Civil Engineering Curriculum

As part of his contribution to the departmental communication assessment effort, a professor in the Civil Engineering department wished to incorporate written communication into his Engineering Statics course. Engineering Statics is required of all students majoring in engineering. Topics covered are two- and three-dimensional force systems, equilibrium, structures, distributed forces, shear and bending moment diagrams, friction, and area moments of inertia. The course also emphasizes free-body diagrams. The professor, who requested the assistance of the technical communication faculty and whose engineering background lay in structural analysis, structural design, solid mechanics, and finite element analysis, was then an untenured professor in his department.

The professor saw the need to incorporate writing into his course for several reasons. First, he believed that writing could help students understand the reasoning behind their solutions to a homework problem, since students often blindly plug numbers into formulae. Consequently, he saw writing as a way to help students understand what they do and do not know. Second, he believed that requiring students to use writing to solve numerical problems could help them develop the ability to communicate a problem's solution to another person, a skill that the professor sees as necessary within the professional engineering workplace. While the professor saw the potential of writing to support students' educational and cognitive development, he was also concerned, however, about the potential risks of incorporating communication into his technical course. Could this assignment be implemented without compromising course content? Would this assignment place a significant burden on students (increasing their time solving homework problems) and on the professor (increasing his time evaluating these written problem solutions)? Further, how could this professor use the Institute-level assessment model (with the focus on outcomes, performance criteria, and rubrics) to inform his work at the course and program level?

Description of the Assignment

Working with members of the technical communication faculty, the civil engineering faculty member developed a new assignment for his Engineering Statics class. As part of a homework problem set, students were asked to provide a written description of one of the problems. Specifically, the assignment stated, "For the specified problem, describe the steps followed in order to set up and solve the problem." The particular problem was always selected by the professor so that every student was describing the same problem. The instructor was careful to choose problems for which answers were provided in the textbook. Therefore, students knew whether they had achieved the correct answer before they began the written description. The complete assignment handout is located in Appendix B. The annotations in brackets and italics were provided by the instructor to guide students' understanding of what the particular response lacked.

The students received the assignment description on the first day of the course. The handout describes the self-assessment and communication learning outcome. In addition, the handout provides examples of well, adequately, and poorly written descriptions for an example problem. These examples were written by the professor. Students were instructed to provide a written description of the steps used to solve the specific problem, not steps to solve the type of problem in general. The written description needed to be no more than one-half of a page in order to promote concise communication. The description could be typed or handwritten.

Assignment Grading

The assignment description handed out at the beginning of the term also included the four objectives expected of the students. They were formulated as grading criteria and were used consistently each time the assignment was used. The four criteria are:

1. Has the student provided sufficient detail that the professor can reproduce the approach to the solution?

2. Has the student demonstrated an understanding of what is being done in the solution process?
3. Is the description written such that the professor can understand what the student means?
4. Is the description focused on the approach to the solution of this problem, not the specific numbers of the solution?

Although student graders were used to evaluate the numerical solution to the homework problems, the instructor chose to evaluate the written descriptions himself. During the first two terms, the instructor critiqued each assignment, then assigned scores for each of the four criteria based on full, partial, or no credit. For the last two terms, the instructor used a grading rubric (shown in Figure 2). The instructor

Criteria	Full Credit (4 pts)	Partial Credit (2 pts)	No Credit (0 pts)
Has the student provided sufficient detail that I could reproduce the approach to the solution?	• Identify sequence by which unknowns are being found. • Terms used in each equation are identified (e.g., forces that contribute moment in moment equilibrium). • Body or particle for FBD is identified.	• One necessary equation is not identified. • Terms used are not identified for one equation. • Body or particle for FBD not clearly identified.	• Several necessary equations are not identified. • Terms used are not identified for multiple equations.
Has the student demonstrated an understanding of what is being done in the solution process?	• Approach described is fundamentally sound. • Each equation used is described in words, not with algebra.	• One error in the approach. • One equation described algebraically.	• Multiple errors in approach. • Multiple equations described algebraically.
Is the description written such that I can understand what the student means?	• Description begins with the objective of the problem. • Description no longer than one-half page (if typed, single spaced lines). • Handwriting is legible. • Pronouns have clear meanings (i.e., "that", "it" are easily interpreted). • All variable names used in the description are defined.	• Description does not begin with objective of the problem. • Description more than one-half page, but less than full page (if typed, single spaced lines). • One or two sentences do not make sense because of handwriting, ambiguous pronouns, and/or undefined variable names. • One variable used in the description not defined.	• Description more than one full page (if typed, single spaced lines). • More than two sentences do not make sense because of handwriting, ambiguous pronouns, and/or undefined variable names. • Multiple variables used in the description not defined.
Is the description focused on the approach to the solution of this problem, not the specific numbers of the solution?	• No quantities (e.g., 100 lb, 20°, 3 m) are used in the description. • Details are provided about solving this particular problem.	• One quantity is provided in the description. • Description is about how to solve this type of problem in general.	• Several quantities are provided in the description.

Figure 2. Civil Engineering assignment evaluation rubric.

developed the rubric in consultation with technical communication faculty to help ensure consistent grading, to possibly reduce the time spent grading, and to provide students with specific guidance on how to do well on the assignment. After the first two terms, the instructor reflected on what he looked for when assessing each criterion and formalized those attributes into the grading rubric. During the terms when the instructor used the rubric, he made it available to the students and encouraged the students to score their own assignments before submitting them.

Support to Students

In the process of developing and implementing this assignment, the instructor provided a variety of in-class supports to help students improve their performance. The instructor reviewed high and low scoring descriptions at the beginning of class. For the review, he had the class read the low-scoring example and score it themselves with the rubric. He polled the class for final scores, then asked students why it earned that rating. He then had the class read the high-scoring example and repeat the process. That term he conducted in-class reviews after the first, second, and third writing assignments (Homework Assignments #2, #4 and #6).

During that same term, the instructor conducted an in-class writing workshop prior to the fifth writing assignment (Homework Assignment #10). The in-class workshop took the entire class period. During that period, students wrote a description of the selected homework problem or a class example problem. After 20 minutes, they were instructed to exchange their drafts with someone in the class and critique the description based on the grading rubric. They continued to exchange until at least three people had reviewed and commented on their descriptions.

Impact on Student Learning

The purpose of this assignment was to improve both students' writing abilities and their cognitive skills. In this assignment, students cannot recite values or formulas; they must describe the process. Therefore, we wondered if students achieved the objective of recognizing the difference between understanding how to solve a problem and blindly plugging numbers into formulas. Support for this conclusion comes from several comments by students in their course evaluations:

> "I learned so much in this class that I had never even thought about before." (Fall 2003)

> "[The instructor] can make people think and teaches in a way to induce problem-solving behaviors as opposed to the 'plug and chug' method." (Fall 2003)

> "I have also learned how to effectively convey my ideas and problem strategies in a shortened format." (Spring 2005)

In Spring 2005, the professor surveyed students who had taken the first class in which this assignment was used two years earlier (Spring 2003). Therefore, the students were all juniors reflecting on their experience. Two of the questions addressed how well the writing assignments helped them:

"I found that the written description problems in Engineering Statics helped me better understand and remember how to perform statics problems...."

Very much - 2   Some - 14   Little - 3   None - 1

"I find that the written description problems in EM120 have had ... impact on how I annotate calculations on homeworks and projects in my various courses."

Very much - 2   Some - 12   Little - 3   None - 2

Impact on Instructor Workload

Overall, the instructor found that the addition of written problem solutions did not impact course content or his grading burden negatively. The instructor was able to maintain the same course syllabus even with the addition of the assignment and the writing support to students. The instructor used time available in "problem-solving" class periods to provide the writing support to students. He did not reduce the length of homework assignments that included the problem. The instructor also did not experience a significant workload to grade the assignments. The first term that the instructor used the grading rubric, he devoted four hours per assignment to grading the writing portion. The time dropped significantly during the next term. The reduction in time required is probably due to increased familiarity with the rubric. With the rubric and clear guidance on what is expected, we believe that graders or teaching assistants could perform the grading duties. Therefore, the increase in instructor workload would only be in training the graders and providing quality control.

Communication in the Chemical Engineering Curriculum

Like the Curriculum Map for the civil engineering program, the map for the chemical engineering program identifies multiple places for students' communication skills development. In particular, the Unit Operations (UO) laboratory represents an important site for the development of technical and non-technical skills in chemical engineering students. Coming in the final year of students' course work, the projects of UO lab give students the opportunity to combine experimental experiences with team work and communication, a combination that chemical engineering educators would agree is crucial to success in the workplace.

Unfortunately, the UO lab as it is commonly designed in many engineering programs may not provide students with adequate support for developing non-technical skills, particularly communication; as experts in chemical engineering, faculty may feel less comfortable with emphasizing writing to their students and may indeed lack specific pedagogical strategies that can help students become more effective communicators. Our second case study emerged from this context, recognizing that the lab environment offered particular opportunities and challenges for improving

137

students' communication skills. The primary coordinator for the course approached the technical communication faculty for suggestions regarding strategies for improving students' written communication. Based on the nature of the course, we suggested the inclusion of a Peer Review component in the course to provide students with important feedback from the instructor and other students on their communication work. The course coordinator was at the time, an untenured assistant professor in the chemical engineering department at Rose-Hulman. His area of specialization is process systems engineering and process modeling and optimization.

The UO lab at Rose-Hulman is organized around the following educational objectives: broad range of equipment and instrumentation; designing and planning experiments; working in a team; analyzing experimental data; and written and oral communication. The course length is one year, during which students complete seven different projects with three different types of reports. Each student is required to write an individual report for each project. The volume of writing required of students in the course might suggest that students are given adequate opportunities to improve their written communication. The chemical engineering faculty member who worked on this project believed, however, that while students wrote a lot in the course, their writing problems continued. In particular the instructor saw four categories of writing problems as they related to three major sections of the required reports, as well as a fourth problem that emerged in every report section. These writing problems are categorized in Table 1.

Table 1

Categories of Writing Problems Identified in Students' Civil Engineering Reports

Introduction Section	Discussion of Results Section	Conclusions Section	Clarity and Conciseness
1. Experiment objectives unclear	1. Data is "what was expected" or "pretty good"	1. Stated conclusions not related to experiment objectives	1. A global problem affecting all sections of the report in general
2. Rambling overview	2. Meaning of data and trends not discussed	2. Conclusions disconnected from results	
		3. Just summaries provided	

The instructor developed several theories in an attempt to locate the source of these writing problems. Students perceived that writing was not as significant as technical content in their reports, and their perception was reinforced by the fact that poor writing had a small effect on their final grade for the project. In addition, students were given inadequate time to write, revise, and review their writing, waiting instead until the last minute before the due date to begin the writing component of the project. The instructor also found that students were not generally offered good models of previous reports on which to base their own work. Students were unable or unwilling, therefore, to identify and correct their own writing problems.

The instructor determined that the best way to encourage students to work on their communication skills was to show them how important he thought communication was. As a way to demonstrate his emphasis on communication, the instructor developed three new course objectives:

1. Devote laboratory time to discuss writing, including evaluating and discussing samples of previous reports that were successful.
2. Require a formal peer review of documents, including instructor guidance on proper reviewing techniques while also allowing adequate time in the course for making revisions.
3. Discuss observations from peer review by using additional writing samples from volunteers.

These objectives are discussed below. In addition to these changes, the chemical engineering faculty member enlisted the assistance of members of the technical communication faculty; together they developed specific writing assignments and pedagogical strategies that could assist students with the development of their communication skills.

Description of the Assignment

Many engineering faculty believe that students should develop good communication skills and use them in their written work. And yet, few faculty are willing to model communication for students by devoting class time to discussions of good writing. In this project, faculty members wished to show, rather than just tell, students that communication is important; to this end, the chemical engineering faculty member devoted class time to discussing the elements of effective communication and illustrated those elements with models of student papers written in previous classes. These examples were collected by the instructor and were used with the permission of previous students. A member of the technical communication faculty attended the first discussion session as an observer.

During the in-class discussion, the chemical engineering faculty member offered a limited set of problem areas students should address in their revision process. This ensured that students approached the writing with a sense of what represented higher-level problems in areas like organization, clarity, and conciseness, versus what represented lower-level problems like comma placement. We believe that students should address both kinds of problems in their writing and revising, but many students believe that all they must do to improve their writing is correct their grammar. In this project, the instructor wished students to focus first on the higher-level problems. Using the student examples, the instructor identified strengths of the reports and indicated areas that represented opportunities for improvement:

1. **Wishy-washy language,** meaning phrases such as "probably fairly accurate," "results follow what was expected," etc.
2. **Conciseness**
3. **Objectives,** meaning a reason for the experiment that goes beyond a class requirement

4. **Organization of paragraphs** with a clear topic sentence and related sentences within
5. **Prioritization of ideas and information**, meaning deciding what represented information that would be important for the reader to know and should be included in a report.

As the bolded category labels above indicate, the instructor personalized the problem areas by using his own language to describe what he believed was lacking in the samples. This, too, showed the instructor's emphasis on good communication and his personal investment in the project. The chemical engineering instructor believed that poor student writing was due, in part, to the brief time students spent on their reports. The key component the instructor wished to change was the time frame in which students drafted and revised their reports. The peer review component added to the writing assignments meant that each student was required to start his/her report earlier than was normal and to devote time to reviewing and revising the report before handing it in to the instructor. At the suggestion of the technical communication faculty, the instructor also drafted a Peer Review sheet containing instructions to student authors for writing particular sections of the reports, as well as providing specific questions the student reviewers needed to answer to complete Peer Review. In this way, students could use the sheet both to guide their own writing and to conduct an effective review of another student's writing. The complete Peer Review sheet is included in Appendix C.

The Peer Review procedure was composed of four steps:

Step 1: First, each student author gave a hard copy of his/her report draft to two student reviewers. These reviewers were members of different experiment groups, so each reviewer was reading a report on a laboratory in which he/she did not participate. This practice ensured that the report reader did not have firsthand knowledge of the experiment and would be less willing to fill in omitted information or make assumptions not offered by the author.

Step 2: In order to complete the review, student reviewers were required to comment specifically on the three sections that were common to all report types: Introduction, Results and Discussion, Conclusions and Recommendations. The instructor developed specific questions pertinent to each section; for example, the Results and Discussion section on the Peer Review sheet included questions about the kinds of data collected and the format in which the data were presented. While some questions were specific to a particular section, the issue of clarity and conciseness was important for each section, and student reviewers were asked to address them throughout the report drafts. A student reviewer wrote his/her comments directly on a student author's draft, then summarized those comments in a memo to the student author.

Step 3: At the end of the Peer Review period, the commented draft and the summary memo were returned to the student author. After each author read the comments from his/her two student reviewers, the entire class met to discuss and/ or clarify the comments. In this session, the instructor was able to reinforce his observations from the first class discussion, illustrating the same principles of good communication, but this time with the students' reports as models.

Step 4: At the end of the process, students were required to submit both their report drafts (marked with student reviewer comments) and the summary memo with the final version of their reports. In addition, the student author was required to submit a summary that described how he/she incorporated the student reviewers' comments.

Assignment Grading

In measuring the impact of the Peer Review Project in the UO lab course, we have focused on the way in which the process improved students' communication skills, determining if they have become better writers as a result. At this stage of our project, we rely on the chemical engineering faculty member's sense that the reports have improved in the four categories of problems identified earlier. Overall, the instructor observed improvements in all four categories. In addition to considering students' improvement as authors, we were also interested in students' improvements as reviewers. We find that a student who can identify a problem in another student's draft is more likely to recognize a comparable problem in his/her own work. The technical communication faculty analyzed the comments provided by student reviewers on the report hard copies. Comments categories are provided in Table 2.

Table 2
Analysis of Student Reviewers' Comments

Sentence-level edits	Audience accommodation	Organization	Conciseness	Graphical information
1. Reviewer suggested a different word choice	1. Reviewer identified parts of the report in which the writer had not considered his/her audience. i.e. by omitting key data, etc.	1. Reviewer made concrete suggestions to the author about moving particular paragraphs or reorganizing report	1. Reviewer suggested ways to reduce wordiness in a report section	1. Reviewer suggested changes that should be made to the presentation of data and results
2. Reviewer corrected errors in grammar, spelling, and/or punctuation				

Impact on Student Learning

Our observations were reinforced by comments we collected from the students themselves as part of the course evaluation. In considering themselves as reviewers, students wrote that the Peer Review Project had the following results:

1. A student looked at her own writing in order to determine if she had committed the errors she pointed out in the writer's draft.
2. Another student felt no hesitation in writing comments on drafts.

3. Several students were willing to share the instructor's suggestions from their own reports (i.e., one student took a suggestion the course instructor made to him and shared it with the student author whose report he was reviewing).
4. Students used their own reports as models.
5. Some students cited class discussion as an indication of what the writer should do and what the instructor expects.
6. Many students started their summary memos with a positive comment.
7. Only two students in the project group offered a minimal review—just a few "you did great" statements.
8. Most students performed a detailed review of grammar and sentence structure.
9. Despite their careful review of grammar, etc., all students kept their review focused primarily on technical content.

The two sets of summary comments—from the reviewers and from the author—represented an important closing of the loop between reviewer and author. In addition, the instructor also closed the loop between Peer Review and final evaluation by using the same set of evaluation criteria in both. We believe this helped to prevent some common disconnections that students see in the Peer Review processes.

In addition to this analysis, we also collected student responses to Peer Review assignment. We were interested in knowing if students saw value in completing Peer Review and if they saw improvements in their writing as a result. Student comments are listed below:

- "Peer evaluations were a lot of extra work, but overall very helpful."
- "Peer review of reports good idea, helps to improve writing."
- "Grading was pretty rough. I liked the peer evaluation, it cut down on the rush of the project as one could space reworks and rereading down."
- "I liked the student eval idea...it took a lot of stress out of lab."

In general, student response to the activity was positive. In particular, students noted that they had two opportunities for improvement: once based on Peer comments and again based on the documents they reviewed. Students also indicated that reading other students' writing raised their awareness of best practices in the different types of reports—for instance, effective and appropriate discussion of results. Some students also remarked that their ability to discuss and draw conclusions from data improved significantly. As the chemical engineering instructor noted, the average score of the reports improved by nearly a letter grade compared to the initial drafts.

Conclusion

The move to student learning outcomes assessment for purpose of accreditation has prompted ongoing discussions among engineering educators. They are not in agreement regarding the impact of the new process by which their programs will be accredited. For instance, at a recent meeting of the American Society for Engineering Education Illinois/Indiana Section meeting, a panel of leading experts in the field of engineering education accreditation discussed the topic "What Do We Gain by Assessment? Cost/Benefit Perspectives" (Williams, 2008). Questions from the audience ranged from whether the impact of outcomes assessment on students and programs is measurable to whether the level of effort required by outcomes assessment is sustainable for faculty and their departments. In addition, a study conducted at the Pennsylvania State University entitled "Engineering Change: A Study of the Impact of EC 2000" (Lattuca, Terezini, & Volkwein, 2006) has also attempted to measure both quantitatively and qualitatively the costs of outcomes assessment. Suffice it to say, however, that the final measure of the impact of outcomes assessment is yet to be made. As one panelist put it, however, the continuing challenge is to make assessment meaningful to faculty and students through improvements to curricula and learning.

The challenge for those working in the field of institutional research and assessment may continue to evolve. Faculty members require assistance to complete data collection and analysis in the most efficient manner possible. Those responsible in their engineering departments to collect and analyze data, as well as to write the Self Study Report, may have no experience in the field. For these reasons, institutional researchers may offer valuable insights into assessment processes.

REFERENCES

ABET, Inc. (2007). *Criteria for accrediting engineering programs: Effective for evaluations during the 2008–2009 accreditation cycle.* Retrieved July 31, 2009, from http://www.abet.org/Linked%20Documents-UPDATE/Criteria%20 and%20PP/E001%202008-09%20EAC%20Criteria%2012-04-07.pdf

America's Best Colleges. (2008). Washington, DC: U.S. News & World Report LP.

House, R., Watt, A., & Williams, J. (2007, October). Mapping the future of engineering communication: Report on a research study of engineering faculty and their teaching of writing as a function of the ABET/EAC criteria. Paper presented at the International Professional Communication Conference, Seattle, WA.

Lattuca, L. R, Terezini, P. T., & Volkwein, J. F. (2006). *Engineering change: A study of the impact of EC2000.* Baltimore, MD: ABET, Inc.

Peterson, G. (2006). ABET's legacy: Responding to challenges, adapting to change. *The Interface,* (2), 1–3.

Williams, J. (Moderator). (2008, April). *What do we gain by assessment? Cost/ benefit perspectives.* Panel discussion conducted at the American Society for Engineering Education Illinois/Indiana Section Conference, Terre Haute, IN.

BIBLIOGRAPHY OF RESOURCES FOR ASSIGNMENT
AND ASSESSMENT DEVELOPMENT

Angelo, T. A., & Cross, K. P. (1993). *Classroom assessment techniques: A handbook for college teachers (2nd ed.)*. San Francisco: Jossey-Bass.

Bielaczyc, K., Pirolli, P. L. & Brown, A. L. (1995). Training in self-explanation and self-regulation strategies: Investigating the effects of knowledge acquisition activities on problem solving. *Cognition and Instruction, 13*(2), 221–252.

Bloom, B., Englehart, M., Furst, E., Hill, W., & Krathwohl, D. (1956). *Taxonomy of educational objectives: The classification of educational goals. Handbook I: Cognitive domain*. New York: Longmans, Green.

Brent, R., & Felder, R. M. (1992). Writing assignments—Pathways to connections, clarity, and creativity. *College English, 40*(2), 43–47.

Brinkman, G. W., & van der Geest, T. M. (2003). Assessment of communication competencies in engineering design projects. *Technical Communication Quarterly, 12*(1), 67–81.

Brown, A. L. (1975). The development of memory: Knowing, knowing about knowing, and knowing how to know. *Advances in Child Development and Behavior, 10*, 103–152.

Carvill, C., Smith, S., Watt, A., & Williams, J. (2002, June). *Incorporating writing assignments in technical courses*. Paper presented at the American Society for Engineering Education Annual Conference, Montréal, Quebec, Canada.

Fei, S. M., Lu, G. D., & Shi, Y. D. (2007). Using multi-mode assessments to engage engineering students in their learning experience. *European Journal of Engineering Education, 32*(2), 219–226.

Felder, R. M., & Silverman, L. K. (1988). Learning and teaching styles in engineering education. *Engineering Education, 78*(7), 674–681.

Flavell, J. H. (1976). Metacognitive aspects of problem solving. In L. Resnick (Ed.), *The nature of intelligence* (pp. 231–235). Hillsdale, NJ: Lawrence Erlbaum Associates.

Gandolfo, A. (2001). Motivating students for life-long learning: Developing metacognition. *Journal of Professional Issues in Engineering Education and Practice, 127*(3), 93–97.

Gruber, S., Larson, D., Scott, D., & Neville, M. (1999). Writing4Practice in engineering courses: Implementation and assessment approaches. *Technical Communication Quarterly, 8*(4), 419–441.

Harvey, R., Johnson, F. S., Newell, H. L., Dahm, K., Marchese, A. J., Ramachandran, R. P., et al. (2000). Improving the engineering and writing interface: An assessment of a team-taught integrated course. *Proceedings of the American Society of Engineering Education Conference*, 3233–3247.

Held, J. A., Olds, B., Miller, R., Demel, J. T., Fentiman, A., Cain, K., et al. (1994). Incorporating writing in engineering classes and engineering in writing classes. *Proceedings of the Frontiers in Education Conference, 618–622.*

Herrington, A. J. (1981). Writing to learn: Writing across the disciplines. *College English, 43*(4), 379–87.

Hopkins, C. D., & Antes, R. L. (1990). *Educational research: A structure for inquiry (3rd ed.)* Itasca, IL: F. E. Peacock.

Karelina, A., & Etkina, E. (2007). When and how do students engage in sense-making in a physics lab? *Proceedings of the American Institute of Physics, 883*(1), 93–96.

Koch, A. (2001). Training in metacognition and comprehension of physics texts. *Science Education, 85*(6), 758–768.

McLeod, S. H., Miraglia, E., Soven, M., & Thaiss, C. (Eds.). (2001). *WAC for the new millennium: Strategies for continuing writing-across-the-curriculum programs.* Urbana, IL: National Council of Teachers of English.

Miller, R. L., & Olds, B. M. (1999, June). *Performance assessment of EC-2000 student outcomes in the Unit Operations Laboratory.* Paper presented at the American Society for Engineering Education Annual Conference, Charlotte, NC.

Myers, I. B. & McCaulley, M. H. (1985). *Manual: A guide to the development and use of the Myers Briggs Type Indicator.* Palo Alto, CA: Consulting Psychologists Press.

Newell, J. A. (1997, June). *The use of peer-review in the undergraduate laboratory.* Paper presented at the American Society for Engineering Education Annual Conference, Milwaukee, WI.

Paris, S. G., & Jacobs, J. E. (1984). The benefits of informed instruction for children's reading awareness and comprehension skills. *Child Development, 55,* 2083–2093.

Peck, A., Nydahl, J. E., & Keeney, C. K. (1999). Effective strategies of motivating engineering students to develop their technical writing skills. *Proceedings of the American Society for Engineering Education Annual Conference, 1989–1999.*

Russell, D. R. (1994). American origins of the writing-across-the-curriculum movement. In C. Bazerman, & D.R. Russell (Eds.), *Landmark essays in writing across the curriculum* (pp. 3–22). Davis, CA: Hermagoras Press.

Russell, D. R. (2001). Where do the naturalistic studies of WAC/WID point? A research review. In S.H. McLeod, E. Miraglia, M. Soven, & C. Thaiss (Eds.), *WAC for the new millennium: Strategies for continuing writing-across-the-curriculum programs.* Urbana, IL: National Council of Teachers of English.

Sharp, J. E., Harb, J. N., & Terry, R. E. (1997). Combining Kolb learning styles and writing to learn in engineering classes. *Journal of Engineering Education, 86*(2), 93–101.

Sharp, J. E., Olds, B. M., Miller, R. L., & Dyrud, M. A. (1999). Four effective writing strategies for engineering classes. *Journal of Engineering Education, 88*(1), 53–57.

Swanson, H. L. (1990). Influence of metacognitive knowledge and aptitude on problem solving. *Journal of Educational Psychology, 82*(2), 306–314.

Swarts, J., & Odell, L. (2001). Rethinking the evaluation of writing in engineering courses. *Proceedings of the Frontiers in Education Conference,* T3A-T3A/30.

Wade, S. E., & Reynolds, R. E. (1989). Developing metacognitive awareness. *Journal of Reading, 33*(1), 6–14.

White, B. Y., & Frederiksen, J. R. (1998). Inquiry, modeling, and metacognition: Making science accessible to all students. *Cognition and Instruction, 16*(1), 3–118.

Young, A., & Fulwiler, T. (Eds.). (1986.) *Writing across the disciplines: Research into practice.* Upper Montclair, NJ: Boynton/Cook.

APPENDIX A

ROSE PORTFOLIO SYSTEM (REPS)
ASSESSMENT METHODOLOGY

Within the field of portfolio assessment, there are many methodologies currently in use. For some institutions and programs, the focus of the portfolio is on a student's personal reflection, and the portfolio is used as a showcase for the best work a student can do. In other cases, the focus is on assessment but without much participation from the student; a statistical sample of students is selected and their work is collected without input from the student. Our assessment methodology focused on engaging students in their own learning while still providing us with rich data for the purpose of evaluation and improvement.

RosE Portfolio Rating Process

At the end of the academic year, a team of faculty portfolio raters are trained; they then rate all submissions to the RosE Portfolio System over a two-day Rating Session, using the assessment rubrics. Once the ratings are completed, the portfolio rating results are compiled and analyzed by the Office of Institutional Research, Planning and Assessment. Each department then receives a report that contains detailed portfolio results for all student majors (from freshman through to seniors). Departments use this data to make improvements in their curricula to address any deficiencies in student achievement.

In order to determine students' success in achieving the Institutional student learning outcomes, all student submissions to the RosE Portfolio System are assessed each year by a team of trained faculty raters. The purpose of the RosE Portfolio Rating Session is to assess evidence of student learning in six non-technical Institute outcomes: Ethics, Contemporary Issues, Global, Culture, Teams, and Communication. Evidence of student learning in these six outcomes is collected each year through assignments made by faculty in technical and non-technical departments. For example, some engineering faculty require that students submit documents from capstone senior design courses as evidence for the Teams outcome. Humanities and Social Sciences faculty require that students submit documents produced in their courses for evidence of the Global and Culture outcomes. Definition of performance criteria and rubrics, collection of documents, and assessment and evaluation of evidence for technical learning outcomes is the province of technical departments (although many departments use the same portfolio collection and assessment methodology described below).

Rating submissions to the RosE Portfolio has followed the same basic methodology since the system was initiated in 1998. Rose-Hulman faculty members (usually up to 14 each year) are hired as portfolio raters. Attempts are made to involve faculty from many different departments on campus to ensure objectivity in rating and broad-based familiarity and participation in the process. Raters work together for two days in a computer laboratory and are compensated for their work. The Rating Session Coordinator facilitates the process and assigns pairs of raters to rate student submissions for a particular outcome. For example, a mechanical engineering faculty member and a chemistry faculty member may work as a rating pair assessing the student files submitted to Communication Outcome.

The rating process consists of four steps.

1. First, faculty portfolio raters review the rating rubric associated with the learning outcome. The rating rubrics were developed by faculty members who serve on the Commission for the Assessment of Student Outcomes (CASO), the Institute-wide committee charged with maintaining the outcomes assessment process. Each year faculty portfolio raters review the rating rubric, as well as the comments made by the faculty portfolio raters who evaluated the same outcome in previous years. As part of their training to be raters, the rating team discusses the rubric while comparing it to student documents that were rated during previous rating sessions. The purpose of this work is to ensure calibration: between the two faculty raters and between the current faculty raters and each previous faculty rater team. Calibration like this helps ensure consistency in rating from year to year.

2. Second, REPS requires that each rater team rate a set of three shared documents. The rating is made on the basis of a pre-established Rating Rubric; raters answer "Yes" or "No" for a single rating question: "Does this document meet the standard expected of a student who will graduate from Rose-Hulman?" Student achievement is measured as either "Yes/Pass" or "No/Fail." Raters also have the opportunity to mark the document as "Yes/ Pass/Exemplary" to designate student submissions that represent superior achievement for a particular outcome. In order to ensure consistency in rating between the raters, REPS uses an Inter-Rater Reliability (IRR) process. When they read and evaluate the set of three shared documents, the raters must agree in their rating. If their ratings are not identical, REPS prohibits them from continuing on with the rating process. Raters then discuss their ratings, checking their evaluation against the Rating Rubric for the outcome; they then come to agreement on how they will evaluate the shared document set. IRR is a key component of REPS; it ensures that raters look for the same qualities and features in order to rate documents. This helps the faculty raters to calibrate their ratings against each other and ensures consistency in rating.

3. Third, if the raters agree in their IRR, the system then allows them to proceed with a set of 10 documents, each rater reading and rating a different set of 10 documents. REPS records their rating for each document. The system also introduces a shared file every 10 documents in order to check that the raters have maintained their Inter-Rater Reliability. Failure to rate the shared

document identically will cause the system to stop the raters so that they can recalibrate their evaluation before moving on to another document set. Thus, IRR continues to validate rating throughout the rating process.

4. Fourth, the raters can provide comments about the rating session or about the student submission in the Comment boxes. In addition to the work of rating, faculty raters also record the rubrics they used and collect sample documents in order to provide next year's raters with material for calibration. They may also suggest changes to rating rubrics or to learning outcomes, although revisions must be reviewed and approved by CASO before they are implemented into REPS.

APPENDIX B
CIVIL ENGINEERING STATICS ASSIGNMENT:

For the specified problem, describe the steps followed in order to set up and solve the problem. Use no more than half of a page. It may be typed or handwritten. Use the template provided on the course website.

Objectives:

The goal of this course is to understand the material, not just to plug numbers into equations. An effective way to demonstrate understanding of the material is to describe how you use it.

Another motivation for these assignments is to develop the ability to articulate your thought process in an efficient and comprehensible manner. On real projects, engineers' calculations are archived for many years. If there is ever a problem, the calculations are reviewed. Brief notes on the calculations can make the difference when a review board is determining liability. In addition, it is a distinct advantage to be able to articulate your thought process clearly and concisely when working with other engineers.

Grading Criteria:

1. Has the student provided sufficient detail that I could reproduce the approach to the solution?
2. Has the student demonstrated an understanding of what is being done in the solution process?
3. Is the description written such that I can understand what the student means?
4. Is the description focused on the approach to the solution of this problem, not the specific numbers of the solution?

Examples:

The following paragraphs are examples of descriptions of the solution shown on the attached pages.

Good:

The objective is to determine the moment of F about the OA axis. First, calculate the position vector, r, from the origin to the point where F acts. This is done by subtracting the Cartesian coordinates of the origin from the coordinates of the point where F acts.

Find the moment of F about the origin by crossing r into F. Use the matrix approach to find the cross product. Add products obtained by multiplying diagonals down to the right. Subtract products obtained by multiplying diagonals down to the left. The result is a moment vector in Cartesian coordinates.

To obtain the moment about the OA axis, take the dot product of the unit vector along OA and the moment vector. To obtain the unit vector along OA, calculate a position vector, r_{OA}, from the origin to point A. Calculate the length of r_{OA} by taking the square root of the sum of each Cartesian coordinate of r_{OA} squared. The resulting length is a scalar, not a vector. The unit vector is obtained by dividing each coordinate of r_{OA} by the length of r_{OA}. The dot product is obtained by multiplying x-coordinates of the unit vector and the moment vector and summing that product with the products of the y-coordinates and z-coordinates. The resulting moment value is a scalar. To convert the value to a Cartesian vector, multiply the unit vector by the scalar moment value. The result is the moment of F about the OA axis in Cartesian coordinates.

Minimally Adequate:

The objective is to determine the moment of F about the OA axis. First, calculate the position vector, r, from the origin to the point where F acts. **[How is this done?]**

Find the moment of F about the origin by crossing r into F. Use the matrix approach to find the cross product. **[How is this done?]**

To obtain the moment about the OA axis, take the dot product of the unit vector along OA and the moment vector. Calculate a unit vector between two points along OA. Calculate the dot product, which is a scalar. Multiply the unit vector by the scalar moment value to obtain the moment of F about the OA axis.

Poor:

First, calculate the position vector, r, from the origin to the point where F acts. **[What is the objective?]**

Find the moment of F about the origin by crossing that into it. **[I can't understand what this is saying.]** Use the formula on page 122 to calculate the moment. **[Does not demonstrate understanding of what is being done in the solution process.]**

To obtain the moment about the OA axis, take the dot product of the unit vector along OA and the moment vector. Calculate a unit vector between two points along OA. Calculate the dot product, which is a scalar. Multiply $0.7071\hat{\imath}$ by 56.6 N*m to obtain 40.0 N*m $\hat{\imath}$ for the x-component of the moment about the aa axis. Similarly multiply $0.7071\hat{\jmath}$ by 56.6 N*m to obtain 40.0 N*m $\hat{\jmath}$ for the y-component of the moment. **[Too specific. Description should be focused on the process, not the specific numbers.]**

GIVEN: Force F applied as shown below.

FIND: Determine the moment of F about the OA axis.

ASSUMPTIONS:
    None.

FIGURE:

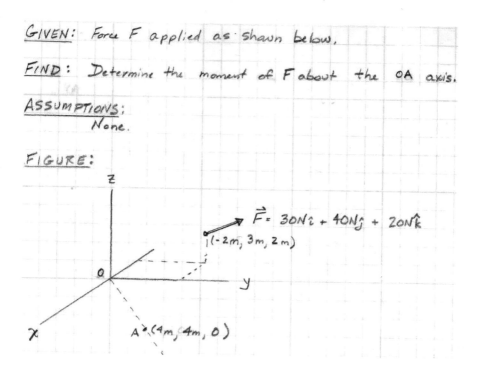

FBD's / CALCULATIONS:

Find position vector from a point on the OA axis to the
point where $\vec{F}$ acts. Use the origin for simplicity.

$$\vec{r} = (-2m - 0)\hat{\imath} + (3m - 0)\hat{\jmath} + (2m - 0)\hat{k} = -2m\hat{\imath} + 3m\hat{\jmath} + 2m\hat{k}$$

Find the moment of $\vec{F}$ about a point along the OA axis, the origin.

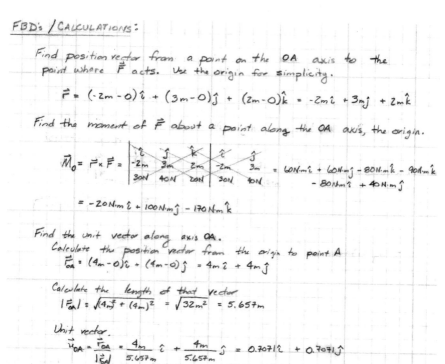

Find the unit vector along axis OA.
    Calculate the position vector from the origin to point A
    $$\vec{r}_{OA} = (4m - 0)\hat{\imath} + (4m - 0)\hat{\jmath} = 4m\hat{\imath} + 4m\hat{\jmath}$$

Calculate the length of that vector
    $$|\vec{r}_{OA}| = \sqrt{(4m)^2 + (4m)^2} = \sqrt{32m^2} = 5.657m$$

Unit vector.
    $$\vec{u}_{OA} = \frac{\vec{r}_{OA}}{|\vec{r}_{OA}|} = \frac{4m}{5.657m}\hat{\imath} + \frac{4m}{5.657m}\hat{\jmath} = 0.7071\hat{\imath} + 0.7071\hat{\jmath}$$

153

Find the moment of $\bar{F}$ about the OA axis.

$$M_{OA} = \vec{u}_{OA} \times \vec{M}_O = 0.7071(-20 N \cdot m) + 0.7071(100 N \cdot m) + 0(-170 N \cdot m)$$

$$= 56.6 N \cdot m$$

$$\vec{M}_{OA} = M_{OA} \vec{u}_{OA} = 56.6 N \cdot m (0.7071) \hat{\imath} + 56.6 N \cdot m (0.7071) \hat{\jmath}$$

$$\boxed{\vec{M}_{OA} = 40.0 N \cdot m \; \hat{\imath} + 40.0 N \cdot m \; \hat{\jmath}}$$

154

APPENDIX C

CHEMICAL ENGINEERING UNIT OPERATIONS
LAB PEER REVIEW SHEET

Name:_____   Project:_____

Introduction • What is the paper is about? • What are the objectives (purpose)? • Are the objectives identified in the opening paragraph? Clarity & conciseness of section	100-60-25
Results and Discussion • What data was collected? • What does the data mean and what general trend does it shows? • Are visual aids (tables and graphs) clear, easy to read, and properly labeled? • Is each visual aid discussed in the text? Clarity & conciseness of section	150-105-40
Conclusions and Recommendations • What are the conclusions and do they directly address the objectives? • Are all the objectives addressed? • Do all the ideas in this section flow logically from the discussion of results? Clarity & conciseness of section	60-40-15
Format for specific type of report and summary (progress reports)	30-20-20

Procedures, Equipment & Materials or description	20-20-0
Sample calculations	35-0-0
References	5-5-0
Quality of feedback given on reviews	

Criteria for peer evaluation of UO reports

Although three different types of reports are written for each laboratory experiment, several of the most important criteria are common to all. The major difference among the reports relates to the amount of detail that should be presented.
For example, the formal report should have a section detailing the theory and experimental setup. On the other hand, the memo report should concentrate almost exclusively on the important findings, results and conclusions.
As you evaluate one another's reports, comment specifically on the following topics. Make comments directly on the draft, and summarize your comments on a separate page. This page should be turned in along with the original, markedup draft by the writer of the paper. In addition, the writer should briefly describe how the reviewer's comments were incorporated into the final draft.

Introduction
Each type of report should contain an introduction. In the memo report this may just be a few sentences of the opening paragraph. In the formal report, this will likely be an entire section that includes an extensive discussion of the underlying theory. In all cases, the introduction should contain the objectives of the experiment and, hence, this report.
- What is the paper is about?
- What are the objectives (purpose)?
- Are the objectives identified in the opening paragraph?
- Comment on the clarity and conciseness of this section.

Results and Discussion

This section requires that graphical information (tables, graphs, charts) be combined with text. The results should be presented in an easy to understand manner (e.g., tables and graphs), and they should be described in the text so that a reader can readily understand what the data represent. In all cases measured values should be clearly differentiated from calculated values. Units should always be included. When discussing the results, <u>the writer should direct the reader to interesting trends that the data show</u>. The writer should not assume that the reader can look at a graph and instantly interpret the results. The emphasis should be on what the results mean. If appropriate, comparison with literature values or theoretical values can be made. When making a comparison, be realistic—the writer's credibility suffers when stating that data matches theory when it really does not.

- What data was collected?
- What does the data mean and what general trend does it shows?
- Are visual aids (tables and graphs) clear, easy to read, and properly labeled?
- Is each visual aid adequately discussed in the text?
- Comment on the clarity and conciseness of this section.

Conclusions and Recommendations

This section should follow logically from the discussion of results. No new ideas should be introduced here without being introduced during the discussion of the results. The conclusions should relate to the objectives of the experiment and the purpose of the report. Recommendations may indicate additional work that could be done to test hypotheses that were developed through analyzing the data or may indicate ways in which the experiment can be improved.

- What are the conclusions and do they directly address the objectives?
- Are all the objectives addressed?
- Do all the ideas in this section flow logically from the discussion of results?
- Comment on the clarity and conciseness of this section.

CHAPTER 9

WRITING, ASSESSMENT, AND NEW TECHNOLOGIES

Anne Herrington and Charles Moran
University of Massachusetts Amherst

As institutional researchers and writing specialists, we share an understanding of the value of assessment, whether that be direct classroom assessment for instruction (e.g., a writing teacher's response to individual students' first drafts) or program assessment (e.g., review of a student portfolios, mean scores on items of the National Survey of Student Engagement). For the most part, such assessments are chosen and even developed by faculty and assessment officers to serve specific classroom or programmatic purposes that they have identified. Currently, however, there is increased external pressure for standardized assessment and increased marketing of commercial assessment products, many capitalizing on the affordances of new electronic technologies. The impact of these pressures is to shift more of the decision-making regarding assessment out of local hands. For writing, the major impact has been the use of automated assessment programs that are designed to evaluate features of writing. In this chapter, we will consider use of these programs for two distinct purposes, classroom assessment of individual students and large scale program assessment. In each case, we will examine a standardized, externally developed assessment instrument versus locally developed options, considering each in relation to accepted principles of sound assessment and conceptions of writing. Our purpose, admittedly, is to caution against reliance on the standardized programs and to advocate locally developed and implemented approaches that are consistent with best practices for assessment, linked to local curricula, and congruent with the rhetorical activity of writing. Our hope is that the chapter will persuade you of the value of the kind of locally developed options described in other chapters of this collection and leave you with ideas for your own campus-based work. First a bit of context.

Externally Imposed Assessment Pressures

Political pressure for outcomes assessment of higher education learning has been mounting in recent years, fueled in no small measure by assessment pressure on public K-12 education and the 2006 report commissioned by the U.S. Secretary of Education, Margaret Spellings. This broad-ranging report, *A Test of Leadership: Charting the Future of U.S. Higher Education*, included recommendations in the area of assessment for "measurement of student achievement . . . on a 'value-added' basis that takes into account students' academic baseline when assessing their results" (U.S. Department of Education, 2006, p. 4). It also calls for transparency in reporting assessment procedures and results and comparability among schools (U.S.

159

Department of Education, 2006, p. 4). In the face of this pressure, some of the major higher education organizations—particularly those representing public education—have voiced similar recommendations. Most recently, for instance, the American Association of State Colleges and Universities (AASCU) and the National Association of State Universities and Land-Grant Colleges (NASULGC) are promoting a Voluntary System of Accountability for Undergraduate Education (VSA). In addition to making such information as costs, financial aid, student demographics, and graduation rates easily accessible using a standardized template, the VSA College Portrait calls for standardized assessment data on learning outcomes that enable comparison among institutions and calculation of "learning gains or value-added scores" for critical thinking and written communication (2008, p. 2). The call for comparability is key to the pressure for standardization, obviously, because locally developed and evaluated assessments do not lend themselves to comparison across institutions. In contrast to AASCU and NASULGC, the Association of American Universities (AAU) and the National Association of Independent Colleges and Universities (NAICU) advocate leaving choice of assessment goals and instruments to local campuses (Lederman, 2007). While we in higher education should be expected to demonstrate that our programs are succeeding in educating our students, we should not accept too quickly the uncritical call for "comparability" as a criterion that trumps principles of sound assessment practice. While the calls for comparability and bench-marking pertain primarily to program and institutional assessments, they have ramifications for classroom instruction and assessment as well.

Ironically, just as AASCU and NASULGC are promoting their VSA, including standardized, comparable outcomes assessment, the U.S. Department of Education seems to be shifting from stressing comparability across institutions and emphasizing transparency instead: that is, each institution making transparent its assessment procedures and results (Schray, 2007). Still, the effect of the original report and these association reports is to focus assessment on standardized products that can be used in uniform ways across institutions and classrooms for comparative purposes. This focus narrows the scope of assessment options, shifting focus away from the kind of site-specific assessments that are closer to principles of best practice for assessment. In short, we share the view expressed in the American Association of Colleges and Universities (AACU) report, *College Learning for the New Global Century*, that standardized tests are a "'low-yield' strategy. . . . at best, a weak prompt to needed improvement in teaching, learning, and curriculum" (2007, p. 40).

Principles for Assessing Writing

College Learning for the New Global Century cautions against a "rush to adopt standardized testing for higher education," advocating instead systematic, "curriculum-embedded assessment," which they see as more likely to yield results that students and faculty will take seriously, and thus be more likely to serve as "a forceful catalyst for significant educational change" (AACU, 2007, p. 41). Such an assessment approach matches closely principles of assessment articulated by both

160

writing specialists and institutional researchers. To illustrate the overlap, we include statements that guide our own practice, both within our professional organization and our university. The first is the position statement on Writing Assessment from the Conference on College Composition and Communication (CCCC, 2006) (see Figure 1). (See Huot, 2002 for theoretical background.) The second is a statement of principles of effective program assessment from our Office of Academic Planning and Assessment (see Figure 2). The overlap is striking. Notice the focus on locally

CCCC Position Statement on Writing Assessment –[excerpts]

- Best assessment practice is undertaken in response to local goals, not external pressures.
- The methods and criteria that readers use to assess writing should be locally developed, deriving from the particular context and purposes for the writing being assessed.
- Best assessment practice engages students in contextualized, meaningful writing.
- Best assessment practice uses multiple measures.
- Best assessment practice supports and harmonizes with what practice and research have demonstrated to be effective ways of teaching writing.
- Assessment programs should be solidly grounded in the latest research on learning, writing, and assessment.
- Best assessment practice is direct assessment by human readers.

Figure 1. Position statement on Writing Assessment from the Conference on College Composition and Communication (CCCC, 2006).

Effective Program Assessment Is Generally:

- Systematic
- Built around the department mission statement
- Ongoing and cumulative
- Multi-faceted
- Pragmatic
- Faculty-designed and implemented

Figure 2. Statement of principles of effective program assessment from the Office of Academic Planning and Assessment (2004). *Program-Based Review and Assessment.* University of Massachusetts Amherst. Adapted from guidelines in the *California State University, Chico, Assessment Plan* (1998) and the *Ball State University Assessment Workbook* (1999).

designed and implemented assessments (as also stressed in the AACU report), linking assessment to institutional/programmatic goals and values, drawing on contextualized, meaningful student performance, and involving faculty in design and implementation. Having site-based assessments increases the likelihood that institutional values and curricula will drive the assessment, instead of the reverse, and that institutionally meaningful information will be derived, thus also increasing the likelihood that faculty and students will actually use the assessment data for formative purposes. A distinct principle in the "Writing Assessment Position Statement" (CCCC, 2006) is that "Best assessment practice is direct assessment by human readers." This principle, consistent with the 2006 CCCC "Position Statement on Teaching, Learning, and Assessing Writing in Digital Environments," reflects the understanding of our professional community that "automated assessment programs distort the very nature of writing as a complex and context-rich interaction between people." We write to impact other people and in anticipation of response; we learn to write by writing and receiving feedback on how our writing is understood and experienced by people.

Defining Learning Outcomes for Writing Assessment

Of course, local definitions of valued outcomes for writing will vary to fit the mission of an institution and specific course and program goals, just as definitions of "critical thinking" will vary. Still, those local definitions should be consistent with accepted, scholarly conceptions of the broad construct to be assessed. For writing, in 2000, the Council of Writing Program Administrators adopted an "Outcomes Statement for First-Year Composition" that provides such a broad definition of the construct of "writing," in terms of valued outcomes. In the most general terms, as we paraphrase, those outcomes include the ability

- to use writing to communicate effectively to various audiences, for various purposes, and in various genres,
- to revise, shape, and edit language to create a final text, and
- to use writing for inquiry, critical thinking, and learning.

Each of these outcomes entails more specific skills, such as the ability to organize, control features of grammar and syntax, integrate one's own ideas with those of others, and adopt tone and line of development for specific audiences. The recognition of writing as a medium for thinking and learning provides the primary rationale for Writing across the Curriculum pedagogy and joins writing with other valued outcomes of liberal education (e.g., "Intellectual and Practical Skills" articulated in College Learning for the New Global Century, including "inquiry and analysis, critical and creative thinking" [AACU, 2007, p. 3]). In other words, writing is at once a set of skills to be taught and assessed in and of itself and a means for engaging in and demonstrating one's abilities at, for instance, critical thinking.

Having established these principles for assessment and a broad definition of the construct "writing" as that which intersects with critical thinking, we move on to our review of two automated programs for the classroom and program assessment of writing.

Criterion™ is marketed by the Educational Testing Service (ETS, 2007a) as a program that can evaluate and respond to student writing particularly in first-year college writing courses, but also for a student's post-secondary academic writing in content courses. Criterion™ is the latest iteration of a project that first surfaced in our literature with the publication in 1968 of *The Analysis of Essays by Computer* by Ellis Page and Dieter Paulus, the report of the U.S. Office of Education-funded Project Essay Grade. Page and Paulus identified 30 quantifiable text-features, including essay length, average word length, amount and kind of punctuation, the numbers of certain words, and number of spelling errors (1968, pp. 21–22). They found that the correlation between the computer-scoring based on these text features and the scoring of a panel of experts was .71, high enough for them to suggest that the computer could be given the job of scoring student writing. Ellis Page surfaced again in 1995, this time with Nancy Peterson, reporting again on Project Essay Grade, now sponsored by ETS. Page and Peterson's claim was again that "in a *blind* test a computer can simulate the judgment of a group of human judges on a brand-new set of essays" (Page & Peterson, 1995, p. 565). For a more detailed account of the early history of computer-scoring of student writing, please see our article in *College English* (Herrington & Moran, 2001).

We fast-forward to the present where this project assumes its contemporary form, Criterion™, marketed by ETS to schools, colleges, and universities as a program to be used not just for scoring writing in mass testing situations, but to be used by students as they write for their teachers in their academic courses. In this model, students write to Criterion™ first, receive scoring and feedback, and then submit their work to their teacher. The CD provided by ETS describes two aspects of the program: e-rater™, the engine that generates a holistic score; and Critique™, the engine that generates what they term "diagnostic feedback." The CD also contains testimonials from teachers, administrators, and students. These testimonials claim that Criterion™ makes it possible to have essays read and responded to "without an inordinate amount of time"; it produces an "immediate result"; that the annotated feedback given by the program is "valuable"; and that Criterion™ is useful to student writers as a "learning tool" in a "virtual writing lab." A student voice tells us, "I also received a lot of great writing feedback, suggestions about grammar and style. It's great practice to know what still needs work, how to re-write it, and resubmit my assignment for a better score" (ETS, 2007c). Criterion™ is made available to college bookstores, so that instructors may require students to buy Criterion™ just as they would require a text or printed book.

Our experience of writing to Criterion™ was disturbing in two ways: writing to the computer, not to a human reader, radically distorted the normal writing situation; and the feedback given to us by the program was vague, generally misleading, and often dead wrong.

On the ETS web site one of us, Charlie, wrote, as asked, a response to this prompt:

Often in life we experience a conflict in choosing between something we want to do and something we feel we should do.

In your opinion, are there any circumstances in which it is better for people to do what they want to do rather than what they feel they should do? Support your position with evidence from your own experience or your observations of other people.

For Charlie's essay in response to this prompt, please see the Appendix.

The Scoring: e-rater™

e-rater™ gave Charlie's essay the following holistic score:

> **ADVISORY**
> **Your essay has triggered the following advisory:**
> > **Your essay does not resemble others that have been written on this topic. This might be an indication that it is about something else or is not relevant to the issues this topic raises.**
> **Please review this essay with your instructor or writing tutor.**

Charlie's reaction to this response was dismay. He had written a piece that was important to him, and, despite the fact that at one level he knew that he was writing to a computer, as a writer, he expected some response to his ideas. This was not "writing as a complex and context-rich interaction between people" (CCCC, 2006). A numerical score would have been inadequate enough, but the "advisory" he received felt like a rejection. Further, the bullet tells him that his essay "does not resemble others that have been written on the topic." This feels like punishment for the critical thinking he was doing as he examined the terms and assumptions of the question. Were he a student writing this essay for a college class, he would learn to hunker down and try to be less thoughtful in his approach, perhaps inventing sometime when he wanted to cheat on a test but realized that he should not. After repeated submissions, he would have learned to write to the test—improving his score, but not his writing, learning to play the e-rater™ game. Here e-rater™ is clearly working against most, and perhaps all, teachers' goals for their students' learning. ETS' principal argument for e-rater™, that its scores are reliable and coincide acceptably with the scores of human readers, are arguments for the use of e-rater™ in mass testing situations, but not as an adjunct to classroom teaching.

Finally, the e-rater™ advisory tells Charlie that his piece might be "about something else" or "not relevant to the issues this topic raises." This is a serious charge, serious in that it is based on an assumption that e-rater™ can read for content. Despite this implied claim that the program can "read" for content, we know that it can not.

The Feedback: Critique™

The feedback provided by Critique™ asserted that Charlie had made one error in grammar, two in usage, and five in mechanics. The grammar error was an alleged sentence fragment. "Let me pick on the last of these 'what-if's' and expand on it a bit." That is not a sentence fragment. So Critique™ can not reliably parse a sentence. The usage errors were described as "missing or extra article." Here is the offending sentence: "There's no reported 'good' outcome of our three-years' pursuit of democracy in Iraq, not even anything approaching the beginnings of a democracy." *Critique*™ tells Charlie, "You may need to use an article before this word," and the word highlighted is <u>good</u>, the fourth word in the sentence. Adding an article before good would make the sentence into nonsense. *Critique*™ tells Charlie, "You may need to remove this article," and the article is the <u>a</u> before <u>democracy</u>, the last word in the sentence. We do not need to remove this article; the sentence stands as is. So *Critique*™ cannot reliably "read" for missing or extra articles. *Critique*™ found five spelling errors: one was <u>do—the</u>, which tells us that *Critique*™ can not handle the dash; another was <u>Shaftesbury</u>, which tells us that *Critique*™ cannot handle proper names; a third was <u>three-years'</u> which tells us either that *Critique*™ cannot handle the hyphen or that it can not handle the apostrophe; the fourth was <u>not-learned</u>, which is another case of not being able to handle the hyphen; and the fourth was <u>Iraquis</u>, listed as the plural of Iraqui in the American Heritage Dictionary, third edition (1992). Lesson learned: *Critique*™'s dictionary does not reliably identify plural nouns.

So in terms of grammar, usage, and mechanics, *Criterion*™ is 0 for 8: in this case, it is wrong <u>all</u> the time. Charlie ran his essay through his word-processor's grammar-check, and found that *Critique*™ was less accurate than this widely available program. His word-processor noted a subject-verb-agreement error that *Critique*™ had missed; it did not wrongly identify the sentence *Critique*™ had marked as a fragment; and it did not mark <u>Iraquis</u> as a spelling error.

We can only imagine how *Critique*™'s feedback would affect a student writer. At the least, it would confuse; at the worst, it would misinform. If we had a teacher in our writing program who misidentified errors of grammar, usage, and mechanics all the time, or even 10% of the time, we would fire that teacher, because misinformation about error is worse than no information at all.

Moving on quickly to the 31 comments on Charlie's style: the program flags every time Charlie uses <u>we</u> in the piece. He used <u>we</u> 27 times in the piece; each was flagged as an error. He argues that on reflection he might remove one or two of these, but that they are generally integral to his argument. The program's advice, "vary your word choice," was not helpful to him. It flags a sentence as "too many long sentences" and says that "this sentence may be a run-on sentence." It is not a run-on sentence, and is one long sentence too many? Finally, the program flags three uses of the passive voice, all of which are just fine as they are. So, the comments on style are misleading, in one case dead wrong, and not useful.

Even more problematic than the feedback on grammar, style, and mechanics is the feedback on Organization and Development. Feedback in this area carries with it the implied assumption that the program can read for meaning, which it cannot. *Critique*™ identifies Charlie's first sentence as his "introduction," and asks, "Is this part of the essay your introduction? In your introduction you should capture the reader's interest, provide background information about your topic, and present your thesis sentence. Look in the Writer's Handbook for ways to improve your introduction." We assume, though we do not have access to the program's formulas, that the program has identified Charlie's one-sentence first paragraph as his introduction and has judged it too short. The advice given is not useful, even if we accept the premise that one-sentence paragraphs are a bad way to start a response to the given prompt. In this category of Organization and Development, Critique™ goes on to identify Charlie's main ideas, which it tells him are the first sentences of the next three paragraphs. Again, though we do not have access to the program's formulas, it seems as if the program identifies as "main ideas" the first sentences of the second, third, and fourth paragraphs of what it must assume to be a five-paragraph theme as "main ideas." The first sentence of Charlie's second paragraph needs to be stretched to become a "main idea"; the first sentence of the second paragraph is clearly not a main idea; the first sentence of the third paragraph is a legitimate "main idea." So score one hit, one miss, and one possible. The advice given, further, is formulaic and inappropriate: "Do you use examples?" and "Look in the Writer's Handbook for ways to develop main ideas." Critique™ then goes on to assume that everything but the first sentence of paragraphs two, three, and four is "supporting ideas," gives generic advice ("give examples"), and finishes up by assuming that the last paragraph is a conclusion, and gives generic advice (e.g. "a conclusion reminds the reader about your thesis").

It is hard for us to see how this "diagnostic feedback," so warmly praised in promotional material and testimonials, could be useful to a writer. It is much easier to see this feedback as harmful. It is harmful in that it is overwhelmingly wrong. It is harmful in that this dreadfully wrong feedback can be given such authority—by the institution that installs the system, and by the instructor who tells his students to purchase access to the program for the writing in their course. It is harmful in that it complicates the work of the teacher, who will need to deal not only with the student's writing but with Criterion™'s responses to that writing and their effect on her students. And finally it is harmful because it discourages inquiry, critical thinking, and stylistic and intellectual risk-taking, all aspects of good writing. In its promotional material, ETS states, tellingly, that "Criterion™ is designed to be used for evaluating writing done under testing conditions—situations in which even the most creative writers concentrate on 'playing it safe'" (ETS, 2007b). Yet Criterion™ is marketed as a tool that students can use in all of their undergraduate and graduate-school writing, writing situations when we would hope that writers would not be "playing it safe." Our experience with Criterion™ underscores the soundness of the claim made in the CCCC Position Statement (2006) that "Best assessment practice is direct assessment by human readers."

Project SAGrader™

SAGrader™, our second automated program for classroom and program assessment, is radically different from Criterion™ in its aims, function, and process of development. Whereas Criterion™ is designed to measure global writing quality and give student writers feedback on grammar, style, and organization, SAGrader™ is designed to be used in subject-area courses to measure and give feedback on students' mastery of content in essay responses to highly constrained topics.

SAGrader™ not only measures mastery of particular content, but it gives substantive feedback to student writers, telling them what they have included and where they have left gaps. It is presented by its developers as a viable, cost-effective alternative to multiple-choice tests in large courses.

Lest all of this seem too good to be true, we need to be clear on what SAGrader™ does not do. It does not give students a "grade" on "good writing"; it does not attempt to point out sentence-level errors; it does not attempt to measure and comment on organization; it makes no claims about natural language processing or its ability to "read" for meaning; and it makes no judgments about style. From our experience with Criterion™, we think that these limitations speak to the SAGrader™ developers' good sense of the limitation of computers as "readers" of written language.

SAGrader™ can do what it does—evaluate and respond to students' mastery of course content—because its knowledge base must be developed locally to suit the particular aims of a particular course. The process of development begins with the teacher, who, under the guidance of the Ideaworks staff, selects an area of course content that will be the subject-area of the to-be-written essay. The teaching/learning goal must be finite and specific—not "Improved appreciation for 19th century American Literature," but perhaps "An understanding of the relationship of the American Transcendentalist movement to British Romanticism." Then, working still with the Ideaworks staff, the teacher develops a "concept map" of this area. Let us say, for example, that the course is not American Literature but Composition Theory, and the particular subject for the week is the students' reading of James Britton's *Language and Learning* (1970). The teacher's aims are, let us further say, to have her students know and understand the basic concepts in Britton's work. To judge whether her students had mastered this course content, and to help her students learn this course content, the teacher, let us again say, asks her students to write a one-page essay to this prompt: "What categories of language function does James Britton establish in *Language and Learning*? And how does he define each? What are other important concepts in his book? Name and discuss two of these." This writing assignment would fall into our understanding of "writing to learn": it is a short writing, one of several in the course, designed not only to evaluate students' learning but to enhance and support this learning.

Given the teacher's aims, and given the writing prompt designed to discover whether her students have met her goals for their learning, the knowledge base will include at least these concepts: Britton's three categories of language function: the transactional, the expressive, and the poetic; the role of the spectator; the role of the participant; world representation; gossip; or play. The teacher would have to furnish definitions of each of the concept terms, and, in addition, allowable variations. For example, in *Language and Learning* Britton defines transactional function as "language to get things done" (1970, p. 125). The teacher would provide this definition, but might decide that allowable variations were "writing to get things done" and "everyday writing." The teacher might decide, as well, that "workplace writing" was not an allowable variation. Finally, the teacher would be asked to give weights to each of the items so that the program could score student responses. With these materials, the Ideaworks staff would set up the knowledge base, and what they term the "development" stage would be complete. For a topic of this complexity and essays of this length, the Ideaworks staff estimates that the teacher would need to spend less than an hour.

Then follows a "training" stage, in which the program is tested in its first run against student essays written to the topic. In this phase, and throughout the program's evolution, students are permitted to challenge its results. The challenges are reviewed by the teacher, and a determination is made: either the student made an error, or the knowledge base in the program was at fault. If the knowledge base was at fault, then it is changed, or "trained." For example, if the student who brought the challenge argued that his definition of transactional writing, "writing to accomplish something tangible," was valid, and the teacher agreed with the student that this was an allowable variation of Britton's definition, then this variation would be added to the knowledge base and all past and future essays would permit this variation. The training phase for this topic, the Ideaworks staff estimate, would take the teacher something less than two hours (Brent, Carnahan, & McCully, 2007, p. 6).

Finally, there is a "monitoring" stage, which continues throughout the program's use. The monitoring stage is really a continuation of the "training" stage, but at a much lower intensity, as student challenges to the program's results diminish in number and the adjustments made to the knowledge base become less frequent. The Ideaworks staff estimates that this monitoring process will take something less than a minute per student essay submitted. At this point we have a program in place that can scan our students' one-page essays on James Britton's *Language and Learning* and give student writers feedback that looks like this:

You have correctly named and defined transactional and expressive writing; you have not named and defined 1 other of Britton's function categories. You have correctly identified "writing in the spectator mode" as a key concept; you have not identified 1 other key concepts. Weighted score: 60.

Given their assumptions about the time taken to develop the knowledge base for *SAGrader*™ and the time taken to hand-score students' writing, the Ideaworks staff calculates that the point at which *SAGrader*™ begins to be quicker than hand-grading and responding, for a writing task of this length and this complexity, is somewhere around 25 submissions. One can argue with their assumptions about the speed of human readers or the predicted development and training time required, but still the numbers look promising: if you have a lecture class of 150 with multiple discussion sections, *SAGrader*™ would permit you to assign multiple short writings instead of multiple-choice tests.

There is, as noted above, substantial teacher-time required for the up-front development and training of the program, but there is time saved in the subsequent evaluation and response to student essays, because the cost to the system of evaluating and responding to a single essay is essentially zero. There is continued monitoring of the program, as the teacher checks its results and responds to student challenges, but the per-submission cost is still low and becomes lower if the teacher permits students to submit multiple drafts to the program and improve their score.

Here efficiency would seem to drive good teaching practice: as students re-write and improve their scores, they are, arguably, learning the course content.

So far, SAGrader™ seems to have what we want in an instrument for assessing writing: it follows good practice in the teaching of writing, as it encourages drafting and revising and gives feedback on content only. It is locally developed and therefore responsive to teachers' goals for their students' learning. It supports the use of writing as a mode of learning, and encourages and enables writing across the curriculum. Used responsibly, as it is at the University of Missouri, where Ed Brent, its principal developer, teaches sociology, it is a very attractive program—not a replacement for, but an aid to, the human reader. The white papers that Ideaworks publishes on its web site, however, suggest that this program can easily be misused. In a section titled "Strategies for Reducing Costs and Increasing Benefits," the authors suggest that "reviewing every student essay by hand will drastically reduce the effectiveness of the program" (Brent et al., 2007, p. 10), and the context suggests that this "reviewing" is a quick skim, not a real reading. This is a suggestion that runs counter to the program developer's practice in his own sociology course, where he or a TA reads every final draft (Brent & Townshend, 2006). The authors further suggest as a cost-reducing stratagem that we "target high-enrollment classes" and "classes with multiple sections." That makes good sense to us. But they continue the series: "Or classes where it can be used in subsequent semesters (Brent et al., 2007, p. 8). Later they suggest that we "Re-purpose questions for use in different assignments from one semester or course to another" (p. 9). Given that developing or revising an SAGrader™ knowledge base costs the instructor time and effort, time-pressures and workload may lead instructors to use the same texts and related SAGrader™ prompts again and again, a high-tech version of the yellowed lecture-notes of yesteryear: static, formulaic, make-work for both sides of the teaching/learning transaction. Further, these same forces, coupled with an administrator's need to standardize across institutions, could lead to a standard Sociology 101 course mandated across a full state-wide system, all courses using the same syllabus, texts, essay prompts, and SAGrader™ routines. But given that anything new can be used for good or for ill, we count on teachers and administrators to use this technology well, in the service of their students' learning. Finally we need to say that in a just world all writing would be meaning-making human communication, not the generation of information to be processed. Unfortunately, in the present political and economic situation, only the elite and expensive private colleges will be able to provide active human readers for all their students' writing. In this context, SAGrader™, properly used, is an attractive option.

Higher Education Learning Outcomes Assessment

How technology will be used and how faculty will be involved for larger scale assessments of learning outcomes are equally pressing issues. Most of our institutions identify a comprehensive set of learning outcomes for our graduates, for both in-depth knowledge of a particular major and broader knowledge, skills, and understandings across disciplines. One conception of these broad outcomes is presented in the American Association of Colleges and Universities report, *College Learning for the New Global Century*, that makes the case for a set of "Essential Learning Outcomes" necessary to "prepare for twenty-first century challenges." The outcomes are organized in the four broad areas of "knowledge of human cultures and the physical and natural world, intellectual and practical skills, personal and social responsibility, and integrative learning" (2007, p. 12). "Intellectual and practical skills" include "inquiry and analysis, critical and creative thinking, written and oral communication, quantitative literacy, information literacy, and teamwork and problem solving." Personal and social responsibility includes, for instance, "civic knowledge and engagement, intercultural knowledge and competence, and ethnical reasoning and action" (p. 12).

Given this broad conception of outcomes for liberal education, it is perhaps ironic that the pressure for accountability using standardized measures reduces these broad outcomes considerably, to focus primarily on critical thinking and writing, as they are defined by standardized tests. These are the skills identified in the VSA as the Core Education Outcomes to be assessed. Further, this document identifies three tests from which participating institutions are to select one for the assessment: American College Testing's Collegiate Assessment of Academic Proficiency (CAAP), ETS's Measure of Academic Proficiency and Progress (MAPP), and The Council for Aid to Education/RAND Corporation's Collegiate Learning Assessment (CLA). Note that MAPP and CLA are also mentioned as exemplars in *A Test of Leadership: Charting the Future of U.S. Higher Education* (U.S. Department of Education, 2006, p. 24). All three promise to enable an institution to compare its results with other comparable institutions, but all fail to meet principles of assessment practice in key ways. Notably, they are not site-based in terms of faculty involvement in design and evaluation of performance, they are not "curriculum-embedded," and for writing, they distort the nature of the activity and do not match with what we know to be effective ways to teach writing. According to Dan Fogel (2007), President of the University of Vermont and Co-Chair of the Core Education Outcomes Task Force for the VSA initiative, they are being recommended as a key component of VSA to serve perceived demands of external audiences; how valuable they will be for specific institutional improvement is still an open question. While some institutions might want to use one of these tests as one *part* of an assessment program, at best, they provide only gross information as to program performance. Our primary concern is that these tests not be used in place of locally based assessments, instead of as a small part of a comprehensive, institutionally developed assessment program that is primarily curriculum-embedded.

Given the limits of space, we will focus on one of these tests, the Collegiate Learning Assessment, or CLA, since it is the newest of the three and also quite different from MAPP and CAAP. Both MAPP and CAAP are primarily multiple-choice exams although both include a written essay component as an option. Of the three, both CLA and MAPP use e-*rater*™ for evaluation of writing, the same scoring engine we have already met in our review of *Criterion*™. CLA differs from MAPP and CAAP in being totally performance based and eliciting written responses for all tasks. It is marketed as enabling both inter-institutional comparisons and judgments of institutional "value-added" through cross-sectional analysis of scores of first year and final year students. The test is marketed as relatively inexpensive, requiring a sample of only 100 first year students and 100 seniors for the basic assessment (Council for Aid to Education, n.d.a).

The test includes two kinds of tasks: The first is a problem-solving "Performance Task" requiring one to reason through a problem set in a specific rhetorical situation and write an analysis of it and recommendation to a decision-maker. The CLA website provides the following example, as we paraphrase: you are the assistant to the president of a small company and are asked to advise her on advisability of purchasing a small plane about which there is conflicting information regarding its performance and safety. Test-takers are to develop their recommendation after reviewing six documents. This task is "meaningful" in that it situates the problem in a hypothetical context. Further, it does seem like an open-ended task that draws on reading, analysis and problem-solving, and writing. Forty-five minutes are allotted for completing the task. It is presently evaluated by human readers, although not faculty on the campus where the assessment is given.

The second type task involves "Writing Prompts" of two kinds: what are called "make-an-argument" prompts and "break-an-argument" prompts. The make-an-argument task presents a simplistically framed task with an assertion such as the following to agree or disagree with: "Public figures such as actors, politicians, and athletes should expect people to be interested in their private lives. When they seek a public role, they should expect that they will lose at least some of their privacy." The break-an-argument task provides an "argument" for the test-taker to critique on the basis of "the soundness of the argument's logic." The argument is only about five sentences long, however—more a paragraph than a developed argument. Test takers have only 30 minutes to do one or the other of these.

Not surprisingly, it is these more reductive writing tasks, not the performance task, that are evaluated by e-rater™. In the CLA documents, the use of e-rater™ is normalized as unproblematic in that there is no justification for the choice of an automated assessment program. Further, we are given little information as to the specific traits that e-rater™ is evaluating. Indeed, no scoring rubric is presented for any of the tasks although in a separate Council for Aid to Education document, *Collegiate Learning Assessment (CLA) Critical Thinking, Analytic Reasoning, Problem Solving, and Writing Skills: Definitions and Scoring Criteria*, the test designers claim that writing is assessed in an integrated way with critical thinking along dimensions of "presentation, development, persuasiveness, mechanics, and interest" (Council for Aid to Education, n.d.b.). We do not question the claim that e-rater™ ratings correlate well with trained human reader-ratings for global judgments of writing done to specific prompts. Our quarrels are with the way e-rater™ distorts the nature of writing, the reductive tasks that are used, and the vague claims made as to what e-rater™ can evaluate. Specifically, we question e-rater™'s capability at assessing "interest" and persuasiveness; in other words, the rhetorical skills of developing a thoughtful argument for an audience of readers.

If CLA is used, an institution receives a report of the performance of first-year students and seniors and judgment of whether the gain in senior scores is significant enough to represent "value-added." The report indicates whether each score is "below expected," "expected," "above expected," or "well above expected," based on the mean SATs for student participants. Scores are also compared with peer institutions that are also using CLA. The validity of such value-added calculations is open to debate. Trudy Banta, Vice Chancellor for Planning and Institutional Improvement at Indiana University-Purdue University at Indianapolis, concludes: "a substantial and credible body of measurement research tells us that standardized tests of general intellectual skills cannot furnish meaningful information on the value added by a college education nor can they provide a sound basis for inter-institutional comparisons. In fact, the use of test scores to make comparisons can lead to a number of negative consequences, not the least of which is homogenization of educational experiences and institutions" (Banta, 2007). Charles Blaich, Director of Inquiries for the Wabash National Study of Liberal Arts Education, also argues that cross-sectional data do not sufficiently control for differences among entering students to enable valid value-added conclusions (2007).

As teachers and writing scholars, our primary concern is with the way that CLA reduces the outcomes of liberal education to problem-solving and impromptu "argument" writing. In marketing the test, however, CLA developers stress that the CLA is to be used as just one part of an "assessment portfolio." If that is so, then CLA might have a role to play with its Performance Task if that kind of problem-solving is valued at an institution and if CLA is coupled with locally developed assessments that provide further insight into other valued general education outcomes, including writing. Still, CLA aims to broaden its place in the "assessment portfolio." In a web conference marketing CLA, participants were told that if an institution wanted to "drill down deeper," for example, to distinguish performance amongst sub-groups of students, they could pay to have a larger sample of students take the CLA. During that web conference, we were also told that CLA is exploring means to assess quantitative skills (as CAAP and MAPP already do) and ethical reasoning. It is this effort, common to all testing corporations, to sell more of their products that works to divert institutional resources away from campus-based assessments.

Still, what should a school do with the results? What if UMass Amherst shows some "value-added" but our scores are only in the middle compared to peer institutions? Should we focus on raising the scores for problem-solving and argument writing? What if that means less attention to other valued outcomes of a liberal education that are *not* assessed by the CLA? For example, at UMass Amherst, one goal of our General Education program is to "provide contexts for questioning the larger society and the student's relation to it." Related to this goal is another for "Social and Cultural Diversity": "to encourage pluralistic perspectives." While the kind of problem-solving represented by the CLA performance task is also valued, if CLA results were to drive our planning, we would be diverted from these other equally valued goals of our General Education program which CLA tasks do not assess (University of Massachusetts Faculty Senate, 2005).

For writing alone, if our institutional scores for argument writing were low, should we focus on teaching the simplistic form of formulaic argument valued by *e-rater*™ and impromptu writing? If the make-an-argument writing scores as judged by *e-rater*™ are not high enough, is not there some logic to deciding that we should use ETS's *Criterion*™ to support instruction in our writing classes? After all, if *e-rater*™ is the high-stakes institutional outcomes judge, then we should have students writing to that same e-rater judge in their classes.

Obviously, there are assessment alternatives to relying on standardized tests such as CLA and MAPP and CAAP, ones that more closely follow best practices for assessment, and some of which use technology to support their work. Many schools have developed local portfolio projects for single courses, programs, or school-wide purposes (see Yancey & Weiser, 1997). Washington State University (2009) includes a Junior Writing Portfolio as one component of its comprehensive, site-based writing assessment program. It is noteworthy for a number of reasons: it is curriculum-embedded, requiring students to submit three papers written for three different courses, as well as do an impromptu writing; it is open to the genres of writing that are included; it encourages students to reflect on their writing skills as they determine which papers to include and involves them in discussions with faculty regarding their choices, both their faculty advisor and teachers of the courses from which they consider submitting a paper; it involves faculty in the process of decision-making and assessment of the portfolios, thus increasing the formative impact of the assessment. Washington State University (n.d.) is also engaged in a project to develop a rubric to guide teaching practice and assessment of critical thinking within courses across the curriculum. The project demonstrates the generative power of involving faculty in the development of the rubric and the way it encourages links between curriculum, pedagogy, and assessment. Electronic technologies can and are being used to facilitate such assessments: for instance, using web platforms to create electronic portfolios. See, for example, the e-portfolio programs at Alverno College (2007), Rhodes State College (2007), and LaGuardia Community College (n.d.). Alverno's Diagnostic Digital Portfolio is a comprehensive assessment program that tracks students progress toward eight core learning goals, including communication, problem-solving, and developing a global perspective. The E-Portfolio program at Rhodes is one component of a more comprehensive assessment program that also includes use of CAAP. LaGuardia's ePortfolio Program illustrates the gradual development of a comprehensive portfolio program, linked initially to learning communities for first year students (see also Cambridge, 2001; Reiss, 2005; and Yancey & Weiser, 1997). The key to all of these programs is faculty being able and willing to participate in design and assessment, thereby closely linking assessment to curricula and instruction. As Donna Engelmann, Professor of Philosophy at Alverno, reports, the Portfolio "works for us because it is imbedded in the teaching and assessment practices of the faculty, otherwise the digital portfolio would be just a repository for documents" (Engelman, 2007).

Public institutions in New York and Virginia demonstrate how state-mandated assessments can still be implemented by adopting common criteria while keeping program assessment local and tailored to specific programs. What is sacrificed in terms of "uniformity" in the assessments is gained by the ability to tailor the assessment to each institution's unique profile and to involve faculty in the assessment. In the State University of New York System, the General Education Assessment Review (GEAR) Initiative mandates campus-based assessments following common implementation guidelines. For the writing assessment, a group of faculty from across the public community colleges, four year colleges and universities developed a common rubric and general guidelines for design and implementation of the campus-based assessments (SUNY GEAR, n.d.) The rubric includes two criteria:

Students will demonstrate their abilities to produce *coherent texts* within *common college level forms*. Students will demonstrate the ability to revise and improve such texts. The guidelines, drawn from the 2006 CCCC Position Statement on Writing Assessment, stipulate, among other things, that the writing to be assessed should "grow out of classroom assignments," "the rubrics and standards of evaluation should be known to students and should be consistent with the evaluation standards in their classrooms," and that "ideally, judgments should always be made on more than one piece of writing" (SUNY GEAR, n.d., p. 1). The criteria more closely resemble those of the Council of Writing Program Administrators (2000) Outcomes Statement in two key ways: The first criterion, instead of mandating a single genre, leaves the choice of genre(s) open to an institution, as appropriate to its mission and curricula Further, requiring that the assessment samples come from classroom assignments ensures that they will be "contextualized, meaningful writing," instead of impromptu writings to artificial prompts. Assessing revision underscores that the ability to revise is an important writing skill. Clearly, in multiple ways, the link between curriculum, classroom practice, and assessment is reinforced with curricular values—not externally determined criteria—driving the assessment. The involvement of faculty in evaluating the writings serves to encourage them to take the results seriously. Pat Belanoff, Chair of the Writing-Discipline Committee, and Kathleen McCoy, a member of the Committee, say that faculty participation in norming sessions and essay evaluation also serves a valuable professional development function and engages faculty in substantive ways in reflective discussions of their curricula and their students' writing skills (Belanoff & McCoy, 2007). Of course, this work requires a commitment of time from faculty and, appropriately, faculty for whom such work is not part of their job responsibility are paid a pre-established rate for the work. We say this to make the broader point that how assessment dollars are spent is an important indicator of institutional values.

The Virginia state-mandated guidelines also enable institutionally developed and executed assessment programs with substantial faculty involvement. As Terry Myers Zawacki and Karen Gentemann explain in their chapter, George Mason University focuses assessment on writing in the major, with faculty in each department responsible for developing rubrics, deciding on appropriate course-linked writing, and carrying out the assessment. The George Mason University "Writing across the Curriculum" (2006) website also demonstrates how both assessment procedures and results can be made publicly accessible, thus meeting the criterion of "transparency."

Having the option to use these alternatives depends on institutions—and public systems—rejecting the call for comparability as *uniformity*; it also depends on faculty joining with academic assessment officers to conduct assessments that are based on sound principles of assessment. In recommending institutionally based assessment programs, the Association of American Colleges and Universities, in the *College Learning for the New Global Century* report calls for locally developed assessments, used to review and revise curricula to, in the words of the report, "deepen learning and to establish a culture of shared purpose and continuous improvement" (2007, p. 26). The key is faculty being able and willing to participate in design and assessment, thereby closely linking assessment to curricula and instruction.

At UMass Amherst, our assessment work for specific sub-programs of general education programs has been varied and quite extensive, as we suspect it is at many schools. Both our First Year Writing Program and Junior Year Writing Programs are evaluated periodically by the University Writing Committee, a standing Faculty Senate Committee with members from disciplines across the university who review syllabi, student course evaluations, staffing patterns, and other samples of materials from classes (Moran & Herrington, 1997). Their review of our First Year Writing Program includes assessing a sample of student portfolios written in our Basic and College Writing courses. Working with our Office of Academic Planning and Assessment, a Writing across the Curriculum Writing Assessment Group with faculty from across disciplines also developed a common rubric to guide course planning and assessment in our Junior Year Writing Program courses (University of Massachusetts Amherst, Writing Across the Curriculum Writing Assessment Group, 2000). Also, under the leadership of Ximena Zuniga, UMass Amherst is participating in "Experiments in Diverse Democracy: A Multi-University Research Evaluation of the Educational Benefits of Intergroup Dialogues" (University of Michigan, 2007), which includes in its assessment plan both extensive questionnaire data on students' perceptions and analysis of student classroom work in an Intergroup Dialogues course. The assessment of other General Education courses has focused almost exclusively on review of course syllabi by our General Education Council to ensure compliance with established guidelines. These range of assessments can and do provide valuable formative information for improving instruction and curricula and should not be discounted in the current pressure for standardized outcomes assessment.

What we have not done is systematically assess student work from these courses in relation to identified goals of our General Education program. That is what the General Education Council, working with the Director of Academic Assessment, is grappling with now. As explained in a Spring 2007 General Education Action Plan:

> If, as some expect, the University will be pressed toward using standardized tests to demonstrate learning in General Education, it behooves us, as a preemptory—or perhaps complementary—strategy, to develop a non-standardized, local means of assessment that can evaluate in a more nuanced way the complex learning that we ask of students in General Education. Arguably, the higher-level intellectual, problem-solving, integrative abilities, and the civic, intercultural, and ethical capacities that General Education tries

175

to promote can be aptly judged only in the rich contexts of inquiry, analysis, critique, and action that our classrooms provide. (University of Massachusetts Amherst, General Education Council, 2007, p. 10)

We are beginning by looking at data already at hand in relation to stated goals of General Education to see what we still need and want to know. For instance, we have previous analyses of course syllabi to draw on, as well as NSSE data, a valuable source of students' perspectives. Our next step is to tackle the question of how to assess aspects of "critical thinking" that we value, drawing on student classroom work. We do not rule out using a standardized instrument for some aspect of the overall assessment, but we do not see it as central. We want our assessment to be based on what is happening in General Education classes and to provide a process that engages faculty in examining student work in a way that gives them a perspective beyond that of their own classrooms. That is a primary motive that drives us to seek campus-based methods that arise from student work in General Education. One technological tool that we are considering using is iMOAT, the MIT Online Assessment Tool (Massachusetts Institute of Technology, 2005). It has been designed primarily for placement assessments using prompts that more closely resemble the intellectual challenges of college-level work, including formulating a viewpoint on the basis of reading multiple sources. In contrast to the CLA performance task, an iMOAT task and reading selections are designed by each program, as is the nature of the writing situation (e.g., whether a time limit for the writing). The iMOAT database serves as the site for students to place their work and for faculty to then evaluate it. In addition to impromptu writing, student writing from one or more of their classes could also be uploaded although the program is not designed to be an e-portfolio. Still, a program could archive student writing, so that, for instance, longitudinal data would be available. If we were to decide to build our assessment around portfolios instead, we would consider some of the models for e-portfolios. It is these sorts of uses of technology that we are drawn to, programs that involve faculty in assessment design and facilitate making student work available to human readers, including faculty for assessment and advising—not the use of computerized programs with reductive tasks and poor proxies for human readers.

Closing

In his 2005 Chair's address to the Conference on College Composition and Communication," Doug Hesse asked, "Who owns writing?" "Who owns the conditions under which writing is taught? . . . Who may declare someone proficient or derelict?" (p. 337). While Hesse argued that teachers of writing, as stewards for student writers, should have this ownership and control, he reviewed other forces in position to own and control writing: education associations that aim to set standards that would define writing and learning outcomes, and computer programs (and their developers) that assess writing and thereby also set values on it. Hesse's three questions could be asked not only about the ownership of writing, but about the ownership of General Education, as we move toward outcomes assessment in this area of the curriculum. Our answer to all three of Hesse's questions: the teaching faculty of an institution, both in their own classes and across an institution. While the teaching faculty at a given school, college, or university might decide to use technology to assist in assessment, both in the classroom and across the institution, and even decide to use some standardized assessments as one part of an "assessment portfolio," we hope we have made the case against relying principally or exclusively on standardized assessment programs or using automated, externally developed writing assessment programs. To return to the 2006 CCCC "Position Statement on Writing Assessment," the "best assessment practice is direct assessment by human readers."

REFERENCES

Alverno College. (2007). *Diagnostic digital portfolio.* Retrieved July 31, 2009, from http://ddp.alverno.edu/index.html

American Association of Colleges and Universities. (2007). *College learning for the new global century.* Washington, DC: Author.

American Association of State Colleges, & Universities & National Association of State Universities and Land-Grant Colleges. (2008). *Voluntary system of accountability (VSA^{SM}): Overview of college portrait.* Retrieved July 31, 2009, from http://www.voluntarysystem.org/docs/cp/CollegePortraitOverview.pdf

American College Testing. (n.d.). *Collegiate Assessment of Academic Proficiency (CAAP).* Retrieved July 31, 2009, from http://www.act.org/caap/index.html

Banta, T. (2007). *A warning on measuring learning outcomes.* Retrieved July 31, 2009, from http://www.insidehighered.com/views/2007/01/26/banta

Belanoff, P., & McCoy, K. (2007, April). *Examining SUNY's assessment program; Writing in an age of assessment.* Paper presented at the annual conference of the State University of New York Council on Writing, University at Albany.

Blaich, C. (2007, June). *Building linkages between standardized and internal measures of student learning; Increasing public trust through high expectations and public disclosure.* Paper presented at the New England Association of Schools and Colleges Commission on Institutions of Higher Education Sponsored Event, Emerson College, Boston, MA.

Brent, E., Carnahan, T., & McCully, J. (2007). *SAGrader™ benefits can outweigh costs in first semester.* Retrieved July 31, 2009, from https://www.sagrader.com/static/content/whitepapers/cost_effective.pdf

Brent, E., & Townshend, M. (2006). Automated essay grading in the sociology classroom: Finding common ground. In P. F. Ericsson, & R. Haswell (Eds.), *Machine scoring of student essays: Truth and consequences.* Logan, UT: Utah State University.

Britton, J. (1970). *Language and learning.* Harmondsworth, UK: Penguin.

Cambridge, B. (Ed.). (2001). *Emerging practices: Electronic portfolio learning for students, faculty, and institutions.* Washington, DC: American Association for Higher Education.

Conference on College Composition and Communication. (2004). *Position statement on teaching, learning, and assessing writing in digital environments.* Retrieved July 31, 2009, from http://www.ncte.org/cccc/resources/positions/digitalenvironments

Conference on College Composition and Communication. (2006). *Writing assessment: A position statement.* Retrieved July 31, 2009, from http://www.ncte.org/cccc/resources/positions/writingassessment

178

Council for Aid to Education. (n.d.a). *Collegiate Learning Assessment (CLA)*. Retrieved July 31, 2009, from http://www.cae.org/content/pro_collegiate.htm

Council for Aid to Education. (n.d.b). *Collegiate Learning Assessment (CLA) critical thinking, analytic reasoning, problem solving, and writing skills: Definitions and scoring criteria.* Retrieved July 31, 2009, from http://www.cae.org/content/pdf/CLA_Scoring%20Criteria.pdf

Council of Writing Program Administrators. (2000). *WPA outcomes statement for first-year composition.* Retrieved July 31, 2009, from http://www.wpacouncil.org/positions/outcomes.html

Educational Testing Service. (2007a). *Criterion™ online writing evaluation.* Retrieved July 31, 2009, from http://www.ets.org/portal/site/ets/menuitem.435c0b5cc7bd0ae7015d9510c3921509/?vgnextoid=b47d253b164f4010VgnVCM10000022f95190RCRD

Educational Testing Service. (2007b). *Frequently asked questions about Criterion™ online writing evaluation.* Retrieved July 31, 2009, from http://www.ets.org/portal/site/ets/menuitem.1488512ecfd5b8 849a77b13bc3921509/?vgnextoi d=f5d9af5e44df4010VgnVCM10000022f95190RCRD&vgnex tchannel=6aae253b164f4010VgnVCM10000022f95190RCRD

Educational Testing Service. (2007c). *Guided tour of the Criterion™ online writing evaluation for higher education.* Compact disk provided by author on July 19, 2007.

Educational Testing Service. (2007d). *MAPP— Measure of Academic Proficiency and Progress.* Retrieved July 31, 2009, from http://www.ets.org/portal /site/ets/m enuitem.1488512ecfd5b8849a77b13bc3921509/?vgnextoid=ff3aaf5 e44df4010VgnVCM10000022f95190RCRD &vgnextchannel= f98546f1674f4010VgnVCM10000022f95190RCRD

Engelmann, D. (2007). *Assessment from the ground up.* Retrieved July 31, 2009, from http://insidehighered.com:80/views/2007/08/14/engelmann

Fogel, D. (2007, June). *High expectations that build "public trust": Increasing public trust through high expectations and public disclosure.* Paper presented at the New England Association of Schools and Colleges Commission on Institutions of Higher Education Sponsored Event, Emerson College, Boston, MA.

George Mason University, Writing Across the Curriculum. (2006). *Assessing student writing competence.* Retrieved July 31, 2009, from http://wac.gmu.edu/assessing/assessing_student_writing.php#part3

Herrington, A., & Moran, C. (2001). What happens when machines read our students' writing? *College English, 63*(4), 480–499.

Hesse, D. (2005). Who owns writing? *College Composition and Communication, 57*(2), 335–357.

Huot, B. (2002). *(Re)Articulating writing assessment for teaching and learning.* Logan, UT: Utah State University.

LaGuardia Community College. (n.d.). *ePortfolio.* Retrieved July 31, 2009, from http://www.eportfolio.lagcc.cuny.edu/

Lederman, D. (2007). *Campus accountability proposals evolve*. Retrieved July 31, 2009, 2007, from http://insidehighered.com/news/2007/06/26/accountability

Massachusetts Institute of Technology. (2005). *Introducing the MIT Online Assessment Tool (iMOAT)*. Retrieved July 31, 2009, from http://icampus.mit.edu/iMOAT/

Moran, C., & Herrington, A. (1997). Program review, program renewal. In K. B. Yancey, & B. Huot (Eds.), *Assessing writing across the curriculum: Diverse approaches and practices* (pp. 123–140). Greenwich, CT: Ablex.

Page, E., & Paulus, D. (1968). *The analysis of essays by computer. Final report of U.S. Office of Education Project No. 6-1318*. Storrs, CT: University of Connecticut. (ERIC Document Reproduction Service No. ED028633)

Page, E., & Petersen, N. S. (1995). The computer moves into essay grading: Updating the ancient test. *Phi Delta Kappan, 76*(7), 561–565.

Reiss, D. (2005). *Webfolio (Electronic Portfolio) Project*. Retrieved July 31, 2009, from http://wordsworth2.net/webfolio/index.htm

Rhodes State College. (2007). *E-Portfolio*. Retrieved August 31, 2009, from http://www.rhodesstate.edu/About%20Rhodes/College%20Offices%20and%20Departments/Academic%20Affairs/Submit%20a%20Writing%20Sample.aspx

Schray, V. (2007, June). *A test of leadership: Charting the future of U.S. higher education*. Paper presented at the regional summit convened by U.S. Department of Education, Hopkinton, MA.

State University of New York, General Education Assessment Review Group. (n.d.). *Report of the Writing-Discipline Committee*. Accessed July 31, 2009, from http://www.cortland.edu/gear/WritingRubrics.Final.pdf

University of Massachusetts Amherst, General Education Council. *Annual Report of the General Education Council AY 2006-07*. [Sen. Doc. No. 08-005]. Retrieved August 20, 2009 from http://www.umass.edu/senate/councils/gen-ed-annual_rpt_0907.pdf

University of Massachusetts Amherst, Office of Academic Planning and Assessment (2001). *Program-Based Review and Assessment: Tools and Techniques for Program Improvement*. Retrieved August 30, 2009 from http://www.umass.edu/oapa/oapa/publications/online_handbooks/program_based.pdf

University of Massachusetts Amherst, Writing Across the Curriculum Writing Assessment Group. (2000). *Establishing learning objectives: Applications for course planning and assessment*. Retrieved July 31, 2009 from http://www.umass.edu/oapa/oapa/publications/online_handbooks/wac_handbook.pdf

University of Massachusetts Faculty Senate. (2005). *Special Report of the Rules Committee concerning the undergraduate general education requirement, Sen. Doc. No. 85-024B*. Retrieved July 31, 2009, from http://www.umass.edu/senate/fs_docs/SEN_DOC_NO_85-024B_GEN_ED.pdf

University of Michigan, Program in Intergroup Relations. (2007). *Experiments in diverse democracy: A multi-university research evaluation of the educational benefits of intergroup dialogues.* Retrieved July 31, 2009, from http://www.igr.umich.edu/experiments.html

U.S. Department of Education. (2006). *A test of leadership: Charting the future of U.S. higher education.* Washington, DC: Author.

Washington State University. (n.d.). WSU *critical thinking project.* Retrieved July 31, 2009, from http://wsuctproject.wsu.edu/index.htm

Washington State University. (2009). *Junior writing portfolio: Proof of readiness to write in the major.* Retrieved July 31, 2009, from http://www.writingprogram.wsu.edu/units/writingassessment/midcollege/

Yancey, K. B., & Weiser, I. (1997). *Situating portfolios: Four perspectives.* Logan, UT: Utah State University.

APPENDIX

Charlie's Response

Should we do what we want to do? Or should we do what we feel we should do?

The answer to this question depends on what our moral compass is telling us to do—the "should" that lurks in the question and in that aspect of our personality and character we might call our "conscience." We can't, however, glibly assume that we share a moral compass. That view was held by Enlightenment philosophers such as the Earl of Shaftesbury, who believed that there was a "moral sense, a 'sixth sense' that was both shared and educable." The "moral sense" was a subset of what was called then, and what we currently call, "common sense"—a sense that was shared, common, across nations, classes, races, and genders.

This lovely idea seems now somehow antique. So if my moral compass tells me to make as much money as fast as I possibly can, should I follow that lead? What if my moral compass tells me to strap explosives under my coat and blow up the Statue of Liberty? What if my moral compass tells me to bomb innocent women and children in Iraq, in the name of Democracy?

Let me pick on the last of these "what-if's" and expand on it a bit. In our excellent adventure in Iraq, we have killed, or caused to be killed, more persons than anyone alleges were killed by Saddam Hussein. We have killed, or caused to be killed, some 2,300 American citizens. We have reduced Iraq's ability to produce the basics for its citizens: water, electricity, sanitation. There is no reported good outcome of our three-years' pursuit of democracy in Iraq, not even anything approaching the beginnings of a democracy.

Yet more than half of our citizens still support this war. Yes, the approval rating of the President and Vice President have declined. But there has been no significant opposition in Congress to the continued pursuit of the way. Democrats have no stated plans for withdrawing from Iraq. In this case, it appears that our moral sense, our common sense, tells us that we should continue in this desperate and destructive adventure, despite lessons apparently not-learned from Viet Nam, and despite the best intelligence that we now have, which tells us that we are losing support in the country we are trying to save, that each bomb that we drop creates more martyrs and more Iraqis who will have us for generations to come.

So the question comes around finally to this: where should we go to find what we should do? Who will tell us? We need to begin to think in global terms. What is, globally, good? Globally, we need to reduce energy consumption, stabilize the globe's population, and reduce the immense gap between the rich and the poor. These goals are pretty universally agreed upon, yet not, by us, in our recent history, acted upon. As Americans, we've been doing what we 'want' to do: shopping, living large, consuming 60% of the world's energy, and trying to maintain this situation by making war on those who would get in our way. It is time that we begin to do what we "should" do, and not what we "want" to do.

CHAPTER 10

ELECTRONIC PORTFOLIOS AND WRITING ASSESSMENT: A WORK IN PROGRESS

Kathleen Blake Yancey
Florida State University

Perhaps more than in other disciplines, portfolios—collections of texts that are subsets of a larger archive, contextualized through a student reflection (Yancey, 1999)—have informed undergraduate education in writing for over 20 years, especially in first-year composition programs. At least, that was the case in print. For many composition scholars, it was thus reasonable to expect that when composition programs increasingly went electronic, either in a more limited word-processed version or in a more capacious visual and audio multi-modal form, e-portfolios would "naturally" follow. As this chapter suggests, however, compositionists have not migrated to digital portfolios, and consequently, there are few models to highlight. Still, reading across extant models of e-portfolios, we can see two choices emerging: a "affordances-invisible" model portfolio writing, but *without* reference to technology or inclusion of multi-media exhibits; and a second, "inflected" model of electronic portfolio requiring some technological sophistication and demonstration, and vested in a digital model of composing.

Brief and Recent Histories of Portfolios

The history of print portfolios is located in two motives: a search to create an assessment congruent with new understandings and pedagogies of composing (Yancey, 1999), and a search for a new kind of exit assessment, rather than a single-essay-as-exit-test (Belanoff & Elbow, 1986). Directly or indirectly, assessment has been at the center of print portfolios, and as part of that effort, new and different criteria were identified. In place of separate features for a single text like "organization" and "focus," for instance, the criteria associated with portfolios often bridged individual texts. Such features derived from classroom practice—"use of processes" and "ability to write across genres"—and collectively spoke in a dynamic way to a composer's practices in not one, but a *diverse* set of rhetorical situations. In addition, the genesis of the portfolio introduced a new dimension: the voice of the student in a reflective letter or essay. This reflection allowed the student to perform any number of tasks, for example, accounting for processes contributing to the composition of texts; explaining his or her own growth over a period of time; and speaking to key concepts like genre. In terms of consequential validity, many scholars find in the portfolio reflection the best opportunity for learning, an insight that has been sounded in the literature on transfer (see Bransford, 2000, for example).

In some ways, the adoption of electronic portfolios seemed, at least at first, to follow a parallel path in a search for congruence. And the logic seemed impeccable: with students creating digitized texts, asking them to create digital portfolios made more sense than having them print out digital texts and compile them into a paper notebook. Margaret Price, in explaining why Spelman College migrated to e-portfolios, puts a specific face on the logic:

> SpEl.Folio grew out of the college's Comprehensive Writing Program (CWP) in part because the CWP has been using an interdisciplinary writing portfolio for more than a decade. In its original paper form, the portfolio was designed to foster reflection and assessment of students' writing in their first year. Each portfolio contained several essays from a student's first-year classes, as well as a reflective letter. Portfolios were collected in paper form (housed in manila folders) and assessed by a jury of faculty from across the disciplines. In 2004, as we began to investigate the possibilities of a shift to an electronic version of the First-Year Portfolio, we held a series of group interviews with students and faculty to learn their impressions of the paper portfolio and of a possible migration to electronic form. (Price, 2006)

Upon reflection, however, it seems clear that the impetus for such a shift, at Spelman as at other institutions like Clemson University and Northern Illinois University, was located in looking for a *different* congruence, not one between practice, text, and assessment as in the case of print portfolios, but rather one between *medium* of the texts and the portfolio itself.

It's perhaps because of this history that new assessment criteria for e-portfolios haven't emerged very quickly. It may also be that the e-portfolio is still in search of itself as a genre or even genres. Is it a set of word-processed texts? Is it a set of multi-modal texts, complete with streaming video? Does reflection include more than words? What role does the medium or media play in how we read and then value a portfolio? The single word *e-portfolio* suggests an abundance of possibilities. Regardless of the specific cause, however, leaders of composition programs, by their own accounts, have identified new e-portfolio-motivated practices and new curricular elements as a higher priority than assessment issues, and they often pursue these practices and elements through a program of focused research. At Spelman, for example, e-portfolio leaders Margaret Price and Anne Warner have focused on two areas: (a) student and faculty reactions to and perceptions of the portfolio and (b) curricular revision:

> Some of the findings from the first three years of the project have been unsurprising. For example, the most common concerns expressed by students and faculty are what new technical skills they'll have to learn, and how much extra work electronic portfolios will entail. Two findings, however, have been surprising: first, the persistence of the question, "What is an eFolio?" and second, the revision of curricula at Spelman that has grown along with the SpEl.Folio project. (Price, 2006)

In other words, in print portfolios, the shift from an essay test to a portfolio didn't seem to require research, whereas e-portfolios are sufficiently new that research is a key element in making change.

At Clemson, the initial focus was also on curricular revisions evolving from the e-portfolio context. For example, inspired by the creation of graphic communication major Ashley Schuermann, one early curricular addition was that of writing process maps, which themselves took different forms—pre- and post-maps illustrating progress during a course, and a second version located in the tradition of "verisimilude," as in Figure 1 where Josh Reynolds' map shows procrastination and TV-watching as part of his writing process (Yancey, 2009).

Figure 1. Example of a writing process map (Yancey, 2009, p. 4).

Such maps are important in two ways, at least. First, they provide another means of representing writing process, one that can be matched with verbal accounts and textual evidence such as drafts for a fuller, more complex representation of the process. Second, while the first use at Clemson was to show *change* in process as a result of a course, later application was to use a mapping process to *introduce* curriculum. In using maps to introduce writing processes, faculty invite students to create a tool of analysis literally showing both how students *understand* composing as a process and how they *practice* that process. As important, the e-portfolio is now a space for making curricular change, not only to capture past curricular change.

Other research efforts have been connected to the National (now International) Coalition for Electronic Portfolio Research (www.ncepr.org), which has supported the work of several composition programs, including those at the University of Georgia and Northern Illinois University, each of which indicates other kinds of research projects generated by e-portfolios. The University of Georgia has focused on the role of e-portfolios in fostering revision, for example, outlining through documentation of student revising practices an institutionally specific definition of their first-year writer in terms of *novice* and *expert* (Desmet, Griffin, Miller, Balthazor, & Cummings, 2008). This line of research focused on the effect of e-portfolios connections to composition research conducted by Hansen et al. (2006) and Sommers and Saltz (2004). Michael Day (2006), leading the effort at Northern Illinois University, researched the effects of introducing e-portfolios on both students and Teaching Assistants (TAs). He divided his findings into five parts, including Technology, Rhetorical Issues, Pedagogical Issues, Assessment Issues, and Attitude. While the full set of findings, and even the full set of technology findings, is beyond the scope of this chapter, several of them speak to the exploration of e-portfolios as a new pedagogical device still under development:

- Empathy with students' technological struggles intensifies their desire to teach well.
- Composing an e-portfolio simultaneously with students enables the TAs to improve their technological teaching strategies (see Helen Barrett's similar observation in Tomkins, 2001, p. 98).
- Teaching levels of discourse becomes easier in an electronic environment—e.g., students can easily compare chatroom talk with the language of various, professionally designed websites.
- Writing in electronic environments magnifies the need of the writer to experiment and play (see Matthews-DeNatale, 2000).
- A curriculum must carefully balance multiple, complex activities with the quantity of work expected, especially if learning technology is involved.
- Reflection is a problem-solving activity, especially if it engages both TAs and students in dialogue about uses of technology.

Taken together, the observations here suggest that technology influences more than texts: it influences practices, time, attitudes, and sense of community. At the same time, precisely how these influences work, and what differences they make, requires additional research.

One Option for Assessment of Electronic Portfolios: Technology Invisible

Two efforts connected to composition and intended to document e-portfolio assessment are currently underway. The first of these, a large collaborative postsecondary effort orchestrated by the Association of American Colleges and Universities (AAC&U), is one piece of a three-prong effort funded by the Fund for the Improvement of Postsecondary Education (FIPSE). In the context of the Spellings Commission report and as outlined in the AAC&U (2009) document "Rising to the electronic portfolios can provide assessment data called for by the government at the same time they foster enhanced learning. More specifically, it intends to provide a national articulation of outcomes while speaking to local institutional values. The process includes e-portfolios, scoring guides, and multiple stakeholders:

The curriculum-linked performance rubrics, criteria and e-portfolio component will gather, analyze and draft model rubrics/metrics for the other learning outcomes, including quantitative reasoning, information literacy, intercultural knowledge and competence, global knowledge and competence, and "integrative learning." These models will be used with a sample of student e-portfolios from a select group of 10-12 campuses identified through the audit as leaders in using assessment and e-portfolios to test the reliability and validity of the metrics for measuring learning. The e-portfolios will be examined by a national review panel of faculty, parents, and employers utilizing the model rubric criteria to judge the effectiveness of both the e-portfolio and the metrics for demonstrating student achievement. A leader's guide to the rubric metrics and e-portfolios will be developed. (AAC&U, 2009)

As of summer 2008, the first draft of the writing rubric (shown in Figure 2 and included in Appendix A) had been created and was being used to assess e-portfolios

Written Communication Metarubric First Draft

Association of American Colleges and Universities

This rubric is the very first step in a rubric development process that will produce at least three drafts, each responsive to the feedback of those using it to evaluate eportfolios. Please note any concerns or suggestions you have as you use this rubric and report them on the evaluation form

Criterion	1	2	3	4
Engagement with the subject/s of writing Refers to: ___ Visible interest by the writer in the subject of her/his work reflected in writer's expression of ideas (through language and/or form) What it might look like: ___ Extending ideas in directions that are new to the writer; articulating the relevance of the writing to the writer's experiences or of the writer's experiences to the subject of the writing. Language appropriate to the discipline will reflect the writer's connections to the subject/s.	Writing begins to demonstrate writer's interest in the subject, method, and/or theory of the writing through the focus, method, or application of theory in the writing. Connections are articulated explicitly and directly in the writing as the writer practices with these concepts using language, evidence, and conventions appropriate to the discipline.	Writing illustrates visible signs of connection between the writer's interest in the focus, method, and/or theory of written work. Writing begins to demonstrate attempts to use conventions of engagement with existing work (focus, methods, and/or theories) that demonstrate familiarity with language, evidence, and conventions appropriate to the discipline.	Writing illustrates writer's investment in the subject, method, and/or theory that is visible in focus, method, and/or theory of written work. Language, evidence, and conventions appropriate to the discipline are used to weave visible connections between the writer's interests in the subject, method, and/or theory.	Writing illustrates writer's investment in and compelling contributions to the focus, methods, and/or theories used in the work by framing the subject(s) of the writing using language, evidence, and conventions appropriate to the discipline and demonstrating how the subject(s) have led to new understandings of or knowledge about the subject(s) relevant for the writer and/or others interested.
Intentional use of evidence Refers to: ___ Purpose of evidence in writing; conventions of source use (transitions; paraphrase, summary, and/or direct quotation if written evidence; graphic/photographic text if visual; conventions of citation appropriate to writing/discipline) What it might look like: ___ Use of evidence that is in the work for	Use of evidence demonstrates developing familiarity with definitions of "credible" and "reliable" evidence as appropriate to the discipline. Selection and incorporation of	Use of evidence demonstrating growing proficiency with definitions of "credible" and "reliable" evidence as appropriate to the discipline. Selection and incorporations of evidence	Use of evidence demonstrates writer's familiarity with evidence as appropriate to the discipline. Selection and incorporation of evidence demonstrates writer's application	Use of evidence demonstrates writer's familiarity and engagement with evidence appropriate to the discipline. Selections and incorporation of evidence demonstrates writer's understanding of

Figure 2. First draft of AAC&U metarubric for written communication.

187

at several campuses (see http://www.aacu.org/value/). (The draft preceded an interim version shown in Appendix B and the final version provided in Appendix C. The final rubric includes the same features although collapsed into fewer categories, and with another interesting difference: the reference to e-portfolios in the introductory material in the first document has been deleted in the last.)

The draft includes seven dimensions:

- Engagement with the subject/s of writing;
- Intentional use of evidence;
- Understanding of and thoughtful decisions about structure;
- Connections between interests and writing;
- Awareness and use of genre/disciplinary conventions;
- Reflection/metacognitive awareness; and
- Awareness of and sensitivity to audience expectations.

In addition, each dimension is operationalized in two ways. The first is by what the dimension "refers to." Thus, for example, the dimension "Intentional use of evidence"

Refers to:

Purpose of evidence in writing; conventions of source use (transitions; paraphrase, summary, and/or direct quotation if written evidence; graphic/photographic text if visual; conventions of citation appropriate to writing/discipline).

Each dimension then is operationalized across a developmental range, with four levels (along an ordinal scale). And for each dimension, the second operationalizing, "What it might look like" begins at the entry level. To return to our example of evidence, "Intentional use of evidence," at the entry level,

What it might look like:

Use of evidence demonstrates developing familiarity with definitions of "credible" and "reliable" evidence as appropriate to the discipline. Selection and incorporation of evidence demonstrates writer's understanding of conventions of source use (including role of evidence in writing, use of appropriate representations of evidence, and use of conventions).

At the highest level, students include in their e-portfolios

Use of evidence that is in the work for a clear purpose—as support, illustration, a point against which to argue, a theoretical or methodological framework, for example. This purpose is reflected in the moves into and out of writing (e.g., transitions into and out of the writing that indicate to the reader what purpose[s] the evidence serves), in the manner in which the evidence is incorporated (direct quotation, paraphrase, and/or summary), and in the citational systems used to attribute the evidence to its original source.

Five points about this e-portfolio assessment project are worth noting.

- First, this project complements work completed by compositionists in the Council of Writing Program Administrators (WPA) Outcomes Statement (http://www.wpacouncil.org/positions/outcomes.html), a document intended to identify writing expectations for first-year composition students, regardless of institutional type or specific curriculum (and there are a variety of curricula: see Yancey, 2006). Divided into four categories, the outcomes include "Rhetorical Knowledge; Critical Thinking, Reading, and Writing; Composing Process; and Knowledge of Conventions." In addition, a fifth category addressing students' use of digital technologies in composing was submitted to the WPA Executive Board at the July 2008 meeting. The intent of WPA outcomes, of course, is that students will demonstrate them as one step on a larger collegiate developmental trajectory, and the effect of the AAC&U e-portfolio writing outcomes, in turn, is to provide that trajectory and locate it in a consistent theme across dimensions: disciplinarity in writing.

- Second, the scale is progressive, located in tasks that students can accomplish (rather than in a deficit model identifying what they can't do). This guide thus lends itself both to supporting individual student development based on student performance and to fostering a program assessment that can identify both programmatic successes and opportunities for improvement.

- Third, the student is constructed as a maker of knowledge:

> Writing illustrates writer's investment in and compelling contributions to the focus, methods, and/or theories used in the work by framing the subject(s) of the writing using language, evidence, and conventions appropriate to the discipline and demonstrating how the subject(s) have led to new understandings of or knowledge about the subject(s) relevant for the writer and/or others interested.

Writing, too, is thus understood as more than a tool for repeating knowledge to be consumed, but rather as a medium where the knowledge of a discipline is both created and represented. And in making knowledge, students are encouraged to include their own observations and experiences. Thus, evidence in writing can link to "personal interests to inform and enliven the topic" and include "personal anecdote, references to topics, hobbies, interests, and studies that transcend (appropriately) a narrow interpretation of the assignment."

- Fourth, the e-portfolio itself is constructed as its own text with its own rhetorical demands, and the expectation is that students will demonstrate facility with it. More specifically, students are asked to show an "understanding of a variety of structural possibilities for writing and evidence of conscious choices about structures used in specific genres and in the portfolio as a whole that take into account the rhetorical contexts for the writing (OR: the purposes and audiences for the writing) [including] choices about organization of essays, artifacts, and the portfolio, made within appropriate rhetorical contexts."

- Fifth, in an age of machine scoring, this set of outcomes understands writing as a fundamentally rhetorical exercise, that is, an opportunity to engage with human readers. There is, then, a "recognition that writing will be read by humans with particular preparation or lack of it."

This model of e-portfolio assessment thus presents a strong design, with the student as knowledge-maker at the center. At the same time, it's fair to note that nothing in the AAC&U outcomes stipulates technological expertise or understands composing in a specifically digital way. It doesn't preclude such composing, either, of course. But in this sense, this e-portfolio is technology invisible.

A Second Option for Assessment of Electronic Portfolios: Technology Inflected

A second option is illustrated in an e-portfolio model under development in Virginia Beach City Public Schools high schools. As is the case with several models—Northern Illinois and Spelman, for example—this portfolio model is morphing from print to the electronic. Although the print model is district-wide, the electronic portfolio isn't yet, but the work on it thus far can be characterized as a *remix*—of work in print portfolio assessment; of recent insights from literacy studies; and of a composing reconceptualized as a set of digital practices. It's also fair to say that the current criteria, shown in Figure 3, may not all be included when the pilots are concluded, but the preliminary set of criteria speak to an e-portfolio that is technologically inflected, at least in terms of media and affordances.

Perhaps not surprisingly, the first criterion is *Writing*. It includes three dimensions: development, processes, and achievement, which are the same dimensions used in the Pittsburgh Arts Propel portfolio program in the 1990s, and which here refer to in-school writing. A second criterion is self-sponsored digital literacy practices (*Connection to Appropriate Street Literacy*), such as the use of instant messaging, blogging, listmania, and emailing. This criterion thus connects students' current out-of-school practices to an in-school exercise, encouraging students to make connections between them. *Reflection*, another criterion, is likewise both old and new, including the verbal reflection of print, especially in multiple contexts, as well as reflection taking digital form: visual reflection; audio reflections; highlighting and annotation; and process and concept maps.

A second set of criteria are medium-specific. The first of these is *Links*, which here refers to the hyperlinks inside the portfolio, connecting a student's texts one to the next and to sites on the Internet. These links need to work both forward and backward; they need to be both internal and external, with the suggestion that internal links are at a lower level of competence; and they need to evidence meaningfulness, which all links need. The inclusion of meaningfulness thus acknowledges that all links are not by the fact of their existence meaningful. A second item is *Use of the Visual*, focusing on the design of the portal and related to any theme the composer may create. A third, related criterion is *Screen Literacy*, which includes font style and size as well as use of

```
Scoring Guide:
Writing in a Digital Portfolio

Off Track    Emerging    On Track    Outstanding

    Writing
        Development
        Processes
        Achievement

    Connection to appropriate street literacy
        Use of extra-school language
        IM; blogs; listmania; emails

    Theme
        Integral to learning
        and to the portfolio

    Reflection
        Verbal/Visual/
        Audio
        Highlighting/annotation
        Mapping processes/concepts
        Multiple Contexts

    Navigational design
        Ease
        Choice/arrangements
        Clear directions
        Multiple contexts

    Links
        Forward and backward
        Internal
        External
        Meaningfulness

    Use of visual
        Portal design/theme

    Screen literacy
        Use of screen space
        Font style and size
```

Figure 3. Scoring Guide for Virginia Beach City Public Schools e-portfolio model under development.

screen space. And not least, the fourth criterion is *Navigational Design*, which includes ease of navigation, clear directions, multiple arrangements, and multiple contexts.

The final criterion, *Integral Theme*, is the theme of the e-portfolio, one that, like the links, is meaningful. Put in the language of the guide, the theme is integral to the learning and to the e-portfolio. Print portfolios have been thematized as well, but the material effects of print are different than those of digital and historically have not been included in portfolio criteria. Thus, the departure here is two-fold: attention to both the writing and its representation; and attention to its use of the digital in that representation.

Three aspects of this model of e-portfolio assessment merit additional discussion.

- First, as is often the case in classroom assessments, terms—*development in writing*, for example—are often not well operationalized. It is the intent to provide such definition through classroom usage and through a larger review of models not unlike the review being staged by AAC&U. At the same time, in general, the newer terms are better defined than the more familiar terms. For instance, it's not that links per se are valued, for example, but rather bi-directional links; internal links; and external links. The ability of the new, in this case, the digital, to highlight assumptions in

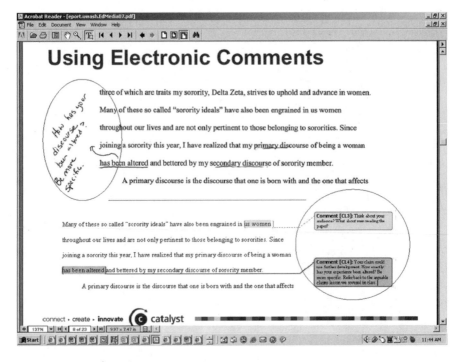

Figure 4. Using electronic comments.

the old may also be at play. Such was the case at another Inter/National Coalition for Electronic Portfolio Research (ICEPR) campus, the University of Washington, where the composition program engaged in a small case study with TAs working with IT staff to create an e-portfolio tool (Lane, 2006). In the process of explaining to the IT staff the assumptions governing the print portfolio in order to build those into the tool, the TAs found that more explanation, precisely the kind of explanation they were providing to the IT staff, would also likely help students, and this explanation thus became part of the e-portfolio environment, as we see in the screenshot in Figure 4, which demonstrates how the e-portfolio tool can be an enviroment rather than a tool for a culminating document.

- Although the Virginia Beach project is not using an e-portfolio tool, but allowing students to use common tools such as Dreamweaver and Mozilla, the curricular leaders have seen some "translation" effect there as well. It was in the translation from print to electronic, in fact, that the criterion *Integral Theme* assumed importance. In the print portfolio, coherence seemed to be provided by the book-like notebook form or chronological arrangement, but without those default organizational schemas and with the affordances of the web, an integral theme provided for more creativity at the same time that it created more of a challenge for students. Put differently, the challenge of e-portfolio possibility brought both theme and arrangement to life.

- Second, the Virginia Beach model deliberately incorporates students' out-of-school composing practices. In so doing, it not only encourages connections between in- and out-of-school literacy practices, but it makes the out-of-school practices visible in a way they ordinarily are not. In addition, through student reflection on those practices, educators can come to understand those from students' perspective. In this sense, students are invited to make quite specific knowledge about composing, drawing on an expertise still in the process of development.

- The inclusion of navigational design in this model also replicates a decision that higher education models have made, but in their case, as a second step. The St. Olaf integrative major e-portfolio model (http://www.stolaf.edu/depts/cis/web_portfolios.htm), for example, began with four criteria: integrative thinking; reflective thinking; thinking in context; and thinking in community. After several years of working with e-portfolios, however, the leaders of the program added three more: focus; visual theme; and navigational design (S. Carlson, personal communication, July 14, 2004). The St. Olaf model, like the Virginia Beach model, is located in common tools and in valuing links, and in such models navigational design is an especially important component. Thus, too, another value of this model of e-portfolio is highlighted: the internal connections students make among their own exhibits as well as the external links that can contextualize those exhibits in multiple ways.

193

This model of e-portfolio assessment constructs composition as a digital enterprise with new opportunities for expression and creativity. The student is constructed as a literacy practitioner both inside and outside school. And at the same time, one might observe that were the level of detail provided in the AAC&U model included in the Virginia Beach model, especially that pertaining to other issues of composing—rhetorical situation, genre, discourse community knowledge—digital technology might not so dominate composing itself in a useful way. As it currently stands, however, this e-portfolio model is technology inflected.

E-portfolios Tomorrow

In 1996, *Computers and Composition* published a special issue on electronic portfolios in composition, and given that it's now 13 years later (and in terms of technological speed, *seems* much more than a mere 13 years), we might expect that electronic portfolios and their assessment would have been fully outlined. At the same time, perhaps it's just as well that the assessment, at least, is not. Instead, what we see in these two models are very different notions of composing located in a very similar construct of composer: someone who makes connections and knowledge in a social environment. A good question, then, is whether at some point we might see a merging of the two models such that we'd have a set of criteria speaking both to evidence and personal investment and to navigational design and visual and verbal themes.

As the future comes upon us, there will be other tasks as well. Astute readers will note that omitted here is any discussion of how these portfolios are read and reviewed and thus how the artifacts themselves are assessed, a non-trivial issue. At this point, there has been scant attention to this topic, but as e-portfolios become more dissimilar one to the next, an exigence requiring attention will be created. Excluded as well are e-portfolio environments where students receive multiple reviews—from peers; from faculty; and from external audiences. And astute readers, especially those with an affinity for the Web, will also notice that the models here are both static collections of digital texts, not the dynamic sort where students can archive many exhibits and then share subsets of them with different audiences, typically in a password-protected environment. The quick explanation for these latter exclusions especially is that these models are not yet operative in the composition world. In part, that's because in composition, the e-portfolio is often understood as a composition itself (Yancey, 2004) whose design is both intentional and stable. The claim underlying such an e-portfolio, in fact, is that the act of creating an interface is itself both a design and an epistemological act, an opportunity for learning. And there is some evidence for such a claim, though not in composition, but from the St. Olaf model and from a psychology e-portfolio project at Clemson University (Stephens, 2008). Still, these exclusions need to be more fully addressed.

It's also the case that these models aren't explicitly informed by Web 2.0, although it's not uncommon for students to link from their school-sponsored e-portfolio to their blog or Facebook account. Interestingly, those social networking spaces are often considered to be more about context than message or text. The relationship between text and context, in fact, provided part of the rationale for using portfolios in the first place: to see a set of final drafts in a larger context, that of earlier drafts and student reflection. Still, as currently implemented, the e-portfolio text-and-context relationship is more internal than external, more enclosed in a school box than continually networked into the world. The Web, however, moves all of us outside the internal to the external; it provides a public audience as well as new materials with which to think and compose. It seems predictable, then, that soon, we will consider how e-portfolios and Web 2.0 might interface.

In the meantime, both of these models of e-portfolios invite students to compose and then to create archives for those texts; to do knowledge-making archival work in those e-portfolios; and to use that opportunity to compose anew.

References

Association of American Colleges and Universities. (2009). *Value-plus: Rising to the challenge*. Retrieved July 31, 2009, from http://www.aacu.org/rising_challenge/index.cfm

Belanoff, P., & Elbow, P. (1986). Using portfolios to increase collaboration and community in a writing program. *Writing Program Administrators, 9*(3), 27–40.

Bransford, J. (2000). Learning and transfer. In Committee on Developments in the Science of Learning, National Research Council (Eds.), *How people learn: Mind, brain, experience, and school* (pp. 51–78). Washington, DC: National Academies Press.

Day, M. (2006). *Final report: National coalition for electronic portfolio research*. Indianapolis, IN: Indiana University-Purdue University-Indianapolis.

Desmet, C., Griffin, J., Miller, D. C., Balthazor, R., & Cummings, R. (2008). Revisioning revision. In D. Cambridge, B. Cambridge, & K. B. Yancey (Eds.), *Electronic portfolios 2.0* (pp. 155–165). Washington, DC: Stylus.

Hansen, K., Reeve, S., Gonzalez, J., Sudweeks, R. R., Hatch, G. L., Esplin, P., et al. (2006). Are advanced placement English and first-year college composition equivalent? A comparison of outcomes in the writing of three groups of sophomore college students. *Research in the Teaching of English, 40*(4), 461–501.

Lane, C. (2006, October). *University of Washington National Coalition for Electronic Portfolio Research: Research findings and evidence*. Retrieved July 31, 2009, from http://www.ncepr.org/finalreports/washingtonfinalreport.pdf

Matthews-DeNatale, G. (2000). Teach us how to play: The role of play in technology education. In S. Harrington, R. Rickly, & M. Day (Eds.), *The online writing classroom* (pp. 63–81). Creskill, NJ: Hampton.

Price, M. (2006). *What is the purpose of an electronic portfolio? Is the answer the key to your successful implementation?* Retrieved July 31, 2009, from http://www.campustechnology.com/articles/41320/

Sommers, N., & Saltz, L. (2004). The novice as expert: Writing the freshman year. *College Composition and Communication, 56*(1), 124–149.

Stephens, B. (2008). e-Portfolios in an undergraduate research experiences program. In D. Cambridge, B. Cambridge, & K. B. Yancey (Eds.), *Electronic portfolios 2.0* (pp. 103–109). Washington, DC: Stylus.

Tomkins, D. (2001). Ambassadors with portfolios: Electronic portfolios and the improvement of teaching. In B. Cambridge, S. Kahn, D. Tomkins, & K. B. Yancey (Eds.), *Electronic portfolios: Emerging practices in student, faculty, and institutional learning* (pp. 91–105). Washington, DC: American Association for Higher Education.

Yancey, K. (1999). Looking back as we look forward: Historicizing writing assessment. *College Composition and Communication, 50*(3), 483–504.

Yancey, K. (2004). Postmodernism, palimpsest, and portfolios: Theoretical issues in the representation of student work. *College Composition and Communication, 55*(4), 738–762.

Yancey, K. (2006). *Delivering college composition: The fifth canon.* Portsmouth, NH: Boynton/Cook.

Yancey, K. (2009). Portfolios, circulation, ecology, and the development of literacy. In D. N. DeVoss, H. A. McKee, & R. Selfe (Eds.), *Technological ecologies and sustainability.* Logan, UT: Utah State University Press.

APPENDIX A: RUBRIC 1

WRITTEN COMMUNICATION METARUBRIC FIRST DRAFT

This rubric is the very first step in a rubric development process that will produce at least three drafts, each responsive to the feedback of those using it to evaluate eportfolios. Please note any concerns or suggestions you have as you use this rubric and report them on the evaluation form.

Criterion	1	2	3	4
Engagement with the subject/s of writing <u>Refers to:</u> Visible interest by the writer in the subject of her/his work reflected in writer's expression of ideas (through language and/or form) <u>What it might look like:</u> extending ideas in directions that are new to the writer; articulating the relevance of the writing to the writer's experiences or of the writer's experiences to the subject of the writing. Language appropriate to the discipline will reflect the writer's connections to the subject/s.	Writing begins to demonstrate writer's interest in the subject, method, and/or theory of the writing through the focus, method, or application of theory in the writing. Connections are articulated explicitly and directly in the writing as the writer practices with these concepts using language, evidence, and conventions appropriate to the discipline.	Writing illustrates visible signs of connection between the writer's interest in the focus, method, and/or theory of written work. Writing begins to demonstrate attempts to use conventions of engagement with existing work (focus, methods, and/or theories) that demonstrate familiarity with language, evidence, and conventions appropriate to the discipline.	Writing illustrates writer's investment in the subject, method, and/or theory that is visible in focus, method, and/or theory of written work. Language, evidence, and conventions appropriate to the discipline are used to weave visible connections between the writer's interests in the subject, method, and/or theory..	Writing illustrates writer's investment in and compelling contributions to the focus, methods, and/or theories used in the work by framing the subject(s) of the writing using language, evidence, and conventions appropriate to the discipline and demonstrating how the subject(s) have led to new understandings of or knowledge about the subject(s) relevant for the writer and/or others interested.
Intentional use of evidence <u>Refers to:</u> Purpose of evidence in writing: conventions of source use (transitions; paraphrase, summary, and/or direct quotation if written evidence; graphic/photographic text if visual; conventions of citation appropriate to writing/discipline) <u>What it might look like:</u> Use of evidence that is in the work for a clear purpose – as support, illustration, a point against which to argue, a theoretical or methodological framework, for example. This purpose is reflected in the moves into and out of writing (e.g., transitions into and out of the writing that indicate to the reader what purpose(s) the evidence serves), in the manner in which the evidence is incorporated (direct quotation, paraphrase, and/or summary), and in the citational systems used to attribute the evidence to its original source.	Use of evidence demonstrates developing familiarity with definitions of "credible" and "reliable" evidence as appropriate to the discipline. Selection and incorporation of evidence demonstrates writer's understanding of conventions of source use (including role of evidence in writing, use of appropriate representations of evidence, and use of conventions).	Use of evidence demonstrates growing proficiency with definitions of "credible" and "reliable" evidence as appropriate to the discipline. Selection and incorporation of evidence demonstrates writer's understanding of conventions source use and ability to directly apply the focus, methods, or theories to their own written work.	Use of evidence demonstrates writer's familiarity and engagement with evidence as appropriate to the discipline. Selection and incorporation of evidence demonstrates writer's application of conventions of source use to serve a variety of purposes within the writing.	Use of evidence demonstrates writer's familiarity and engagement with evidence appropriate to the discipline. Selection and incorporation of evidence demonstrates writer's understanding of conventions of source use and ability to use evidence in order to engage in dialogue with the focus, methods, or theories of the writing – e.g., to extend the writer's ideas and demonstrate disciplinary engagement as appropriate to the discipline.

WRITTEN COMMUNICATION METARUBRIC FIRST DRAFT (Continued)

Criterion	1	2	3	4
Understanding of and thoughtful decisions about structure Refers to: Understanding of a variety of structural possibilities for writing and evidence of conscious choices about structures used in specific genres and in the portfolio as a whole that take into account the rhetorical contexts for the writing (OR: the purposes and audiences for the writing). Choices about organization of essays, artifacts, and the portfolio, made within appropriate rhetorical contexts. What it might look like: Acknowledgement of readers' needs and of the purposes of the writing (and portfolio). Structural conventions of chosen genres (e.g., elements of multigenre essay, reflective writing, argumentative essay) are used appropriately and purposefully as evidenced in elements signaling focus, connection between components of the essay, transitions, etc.	Structural choices to demonstrate that writer is beginning to consider audience expectations and consider relationships between those expectations and choices made in the work.	Structural choices demonstrate that writer is analyzing audience expectations and applying that analysis to choices made within the work. Safe organization interferes with engagement, although transitions indicate writer is thinking about moving from part to part.	Structural choices demonstrate that writer understands audience expectations and discipline-based motivations for these expectations. Understanding is demonstrated throughout choices made in the work. Good transitions indicate movement from section to section; transitions indicate rhetorical shifts as well as content shifts (i.e. help readers process as well as help divide content)...my brain is wearing out!!!	Structural choices demonstrate that writer understands connections between audience expectations and disciplinary contexts and has purposefully employed both structures and contexts in the organization of the work. Organization of the writing indicates writer's sense of the purposes of and intentions for the structure of the writing. Structural elements emerge from the content of and purposes for the work Conventions of structure enhance readers' experiences of the writing.
Connections between interests and writing Refers to: Evidence in the writing that the writer has become involved in the assignment or subject to the degree that he or she can draw upon personal interests to inform and enliven the topic. What it might look like: Development might include personal anecdote, references to topics, hobbies, interests, and studies that transcend (appropriately) a narrow interpretation of the assignment.	Writing suggests that the writer's interest focuses mainly on the fulfillment of the assignment but may be beginning to explore additional connections.	Writing demonstrates the writer's willingness to risk making one or more connections between the topic and personal interests.	Writing connects the writer's interests to the topic in significant ways, demonstrating willingness to delve into personal dimensions and interests to develop fresh ideas.	Writing successfully and appropriately integrates writer's personal interests in various ways, adding breadth and depth by informing the paper with unique insights and experiences.
Awareness and use of genre/disciplinary conventions Refers to: Style, mechanics, grammar, and usage, as well as disciplinary- and task-specific expectations for choices in documentation, point of view, diction, and format What it might look like: Besides "correctness," the writing demonstrates the writer's developing awareness of and ability to balance written communication's allegiances to specific disciplinary expectations, to personal expression, and to the ability to speak to wider audiences.	Writing begins to employ appropriate choices in format, style, and documentation. Writing shows an awareness of standards for grammar, mechanics, and usage.	Writing demonstrates appropriate choices in format and style. Documentation is consistently incorporated. Grammar, mechanics, and usage are generally competent.	Writing demonstrates, on the part of the writer, consistent awareness of and attention to the expectations and conventions inherent in the specific writing tasks, Style and format are appropriate to the assignment, and grammar and usage are well controlled. Documentation is competent.	Writing demonstrates full and accurate employment of all relevant genre/disciplinary conventions, including documentation, grammar, usage, and mechanics. Format is appropriate to assignment. Style is fresh and sophisticated but fully appropriate to both the discipline and the assignment involved.

Reflection/metacognitive awareness Refers to: Awareness on the part of the writer of conscious actions in composing. Might look like: Confident voice demonstrated by purposeful language and a sense of ownership of the material. Exhibits control of rhetorical choices.	Writing appears to be generic in response to the assignment.	Writer may demonstrate a sense of writerly identity through voice.	Writer demonstrates a sense of writerly identity that promotes reader engagement through insight and self-awareness.	Writer overtly claims a reflective or metacognitive stance, using language that expresses insight, queries own thinking, and engages the reader in dialogue or dialectic toward new knowledge.
Awareness of and sensitivity to audience expectations Refers to: Recognition that writing will be read by humans with particular preparation or lack of it. Might look like: Anticipation of reader needs, including providing definitions of technical language, relevant background (including conceptual material), imagining reasonable questions, and anticipation of counter arguments.	Writer gives some cues to readers that invite them to be part of the audience.	Writer conceives of audience according to the categorical specifics of the assignment and tries to meet reader needs.	Writer demonstrates a sense of reader needs and expectations and attempts to engage readers on those terms.	Writer uses rhetorical devices to anticipate reader needs, offer assurance, and clearly engage or challenge reader expectations.

APPENDIX B: RUBRIC 2

SPRING 2009 DRAFT FOR PUBLIC RELEASE OF WRITTEN COMMUNICATION VALUE RUBRIC

Association of American Colleges and Universities

This rubric is a step in a rubric development process that will produce a final draft by September 2009. All drafts are revised in response to the feedback received from VALUE Leadership and Partner campuses. The final feedback deadline for the VALUE Initiative is July 3, 2009. For more information or to give feedback, please email Wende Morgaine, VALUE Initiative Manager, at wendemm@gmail.com. Thank you!

The VALUE rubrics emerge from a process that examined many campus rubrics for each outcome and from the knowledge of faculty experts. They articulate fundamental criteria for each outcome demonstrated at progressively more sophisticated levels. The rubrics are intended primarily for institutional level use in evaluating and discussing student learning. The core expectations articulated in the VALUE rubrics can be translated into the language of individual campuses, disciplines or even courses. At the same time, the VALUE rubrics position learning at all undergraduate levels within a basic framework that is shared nationally.

This writing rubric is designed for use in a wide variety of educational institutions. Perhaps the most clear finding to emerge from decades of research on writing assessment is that the best writing assessments are locally determined and sensitive to local context and mission. Users of this rubric should, in the end, consider making adaptations and additions that clearly link the language of the rubric to individual campus contexts.

This rubric focuses assessment on how specific written products, compiled in a portfolio or on their own, respond to specific contexts. The central question guiding the rubric is "How well does writing respond to the needs of audience(s) for the work?" In focusing on this question the rubric does not attend to other aspects of writing that are equally important: issues of writing process, writing strategies, writers' fluency with different modes of textual production or publication, or writer's growing engagement with writing and disciplinarity through the process of writing. Instead, this rubric encourages faculty to evaluate how well writing responds to audience expectations.

In order to use this rubric, assessors must have information about the assignments or purposes for writing guiding writers' work. We also recommend that portfolios include a reflective component that addresses such questions as: What decisions did the writer make about audience, purpose, and genre as s/he compiled the work in the portfolio? How are those choices evident in the writing – in the content, organization and structure, reasoning, evidence, mechanical and surface conventions, and citational systems used in the writing? These reflective components will enable readers to have a clear sense of how writers understand the assignments that have shaped the portfolio's contents. Readers may take these into consideration as they assess the materials in the portfolio, as well.

This rubric includes four categories for assessing student work: Beginning, Developing, Competent, and Accomplished. Institutions might choose to associate these with a four-year course of educational development; alternatively, they may choose to benchmark these stages of writing at other points in a students' educational career. Writing is an iterative, recursive process where students return to and build upon familiar and new knowledge; these categories are intended to represent a developmental progression through writing. Faculty interested in the research on writing assessment that has guided our work here can consult:

- The National Council of Teachers of English/Council of Writing Program Administrators' White Paper on Writing Assessment (2008; http://www.wpacouncil.org/whitepaper)
- The Conference on College Composition and Communication's Writing Assessment: A Position Statement (2008; http://www.ncte.org/cccc/resources/positions/123784.htm)

Definition

Written communication is the development and expression of ideas in writing. Written communication involves learning to work in many genres and styles. It can involve working with many different writing technologies, and mixing texts, data, and images. Written communication abilities develop through iterative experiences across the curriculum.

Glossary

The definitions that follow were developed to clarify terms and concepts used in the rubric.

- Genre conventions: Formal and informal rules for particular kinds of texts and/or media that guide formatting, organization, and stylistic choices, e.g. lab reports, academic papers, poetry, webpages, or personal essays.
- Disciplinary conventions: Formal and informal rules that constitute what is seen generally as appropriate within different academic fields, e.g. introductory strategies, use of passive voice or first person point of view, expectations for thesis or hypothesis, expectations for kinds of evidence and support that are appropriate to the task at hand.
- Use of sources: Use of primary and secondary sources to provide evidence and support arguments, and to document critical perspectives on the topic. Writers will incorporate sources according to disciplinary and genre conventions, according to the writer's purpose for the text. Through increasingly sophisticated use of sources, writers develop an ability to differentiate between their own ideas and the ideas of others, credit and build upon work already accomplished in the field or issue they are addressing, and provide meaningful examples to readers.
- Sources: Refers to texts (written, oral, behavioral, visual, or other) that writers draw on as they work for a variety of purposes – to extend, argue with, develop, define, or shape their ideas, for example. Evidence is source material that is used to extend, in purposeful ways, writers' ideas in a text.
- Context of and purpose for writing: The context of writing is the situation surrounding a text: who is reading it? who is writing it? Under what circumstances will the text be shared or circulated? what social or political factors might affect how the text is composed or interpreted? The purpose for writing is the writer's intended effect on an audience. Writers might want to persuade or inform; they might want to report or summarize information; they might want to work through complexity or confusion; they might write for themselves or for an assignment or to remember.
- Content Development: Refers to the ways in which the text explores and represents its topic in relation to its audience and purpose.
- Idiomatic Prose: Writing whose usage is in line with general expectations of the audience.

Evaluators are encouraged to assign a zero to any performance that doesn't meet level one performance.

	4	3	2	1
Context of and purpose for writing	Demonstrates a thorough understanding of context, audience, and purpose that is responsive to the assigned task(s) and focuses all elements of the work	Demonstrates adequate consideration of context, audience, and purpose and a clear focus on the assigned task(s)	Demonstrates some attention to context, audience, purpose, and to the assigned task(s)	Demonstrates minimal attention to context, audience, purpose, and to the assigned tasks(s)
Content Development	Content explores complex ideas that are used to shape compelling work	Content demonstrates consideration of new ideas that are used to shape solid work	Content demonstrates attention to simple ideas that are evident in the work	Content demonstrates consideration of simple ideas that are evident in some elements of the work
Genre and disciplinary conventions	Uses sophisticated genre and disciplinary conventions to organize and present ideas	Uses appropriate genre and disciplinary conventions to organize and present ideas	Uses obvious genre and disciplinary conventions to organize and present ideas.	Attempts to use genre and disciplinary conventions to organize and present ideas
Sources and evidence	Skillfully uses highly relevant sources and evidence to support well developed ideas.	Competently uses relevant sources and evidence to support well developed ideas.	Uses some sources and evidence to support ideas.	Attempts to use sources and evidence to support ideas.
Control of syntax and mechanics	Demonstrates graceful, idiomatic prose that conveys meaning to readers with clarity and fluency and is almost error-free.	Demonstrates idiomatic prose that conveys meaning to readers with some measure of clarity and fluency with few errors.	Demonstrates idiomatic prose that generally conveys meaning to readers with some clarity, although writing may include some errors.	Demonstrates non-idiomatic sentence constructions that sometimes impede meaning, but prose is usually readable, despite numerous errors.

Created by a team of faculty from higher education institutions across the United States.

APPENDIX C: RUBRIC 3

WRITTEN COMMUNICATION VALUE RUBRIC

for more information, please contact value@aacu.org

Association
of American
Colleges and
Universities

The VALUE rubrics were developed by teams of faculty experts representing colleges and universities across the United States through a process that examined many existing campus rubrics and related documents for each learning outcome and incorporated additional feedback from faculty. The rubrics are intended to articulate fundamental criteria for each learning outcome, with performance descriptors demonstrating progressively more sophisticated levels of attainment. The rubrics are intended for institutional-level use in evaluating and discussing student learning, not for grading. The core expectations articulated in all 15 of the VALUE rubrics can and should be translated into the language of individual campuses, disciplines, and even courses. The utility of the VALUE rubrics is to position learning at all undergraduate levels within a basic framework of expectations such that evidence of learning can by shared nationally through a common dialog and understanding of student success.

Definition

Written communication is the development and expression of ideas in writing. Written communication involves learning to work in many genres and styles. It can involve working with many different writing technologies, and mixing texts, data, and images. Written communication abilities develop through iterative experiences across the curriculum.

Framing Language

This writing rubric is designed for use in a wide variety of educational institutions. The most clear finding to emerge from decades of research on writing assessment is that the best writing assessments are locally determined and sensitive to local context and mission. Users of this rubric should, in the end, consider making adaptations and additions that clearly link the language of the rubric to individual campus contexts.

This rubric focuses assessment on how specific written work samples or collectios of work respond to specific contexts. The central question guiding the rubric is "How well does writing respond to the needs of audience(s) for the work?" In focusing on this question the rubric does not attend to other aspects of writing that are equally important: issues of writing process, writing strategies, writers' fluency with different modes of textual production or publication, or writer's growing engagement with writing and disciplinarily through the process of writing.

Evaluators using this rubric must have information about the assignments or purposes for writing guiding writers' work. Also recommended is including reflective work samples of collections of work that address such questions as: What decisions did the writer make about audience, purpose, and genre as s/he compiled the work in the portfolio? How are those choices evident in the writing – in the content, organization and structure, reasoning, evidence, mechanical and surface conventions, and citational systems used in the writing? This will enable evaluators to have a clear sense of how writers understand the assignments and take it into consideration as they evaluate.

The first section of this rubric addresses the context and purpose for writing. A work sample or collections of work can convey the context and purpose for the writing tasks it showcases by including the writing assignments associated with work samples. But writers may also convey the context and purpose for their writing within the texts. It is important for faculty and institutions to include directions for students about how they should represent their writing contexts and purposes.

Faculty interested in the research on writing assessment that has guided our work here can consult the National Council of Teachers of English/Council of Writing Program Administrators' White Paper on Writing Assessment (2008; http://www.wpacouncil.org/whitepaper) and the Conference on College Composition and Communication's Writing Assessment: A Position Statement (2008; http://www.ncte.org/cccc/resources/positions/123784.htm).

Glossary

The definitions that follow were developed to clarify terms and concepts used in this rubric only.

- Content Development: The ways in which the text explores and represents its topic in relation to its audience and purpose.
- Context of and purpose for writing: The context of writing is the situation surrounding a text: who is reading it? who is writing it? Under what circumstances will the text be shared or circulated? What social or political factors might affect how the text is composed or interpreted? The purpose for writing is the writer's intended effect on an audience. Writers might want to persuade or inform; they might want to report or summarize information; they might work through complexity or confusion; they might want to argue with other writers, or connect with other writers; they might want to convey urgency or amuse; they might write for themselves or for an assignment or to remember.
- Disciplinary conventions: Formal and informal rules that constitute what is seen generally as appropriate within different academic fields, e.g. introductory strategies, use of passive voice or first person point of view, expectations for thesis or hypothesis, expectations for kinds of evidence and support that are appropriate to the task at hand, use of primary and secondary sources to provide evidence and support arguments and to document critical perspectives on the topic. Writers will incorporate sources according to disciplinary and genre conventions, according to the writer's purpose for the text. Through increasingly sophisticated use of sources, writers develop an ability to differentiate between their own ideas and the ideas of others, credit and build upon work already accomplished in the field or issue they are addressing, and provide meaningful examples to readers.

- Evidence: Source material that is used to extend, in purposeful ways, writers' ideas in a text.
- Genre conventions: Formal and informal rules for particular kinds of texts and/or media that guide formatting, organization, and stylistic choices, e.g. lab reports, academic papers, poetry, webpages, or personal essays.
- Sources: Texts (written, oral, behavioral, visual, or other) that writers draw on as they work for a variety of purposes – to extend, argue with, develop, define, or shape their ideas, for example.

Definition

Written communication is the development and expression of ideas in writing. Written communication involves learning to work in many genres and styles. It can involve working with many different writing technologies, and mixing texts, data, and images. Written communication abilities develop through iterative experiences across the curriculum.

Evaluators are encouraged to assign a zero to any work sample or collection of work that does not meet benchmark (cell one) level performance.

	Capstone 4	Milestones 3	Milestones 2	Benchmark 1
Context of and purpose for writing Includes considerations of audience, purpose, and the circumstances surrounding the writing task(s).	Demonstrates a thorough understanding of context, audience, and purpose that is responsive to the assigned task(s) and focuses all elements of the work.	Demonstrates adequate consideration of context, audience, and purpose and a clear focus on the assigned task(s) (e.g., the task aligns with audience, purpose, and context).	Demonstrates awareness of context, audience, purpose, and to the assigned task(s) (e.g., begins to show awareness of audience's perceptions and assumptions).	Demonstrates minimal attention to context, audience, purpose, and to the assigned task(s) (e.g., expectation of instructor or self as audience).
Content Development	Uses appropriate, relevant, and compelling content to illustrate mastery of the subject, conveying the writer's understanding, and shaping the whole work.	Uses appropriate, relevant, and compelling content to explore ideas within the context of the discipline and shape the whole work	Uses appropriate and relevant content to develop and explore ideas through most of the work.	Uses appropriate and relevant content to develop simple ideas in some parts of the work.
Genre and disciplinary conventions Formal and informal rules inherent in the expectations for writing in particular forms and/or academic fields (please see glossary).	Demonstrates detailed attention to and successful execution of a wide range of conventions particular to a specific discipline and/or writing task (s) including organization, content, presentation, formatting, and stylistic choices	Demonstrates consistent use of important conventions particular to a specific discipline and/or writing task(s), including organization, content, presentation, and stylistic choices	Follows expectations appropriate to a specific discipline and/or writing task(s) for basic organization, content, and presentation	Attempts to use a consistent system for basic organization and presentation
Sources and evidence	Demonstrates skillful use of high quality, credible, relevant sources to develop ideas that are appropriate for the discipline and genre of the writing	Demonstrates consistent use of credible, relevant sources to support ideas that are situated within the discipline and genre of the writing.	Demonstrates an attempt to use credible and/or relevant sources to support ideas that are appropriate for the discipline and genre of the writing.	Demonstrates an attempt to use sources to support ideas in the writing.
Control of syntax and mechanics	Uses graceful language that skillfully communicates meaning to readers with clarity and fluency, and is virtually error-free.	Uses straightforward language that generally conveys meaning to readers. The language in the portfolio has few errors.	Uses language that generally conveys meaning to readers with clarity, although writing may include some errors.	Uses language that sometimes impedes meaning because of errors in usage

CHAPTER 11

WAC AND WRITING PROGRAM ASSESSMENT TAKE ANOTHER STEP: A RESPONSE TO *ASSESSMENT OF WRITING*

Brian Huot and Emily Dillon
Kent State University

Introduction

Writing assessment has evolved over the past several years. Brian often tells the story of having been in a tenure-track position as the Director of a Writing Across the Curriculum (WAC) Program for a couple of years when his senior colleague confided in him that she and the rest of her colleagues were concerned about hiring him because he had all this assessment stuff on his vita, as if assessment scholarship was suspect in and of itself. In job announcements, nowadays it is common to see assessment as one of the preferred areas of experience and education. For good or bad, though we think mostly good, assessment occupies a much different position than it did a couple of decades ago. In the first decade of the twentieth century, we have seen the publication of more volumes on writing assessment than in the previous two to three decades before. Of course, the good part is that more and more people in higher education are better at assessing and supporting their programs than ever before. The bad part is that assessment continues to be used as a stick by administrators and politicians to push through what are often not very well thought out educational initiatives. To quote Brian quoting the Wicked Witch of the West from the Wizard of Oz, "assessment must be done delicately" (Huot, 2002, p. 190).

Being asked to respond to this volume on program assessment sponsored and published by the Association for Institutional Research is both a pleasing and daunting task and responsibility. We are pleased because this volume contains some very interesting and important scholarship, both theoretical and empirical, about Writing Across the Curriculum and Writing Program Assessment, and to be invited to respond is honorable work. It is daunting work, as well, because we want to make sure we read and respond in ways that advance the aims of the volume while still acknowledging important principles from the scholarship on WAC, Writing Program Assessment and educational measurement in general. Our response is also limited and or enhanced by our own very different but intersecting positions as scholars. One of us (Brian) has been working in assessment for over twenty years, and the other (Emily) is on the verge of conducting dissertation research into the ways teachers "read" students' multimodal projects. While it would be impossible to situate a specific location or point at which the field now resides, we can look back a decade or so ago to the first volume that focused exclusively on assessing writing across the curriculum. Using Yancey and Huot's *Assessing Writing Across the Curriculum: Diverse Approaches and Practices* (1997) as a springboard helps us to not only gauge the kind of contribution this volume makes but to gauge also the progress we are making as a field.

Situating This Volume

In the preface to *Assessing Writing Across the Curriculum: Diverse Approaches and Practices,* "The WAC Archives Revisited," Toby Fulwiler and Art Young (1997) recount their early efforts in establishing a WAC Program at Michigan Tech, truly one of the early institutional innovators in WAC. One of the interesting things about Fulwiler and Young's narrative is their recollection that almost from the very beginning assessment was seen as an important part of establishing and sustaining a WAC program: "From the start we felt assessment pressure from without and from within" (p. 4). They felt the need for assessment had a positive impact on their program and its development in that it provided the impetus for hiring new faculty who had been educated in composition and rhetoric and for consulting national experts on assessment to help Fulwiler and Young design a multiple-measures assessment plan to gauge the impact of their WAC Program on the teaching and learning at their institution. Eventually, their efforts to measure, "Was what we were doing working?" failed to provide any conclusive evidence such as whether using journals instead of quizzes in a math class improved students' grades on the final exams or whether teachers' positive attitudes toward WAC workshops and teaching innovations translated into better writing for their students. Fulwiler and Young affirm at the end of their preface that "Both our experiences and our instincts tell us that the stories of individual students and teachers, as illustrated in this volume, will yield the most information and the best results" (p. 6). Ironically, this preface signals a disjuncture between the kinds of WAC assessment Fulwiler and Young came to trust and use and the kinds of assessment available in most of the chapters of *Assessing Writing Across the Curriculum: Diverse Approaches and Practices,* the volume for which they wrote the preface. While our time and purpose does not allow for even a cursory review of each chapter, we would not characterize *Assessing Writing Across the Curriculum: Diverse Approaches and Practices* as illustrating the important stories of students and teachers, though we would not claim that the volume excludes them either.

To illustrate the disjuncture between Fulwiler and Young's preface and the volume itself we look at perhaps the most widely cited of all the chapters in *Assessing Writing Across the Curriculum: Diverse Approaches and Practices,* Richard Haswell and Susan McLeod's "WAC Assessment and Internal Audiences: A Dialogue" (1997). It is the only chapter from the volume to be included in a recent anthology on writing assessment, *Assessing Writing: A Critical Sourcebook* (Huot & O'Neill, 2009) and one of only two chapters in the 24-chapter volume to be on WAC Assessment. Haswell and McLeod script a dialogue between an administrator and WAC assessor in which they map out a scheme for providing multiple reports of assessment data for various audiences. They provide a scenario in which four different reports of WAC assessment data are presented to four different audiences from across campus, including in-progress reports to middle-level administrators, a five-minute presentation

208

during the Board of Regents annual meetings, and a final, annual public report. Haswell and McLeod illustrate the rhetorical nature of assessment as each of these different audiences and communicative events require the assessor to report different kinds of information in different ways. Such a complex and nuanced approach does not completely discount the importance Fulwiler and Young give to narrative, but it does situate the use of narrative as only one of many ways we might want to represent our programs and our assessment of our programs. Certainly, *Assessing Writing Across the Curriculum: Diverse Approaches and Practices* signals a break from a strong reliance on narrative and anecdote available from earlier assessment scholarship on WAC such as Fulwiler's influential "How Well Does Writing Across the Curriculum Work" published in *College English* in 1984.

In the introduction that follows Fulwiler and Young's preface, Kathleen Yancey and Brian Huot (1997) frame the volume with the claim "that assessment can enhance WAC programs" (p. 7). Of course, they are careful to define assessment in specific ways that can aid rather than harm an educational program like WAC. Their definition hinges on five grounding assumptions. One, WAC assessment focuses on the whole program. Two, WAC assessment is essentially research into a particular program and is guided (like all research) by specific research questions. Three, WAC assessment assumes the contextual and social nature of literate communication and cannot be focused on discrete skills or atomized pieces of writing or communicating. Four, WAC assessment uses multiple measures and diverse practices to look at a variety of features within a given program. Five, WAC assessment focuses on learning and teaching and must be regular, systematic and coherent. Since *Assessing Writing Across the Curriculum: Diverse Practices and Approaches* contained chapters that reported empirical data, as well as some stories about successful and failed assessment initiatives, it moved WAC assessment into a new era beyond just valuing stories. As WAC and other writing programs become more prominent and important to a range of stakeholders, including teachers, students, and school administrators, it is imperative that we look for new ways to provide evidence that our programs do what we say they do.

Just as *Assessing Writing Across the Curriculum: Diverse Approaches and Practices* moved WAC assessment out of the realm of narrative and into more systematic and researched-based approaches to WAC Assessment, *Assessment of Writing* also signals some new directions and innovations for WAC and Writing Program assessment. One of the major differences this volume brings is that one of the editors and several of the contributors are teachers and researchers in the disciplines themselves. This is not a volume by English teachers for English teachers. Although WAC has always had its share of writing programs within disciplinary programs and its share of scholarship in pedagogical, discipline-based journals, this volume is different. As Brian noted a few years back, writing assessment is an activity that exists within two bifurcated disciplines, creating a literature that is often only half-known to those who work in writing assessment (Huot, 2002). As the editors, Marie Paretti and Katrina Powell, note in their introduction, good WAC and Program Assessment depend upon collaboration. This volume is a collaboration between people who work in rhetoric, composition and writing program administration and people who work in fields that teach discipline-based writing and use writing to teach disciplinary skills and content. Collaboration is also essential for the assessment of Writing Programs and WAC Programs because it is important to include those whose knowledge and experience give the assessment a local expertise while at the same time providing a connection to important principles in institutional research and educational measurement.

In comparing these volumes and looking more broadly at scholarship that addresses WAC and Program assessment over time, we can identify different approaches and the introduction of new ways to assess writing programs overall. But while we have noted some changes over the last two decades, it is also important to note some similarities. As much as things change, they often manage to stay the same as well. For example, Fulwiler and Young (1997) recount that even at the beginning of their work in WAC, they were faced with pressure from within and without to design and implement some kind of assessment to build a case for the efficacy of their WAC Program. *Assessment of Writing*, like all scholarship, is a product of a particular time and context in which faculty and administrators who teach and work in WAC and Writing Programs face a plethora of issues and challenges. This volume is a response to some of those issues and challenges. The most obvious dilemma is that Writing Program assessment mandates often originate with outside forces, such as political or administrative bodies. Writing Program and WAC administrators and teachers can typically feel powerless and resentful toward these outside-mandated assessments. However, as this volume illustrates, it is imperative that administrators and teachers learn to be creative with assessment and make it their own by actively involving Writing Program staff and other stakeholders.

Assessment mandated by an outside source often includes many potential pitfalls. For example, who will design the assessment and make crucial decisions about what student performances will be valued, how they will be assessed, who will do the assessing and what overall interpretations, inferences, and decisions will be made based upon the assessment? Several chapters in this volume, most notably Chapters 2, 3, and 5 provide readers with varying ways to approach these tasks. The value of these chapters goes beyond simple instruction and/or description, since each of the chapters provides a specific context within which an outside mandate can be used to design and implement an assessment program that furthers the overall goals of the WAC and/or Writing Program. As assessment scholars from Huot (2002) to White (1984, 1995) have argued, assessment is an important and necessary component of program administration. A WAC or Writing Program that has been collecting and analyzing assessment data in an ongoing, systematic fashion will be able to respond to an outside mandate for assessment in a very different way than those who have been doing little or no assessment work.

In addition to the need for WAC and Writing Programs to become "responsible" so that they won't have to be "accountable" (Huot & Williamson, 1997) to outside mandates, programs also must face the challenge of a myriad and diverse group of stakeholders who feel some connection or entitlement to assessment decisions and activities. Program leaders often want to include all stakeholders (administrators, teachers, students, etc.) in the assessment design but are at a loss as to how to do so effectively. The authors of many chapters in this volume are inclusive of assessment participants and may give readers some ideas for effectively integrating the voices of various stakeholders. We note, however, that a potential pitfall with the concept of the stakeholder is that all interested parties in a program assessment should not be given equal authority if assessment is to be used to improve the program overall. As Huot (2002) has argued, stakeholders like teachers and students should have a privileged voice in assessment decisions, since they are often most affected by assessment results and the decisions made on behalf of those results.

Another major challenge, and the last we will address in this section before moving on to the chapters themselves, is the fact that most Writing Program Administrators are not required to have much experience with or knowledge of writing assessment. They may therefore find themselves in a unique and uncomfortable position: being told by an outsider to deliver an assessment but having virtually no idea about how to proceed. This volume and those like it provide the program leader looking to improve her understanding of assessment methods and choices with a valuable resource. We are also hopeful that graduate preparation for writing program leaders will include more attention to assessment issues, and there is some indication that graduate education is moving in that direction, with some programs regularly providing coursework and supervision in program administration and assessment.

To summarize our discussion about the challenges and pitfalls in Writing Program and WAC assessment, what we are really calling for when we address the need for programs to be ready for outside mandates is a change in WAC and Writing Program culture that includes assessment. Issues like the need for ongoing assessment to meet the challenges of outside mandates, the recognition that all stakeholders are not equal and the need for better preparation for writing program leaders is really a call for creating a more visible, vibrant and effective assessment culture for all writing programs. In an upcoming *College Composition and Communication* article, Peggy O'Neill, Cindy Moore, and Brian Huot (in press) argue that departments, programs, administrators, and faculty wishing to embrace and use writing assessment to enhance teaching and learning must approach it from a broad-based position that includes an understanding of historical, theoretical, and contextual perspectives. According to O'Neill, Moore, and Huot, only by creating a culture of assessment can a writing program use assessment in important and productive ways.

The Chapters

The next part of our response refers directly to specific chapters, documenting the individual contributions the chapters make to Writing Program and WAC assessment. Following our comments above on Paretti and Powell's introductory chapter, we turn to Chapter 2. In "Common Denominators and the Ongoing Culture of Assessment," Janangelo and Adler-Kassner argue that assessment participants must clearly articulate their goals and beliefs and keep them visible during the course of an assessment. In their text, the authors highlight similarities between several position statements on writing assessment authored by professional organizations in the field including the Writing Program Administrators (WPA), Conference on College Composition and Communication (CCCC), and the National Council of Teachers of English (NCTE). According to the authors, the assessment principles in these documents "reflect the combined wisdom" of professionals in the field and are therefore integral to the design of an effective assessment. Principally, these statements dictate that productive assessments are sensitive to local contexts and to the needs of all stakeholders, and at the same time contribute information to improve teaching and learning. In other words, assessment as it is conceptualized here is not an end in and of itself; instead, assessment is used to provide local, relevant information about the goals and practices of a Writing Program that must be acted upon by those involved.

Like the authors of Chapter 2, O'Neill and Moore also aspire to make writing teachers' beliefs about writing and assessment explicit in Chapter 3. "What College Writing Teachers Value and Why It Matters" argues that it is vital for Writing Studies scholars to articulate their beliefs about writing, writers, writing assessment, and assessment terminology—especially to outsiders who typically have a prominent role in writing assessments but have little content-area knowledge of the field. In a similar vein, Huot has pointed out the long-standing disconnect between writing assessment as it is theorized in Writing Studies and in Educational Measurement, writing that the two disciplines typically "fail to recognize the debts we have to each other or the ways in which work in one area is stunted by its isolation from the other" (2002, p. 45). The authors of Chapters 2 and 3 attempt to bridge this disciplinary segregation by offering Writing Studies' opinions and understandings of writing assessment to those outside the field. This is an important first step but, as Huot contends, Writing Studies scholars should also strive to educate themselves about how those outside the field understand writing assessment to generate "a serious consideration of rival theories, methods, explanations, and actions, so that it includes a consideration of the values, ideas and explanations possible from both camps" (2002, p. 53). One way to think about the need to understand and respect assessment values from other fields is to think, as the editors encourage us in the introduction, of assessment as collaboration, in this case an intellectual, cross-disciplinary collaboration of ideas, concepts, and values.

Thinking carefully about what writing assessment means often leads those involved to ask what they might learn from an assessment, particularly when it has been mandated by outside forces. Zawacki and Gentemann respond to the challenge of involving participants in outside-mandated assessments in Chapter 4, "Merging a Culture of Writing with a Culture of Assessment: Embedded, Discipline-based Writing Assessment." The authors redesigned the WAC program assessment at their institution to involve the faculty who taught the courses being assessed. They discuss how the assessment was conducted, including how faculty collaboratively designed a scoring rubric and holistically scored single samples of student work. By actively involving assessment participants and encouraging dialogue among them, Zawacki and Gentemann discovered that participating teachers were inspired to be more explicit about their expectations for student work, both with their colleagues and with their students. This chapter puts into motion some of the assessment tenets outlined in Chapters 2 and 3, and illustrates how assessment can function as research. Instead of acting as passive bystanders, teachers were involved in the design and execution of the assessment and became "autonomous agents" instead of just "technicians who administer the technological apparatus" (Huot, 2002, p. 151). This move to involve faculty not only ascribes agency to instructors, it also serves to subvert existing power structures in outside-mandated assessments. Teachers who learn how to construct and carry out writing assessment are more likely to take ownership of writing assessment, rather than to feel like writing assessment is something done to them by outsiders.

Like the authors of Chapters 2 and 3, Schneider, Leydens, Olds, and Miller communicate their writing assessment beliefs in Chapter 5, "Guiding Principles in Engineering Writing Assessment: Context, Collaboration, and Ownership." Based upon their own experience as participants in various writing assessments, the writers offer five "guiding principles" for a variety of participants, especially those outside of the field of Writing Studies. The five principles focus on developing assessments from local, contextual issues and emphasize that assessment methods should be derived from programmatic values about writing. As in Chapter 2, the authors of this chapter stress assessment as research; writing assessments develop out of problems that arise within a specific program and are designed to answer participants' questions and to reflect what the program believes good writing is. Seen in this light, assessment is not a product or an "end," but is research and reflection that require participants to take action to improve their programs. This notion of assessment as important, programmatic research situates assessment as a responsibility rather than a burden or a need to be accountable to others. Clearly, Schneider et al. see assessment as an integral component of responsible and respected administrative practice and encourage others to follow their example.

In Chapter 6, "The Scholarship of Assessment: Increasing Agency and Collaboration Through the Scholarship of Teaching and Learning," Phillips and Ahrenhoerster relate how they, like the authors of Chapter 4, handled an outside-mandated assessment. Following the tenets of effective assessment outlined by authors of previous chapters, the researchers demonstrate how participants can be creative with assessment mandates and turn them into useful research about teaching to benefit their program. Required by the Higher Learning Commission (HLC) to conduct a programmatic review, Phillips and Ahrenhoerster organized the assessment around a question of value to them: *How do students perceive peer review?* They distributed a survey to students about peer review and took the results back to teachers and to the outsiders who mandated the assessment in the first place. Phillips and Ahrenhoerster illustrate how an outside mandate can be an opportunity for a program to ask and answer interesting and important questions. Because of the way they responded to an outside call for assessment, they provide an example for readers about how they might go about using an outside-mandated assessment to improve teaching in their program.

As this demonstrates, Writing Program faculty can use outside mandates as an opportunity to research components in their programs that require their attention or pique their interest, a point we wish to highlight here. This use of assessment to do important programmatic work is part of the argument we have been advancing for assessment to become our responsibility rather than something for which we are accountable. This idea of assessment as a responsibility is an important component of a "proactive" rather than "reactive" stance toward assessment. WAC and Writing Program Administrators can preempt assessment mandates from outsiders by actively assessing their own programs without being told to do so. A move like this may give WPAs and instructors more control over their own program and what is going on in it—even when outside mandates do occur: "If we were to become more interested in and responsible for assessment, we would ultimately have better control over the fate of our courses, teachers and programs" (Huot, 2002, p. 173).

In Chapter 7, "Assessing from Within: One Program's Road to Programmatic Assessment," Edgington explains how his Writing Program has learned to become more responsible, rather than just accountable. He describes how his Writing Program faculty utilize surveys and electronic portfolios to monitor the successfulness of their program over time; these methods are used in addition to the school-mandated placement testing system to assess the program. In this context, assessment is about responsibility; it is initiated and designed by local participants and used over time to improve teaching and learning on a local level. When outside-mandated assessments are ordered, the faculty customizes the assessment from "above" by asking for permission to make important decisions. In this way, the faculty demand that they have power over some aspects of their program assessment. Chapter 7 also illustrates that assessment is often a process. Edgington and his colleagues met many disappointments along the way and continued to devise new ways to think about how assessment could help them learn important things about programs and students, ultimately empowering them to make the best possible decisions for teaching and learning.

In Chapter 8, faculty also actively participate in an outside-mandated assessment. "Assessing Engineering Communication in the Technical Classroom: The Case of Rose-Hulman Institute of Technology" involved faculty across the curriculum in generating writing outcomes for a school-mandated assessment. House and his colleagues measured how well students met outcomes using portfolios; teachers were also allowed to choose which assignments they wanted students to include in the portfolios to demonstrate the course outcomes. The use of portfolios and the involvement of students in this assessment design provide the teachers and administrators of this program with important information with which they can make decisions about the teaching and learning of writing and engineering within a specific program. By involving stakeholders the authors of Chapter 8, like the author of Chapter 7, attempt to exert a degree of ownership over an outside-mandated assessment.

In Chapter 9, "Writing, Assessment, and New Technologies," Herrington and Moran return to the importance of local assessment. One of the admirable elements of this chapter is the kind of research Herrington and Moran conduct about different automated scoring programs. Instead of a blanket condemnation of all automated scoring, the authors research different software programs to discover some real differences that allow program administrators to make informed choices about the kinds of automated scoring software they might want to use in their WAC and Writing Programs. The authors argue that while technologies like Criterion™ and SAGrader™ may be useful, localized assessment must always supplement such standardized assessments. While outside-mandated, standardized writing exams might be inevitable, teachers can still insist on localized, non-standardized assessments of writing that "can evaluate in a more nuanced way the complex learning that we ask of students." Local assessments also improve the likelihood that the results will be useful and reflective of local goals and beliefs about effective writing. They remind readers that assessment technologies cannot replace complex, locally based assessments conducted by instructors who know their students—assessments that reflect the equally "complex learning" being assessed.

In Chapter 10, Yancey stresses the importance of involving students as stakeholders as she overviews two types of electronic portfolios for classroom assessment and evidence of outside-mandated learning goals/outcomes, "Electronic Portfolios and Writing Assessment: A Work in Progress." According to Yancey, there are two options for the design of electronic portfolios: those in which technology is made invisible, and those in which it technology is "inflected," and each has its own benefits and drawbacks. The primary difference between the two is the degree to which technology plays an important role in the shape of the portfolio; it is a difference of "attention to both the writing and its representation; and attention to its use of the digital in that representation." Yancey addresses the value of including students as stakeholders in assessment, describing how students might choose the design and content of their portfolios and demonstrate what they feel is their most successful work. While students may not often have an equal "stake" in writing assessment, they certainly have a role in it. Yancey reminds readers of the value of involving student voices in writing assessment, since it typically affects their academic trajectories. Yancey's chapter also reminds us of the great strides we have made in the last decade or so with the development of national initiatives that use electronic portfolios.

Summarizing Our Response

In considering the volume as a whole, it is important to note that although there are several themes that run through these articles, they are nearly all responses to outside-mandated writing program assessments. Fulwiler and Young's (1997) experiences about continuing pressures to assess from the late 1970s and early 1980s seem to be a continuing reality for those of us administrating WAC and Writing Programs. In reflecting on this theme, we find ourselves looking toward the work that remains in writing assessment. In particular, we note that most of the programs in the volume were not conducting the ongoing systematic, rigorous assessments Yancey and Huot recommended over a decade or so ago (1997). While this volume portrays a wide-range of people working on WAC and Writing Program assessment and a strong variety of approaches to that assessment, programs are still working from a position of having to assess when assessment is not always seen as a regular part of the business of administering a WAC or Writing Program. Our earlier observation that things stay the same as much as they change seems to ring true given the fact that most of the programs in this volume have not assimilated a viable, ongoing culture for assessment. We believe that an investment in program assessment furnishes WAC and Writing Program Administrators and instructors more control over their own program and what is going on in it—even when outside mandates do occur (see Chapter 7 for an example).

Finally, while it is important to articulate program goals, even ongoing systematic program assessments should not (and do not) just reflect course or programmatic goals. They also reflect a myriad of beliefs and assumptions about literacy and power. These beliefs and assumptions should be kept in mind when designing assessments. Any assessment can have an impact beyond just its program goals and objectives, promoting specific beliefs, assumptions and consequences about literacy and its teaching. This notion of the overall effect of an assessment is consistent with current validity theory available in the most recent, *Standards for Educational and Psychological Testing* (American Research Association, American Psychological Association, & NCME, 1999). Validity is not concerned with the assessment instrument or test, but rather, "Validity refers to the degree to which evidence and theory support the interpretations of test scores entailed by proposed uses of tests" (ARA, APA, NCME, 1999, p. 9). Similarly, we have to think about what will be done with the results? *Do the results merit selected actions? What effects will those actions have on the program and its administrators, the institution, the teachers, the students?* In other words, validity is about what we do with the results of assessments that we conduct. Very few of the chapters in this volume exhibit an understanding, familiarity or experience with using validity to gauge the effectiveness of the assessments or to conduct validation research that assures the proper and appropriate use of assessment to improve the overall effectiveness of the WAC or Writing Program. We thus argue that in looking forward, writing teachers and program administrators should make an effort to become more familiar with the terminology and beliefs of educational measurement. We cannot expect outsiders to have a vested interest in our discipline—nor can we expect to engage in any generative conversation with those outsiders—unless we also make an effort to learn what they know about assessment, too. Assessment is a powerful discourse and in learning some rudimentary properties, terms and concepts from educational measurement, WAC and Writing Program Administrators can assume a powerful voice in making assessment decisions and in making decisions based upon assessment. Ultimately, we are responsible for understanding and working within the confines of the shared principles stipulated by recognized professional and academic bodies like the ARA, APA, and NCME who write the *Standards for Educational and Psychological Testing* (1999).

Assessment of Writing signals that we have come a step further along than *Assessing Writing Across Curriculum: Diverse Approaches and Practice* published a decade earlier. Marie Paretti and Katrina Powell's edited volume breaks new ground in WAC and Writing Program Assessment. Their vision and the vision of the volume situates the assessment of writing programs, broadly defined, as a collaborative, interdisciplinary venture that can yoke the power of assessment with the local values and cultures of the individual institution, program, teachers and students. In addition, this volume, as we have described and responded to chapter by chapter provides good, usable examples of colleagues working together within a local context and across professional, disciplinary, and academic borders to create a new breed of WAC and Writing Program Assessment. Building upon the gains made in this volume, we look to an even brighter future for WAC and Writing Program Assessment. Specifically, we call for future work in WAC and Writing Program Assessment to ground itself more thoroughly in recognizable educational measurement theory and practice. This next step is absolutely necessary if we are to avoid charges of amateurishness and ineptitude that have already been applied to locally controlled writing and writing program assessments (Scharton, 1996). Understanding and using measurement theory professionally, especially the theories of validity and validation (Kane, 2006), can only make our assessments and our programs stronger, more defensible, and more effective.

REFERENCES

American Educational Research Association, American Psychological Association, & National Council on Measurement in Education. (1999). *Standards for educational and psychological testing*. Washington, DC: American Educational Research Association.

Fulwiler, T. (1984). How well does writing across the curriculum work? *College English 46*(2), 113–125.

Fulwiler, T., & Young, A. (1997). Preface—The WAC archives revisited. In K. B. Yancey, & B. Huot (Eds.), *Assessing writing across the curriculum: Diverse approaches and practices* (pp. 1–6). Greenwich, CT: Ablex.

Haswell, R., & McLeod, S. (1997). WAC assessment and internal audiences: A dialogue. In K. B. Yancey, & B. Huot (Eds.), *Assessing writing across the curriculum: Diverse approaches and practices* (pp. 217–236). Greenwich, CT: Ablex.

Huot, B. (2002). *(Re)Articulating writing assessment for teaching and learning*. Logan, UT: Utah State University.

Huot, B., & O'Neill, P. (2009). *Assessing writing: A critical sourcebook*. Boston: Bedford/St. Martins.

Huot, B., & Williamson, M. M. (1997). Rethinking portfolios for evaluating writing: Issues of assessment and power. In K. B. Yancey, & I. Weiser (Eds.), *Situating portfolios: Four perspectives* (pp. 43–56). Logan, UT: Utah State University.

Kane, M. T. (2006). Validation. In R. L. Brennan (Ed.). *Educational measurement* (4th ed.) (pp. 17–64). Westport, CT: Praeger.

O'Neill, P., Moore C., & Huot, B. (in press). Creating a culture of assessment for writing programs and beyond. *College Composition and Communication*.

Scharton, M. (1996). The politics of validity. In E. M. White, W. D. Lutz, & S. Kamusikiri (Eds.), *Assessment of writing: Politics, policies, practices* (pp. 53–75). New York: Modern Language Association.

White, E. M. (1984). *Teaching and assessing writing*. San Francisco: Jossey-Bass.

White, E. M. (1995). *Teaching and assessing writing* (2nd ed.). San Francisco: Jossey-Bass.

Yancey, K. B., & Huot, B. (Eds.). (1997). *Assessing writing across the curriculum: Diverse approaches and practices*. Greenwich, CT: Ablex.